The Musical Life of Melanie

From the Village to Woodstock and Beyond

Craig Harris
Foreword by Cliff Eberhardt

ROWMAN & LITTLEFIELD
Lanham • Boulder • New York • London

Published by Rowman & Littlefield
An imprint of The Rowman & Littlefield Publishing Group, Inc.
4501 Forbes Boulevard, Suite 200, Lanham, Maryland 20706
www.rowman.com

86-90 Paul Street, London EC2A 4NE

British Library Cataloguing in Publication Information available

Library of Congress Cataloging-in-Publication Data Available

ISBN 9798881801625 (cloth : alk. paper) | ISBN 9798881801632 (ebook)

♾™ The paper used in this publication meets the minimum requirements of American National Standard for Information Sciences—Permanence of Paper for Printed Library Materials, ANSI/NISO Z39.48-1992.

The Musical Life of Melanie

Dedicated to Susan, Zsa Zsa, and Tu
With much love and gratitude to Melanie

CONTENTS

PART 4
CHORDS OF FAME (1969–1973)

PART 5
AGAINST THE TIDE (1973–1978)

PART 6
HITS AND MISSES (1980–1990)

PART 7
SEEDS (2000–2001)

PART 8
LOSS AND SURVIVAL (2001–2023)

FOREWORD

I met Melanie at Folk City in early 1988. There was a show with songwriters including her and me. I was a huge fan, so I was excited to meet her. I played a set, and she came over and sat with me. We really hit it off. A friend of mine, Baker Lee, was playing with her at the time. Then, that August, I was scheduled to play the Philly Folk Festival. I got a call from Melanie's husband, Peter, asking if I would accompany Melanie's set at the festival. Of course, I said, "Yes." I already knew most of her songs.

We met at her hotel before her set and rehearsed (she was never big on rehearsing). After we finished, she asked what I was doing for dinner. My brother Geoff and his family lived nearby, so I said I was going to their house for dinner with them and my mom. Melanie asked if she could join us. So, we all had dinner together. After the festival, Melanie and I toured Europe and the United States. She was a fantastic performer and songwriter. My favorite times were when she wasn't in the spotlight, and I could see her vulnerability. Like Craig Harris's *The Musical Life of Melanie*, I saw her as a little girl wrapped up in a powerhouse. I think of her often like that.

—Cliff Eberhardt

PRELUDE

M elanie Safka took her last breath on January 23, 2024. Transformed into an "overnight sensation" by the Woodstock Music and Art Festival, on August 15, 1969, she maintained artistic integrity, and released meaningful records, for more than half a century. She and her son, Beau Jarred Schekeryk, were working on a new album when she passed.

Inspired by a candle-lighting ceremony before her Woodstock performance, and recorded with the Grammy-winning Edwin Hawkins Singers, Melanie's "Lay Down (Candles in the Rain)" became a groundbreaking gospel-pop hit in late 1970. Its follow-up fared even better. A month after its Christmas 1971 release, "Brand New Key" knocked Don McLean's "American Pie" out of the *Billboard* pop chart's top slot. Remaining at number one for three weeks, it sold over six million copies and inspired scores of parodies. Deanna Carter, the daughter of Louisiana-born guitarist Fred Carter Jr. (Roy Orbison, Conway Twitty, Dale Hawkins, Ronnie Hawkins, Levon Helm, The Band), scored a country hit with it in 1998. It's been heard in countless TV commercials and film soundtracks.

Melanie continued to break fresh ground. Besides Laura Nyro and Joni Mitchell, few women wrote songs or sang with the power Melanie could muster. Joan Baez didn't record an original tune until "Diamonds and Rust" in 1975.

Accompanying herself on acoustic guitar, Melanie became the first solo artist to top the bill at Carnegie Hall, the Metropolitan Opera House, the Sydney Opera House, and London's Royal Albert Hall. She sang for capacity crowds in England, Germany, France, Australia, South Korea, and the Netherlands and toured as an official UNICEF spokesperson.

A headliner at Woodstock reunions (authorized or not), Melanie made "royal" appearances at the Glastonbury Fayre, Strawberry Fields Festival, Meltdown 2007, Woody Guthrie Folk Festival (Woody Fest), the International Music Peace Festival, and Hippie Fest. Defying an injunction, she performed at the canceled Powder Ridge Festival in July 1970. A few weeks later, she followed the European debut of the Who's *Tommy* at the Isle of Wight Festival and earned four standing ovations. She went on to share stages with Phil Ochs, Dave Van Ronk, Stevie Wonder, John Lennon, Yoko Ono, and Bob Dylan.

Twice named "Female Artist of the Year" by both *Billboard* and *Cash Box*, Melanie was the first woman, and only the second pop artist (after the Beatles), to own a major record label (Neighborhood Records). She received an Emmy for songwriting.

Idolized as the "ultimate hippie," Melanie sang about romance and world peace. She promoted vegetarianism ("I Don't Eat Animals"), called for bonding with "someone with the same button on" ("Beautiful People"), and proposed a solution to world hunger ("Animal Crackers"). Ray Charles, Mott the Hoople, the New Seekers, Dion, Nina Simone, Sonny & Cher, Dolly Parton, Cissy Houston, and Olivia Newton-John covered her songs. Björk translated her adaptation of A. A. Milne's "Christopher Robin (Is Saying His Prayers)" into Icelandic. Yugoslavian rockers Bajaga I Instruktori recorded "Look What They've Done to My Song, Ma" in Serbian. Nana Mouskouri covered it in Greek.

Melanie's personality transformed an eclectic range of covers. One of the first to record a James Taylor tune ("Carolina in My Mind"), she gave new meaning to songs by Bob Dylan, the Beatles, and George Gershwin. She broke into the United Kingdom's top ten by covering the Rolling Stones' "Ruby Tuesday."

But things weren't all rosy. At a time when female artists were pressured to be subservient, Melanie was encouraged to put her guitar down, give up writing songs, and stick to saccharine pop tunes. Her resistance made her enemies.

Constantly on tour or in recording studios, Melanie knew little about bankruptcies, foreclosed homes, repossessed vehicles, personal property loss, lawsuits, substance abuse, and countless unpaid studios, engineers, musicians, arrangers, and booking agents until the passing of her husband/manager/producer/booking agent/chauffeur Peter Schekeryk in

October 2010. He was supposed to be handling the business while she focused on music.

I sat in the grandstand at Central Park's Wollman Rink in July 1971, as Melanie melted the heart of the capacity crowd. Forty-four years later, I found myself onstage with her and her son, adding conga rhythms to classics and new tunes.

Melanie and I first spoke in 1987, when I interviewed her for a now-lamented national folk and world music magazine, *Dirty Linen*. When she and her husband came to Boston, I met them at the show. The next day, I picked Melanie and Peter up at their hotel—waiting for hours before they were ready—and drove them to Faneuil Hall to shop for gifts for their son and daughters back home. We went to the Boston Oyster House for lunch. I thought it ironic to share a passion for lobster with the woman who sang "I Don't Eat Animals."

Melanie and I reconnected when I interviewed her for a local newspaper in 2014. Somehow our conversation shifted to what I'd been doing for the past twenty-seven years. After I mentioned that I'd been playing percussion with singer-songwriters and bands, we discussed my being a guest at her upcoming show at the Center for the Arts in Natick. I was ecstatic as I counted down the days. Little did I know that Melanie would require emergency hernia surgery after her plane touched down in Boston. The show was postponed. As Melanie recuperated, we began speaking daily by telephone. After she was well enough to resume performing, I had the opportunity to play several shows with her and Beau. During that time, I spoke with her friends, family, accompanists, employees, and fans, gaining new insights and perspectives. Melanie's phenomenal journey unraveled further with the help of a half-century of newspaper, magazine, and online articles, interviews and reviews, and books.

Part 1

WOODSTOCK (AUGUST 15, 1969)

"LAY DOWN (CANDLES IN THE RAIN)"

Woodstock made all the difference. When she woke in the pre-dawn hours of Friday, August 15, 1969, twenty-two-year-old Melanie Ann Safka was a little-known Greenwich Village folk singer. It would be the last time she would know obscurity. By the end of her half-hour performance at the Woodstock Music and Art Festival: An Aquarian Exposition, later that night, she would be known around the globe by her first name and set on a path that continued until her passing fifty-four years later.

Getting to the festival wouldn't be easy. Traffic had been backing up for more than twenty-four hours. As Melanie and her mother, Polly Altomare Safka (who was driving), inched toward Max Yasgur's dairy farm in Bethel, New York, a small town in the Sullivan County hamlet of White Lake (about one hundred miles north of Manhattan and forty miles from Woodstock), she feared they wouldn't make it in time. The American Automobile Association (AAA) of New York reported, "It's an absolute madhouse."[1]

"Anybody who tries to come here is crazy," insisted the festival's director of security, Wes Pomeroy. "Sullivan County is a great big parking lot."[2]

Melanie had no choice. She had been booked to perform on the festival's opening day for a year. She had been in London, England, working on the soundtrack of *All the Right Noises*, starring Gareth Wright, Judy Carne, John Standing, and Olivia Hussey, appearing in her first film since *Romeo and Juliet*, when songwriter/Capitol Records producer Arthur "Artie" Kornfeld and mop-topped visionary Michael Lang planned it. Their headquarters at 1650 Broadway was in the same building as Peter's

3

office. "Our intentions were always to make [Woodstock] more than just a concert," said Kornfeld. "We wanted to include arts and crafts, yoga, and spiritual direction . . . what was to us, the whole Woodstock Nation."[3]

As soon as he learned of Kornfeld and Lang's plans, Peter shared them with his wife and client. Melanie loved the idea of three days of music, peace, and love. "I was so naive about the whole thing," she confessed, "I thought it was just going to be a couple of thousand people in the countryside."[4]

Crawling along, Melanie assumed the traffic was caused by an accident. When it didn't clear, she began to panic. Exiting the thruway, she and her mother located a pay phone. Melanie called the festival office. The receptionist wasn't surprised by her call and redirected her and her mother to a Holiday Inn, in Liberty, New York, twenty miles northeast of the festival.

One of two off-site headquarters, the 120-room Holiday Inn buzzed with excitement. Sly Stone strolled through the lobby while San Francisco–based musicians including Janis Joplin and members of Jefferson Airplane and the Grateful Dead played cards in the hotel bar. Melanie watched Joplin take a long slug from a bottle of Southern Comfort. "My heart was in my throat," she remembered. "It was only then that I realized this was no little pastoral picnic with people buying arts and crafts."[5]

Thinking about singing for a record-breaking crowd was horrifying, but Melanie scarcely had time to think before a firm command to "Get in the helicopter!" interrupted her thoughts. "What do you mean? What do you mean?" she asked frantically. Her question remained unanswered as she and her mom tried to keep up with their escort. As they attempted to exit the door to the makeshift launch pad behind the hotel, a security guard stopped them, pointed to Melanie's mother, and asked, "Who's she?"

"She's my mom."

"No! No! No! No mothers; just artists and management!"

Melanie headed for the helicopter alone. It would be a tense fifteen-minute flight before the festival came into view. Hovering over the six-hundred-acre farm, peering through the window, Melanie was unsure of what she was seeing. "It didn't look like it could be people," she recalled, "because you didn't see anything that looked like heads. It was just round things. Then [the pilot] showed me the stage from the air, and it looked like a football field. I had never been on anything other than a little box stage in Greenwich Village. I had never done anything like this."[6]

Once the helicopter landed, and she was back on solid ground, Melanie could make out the sound of Richie Havens onstage. As documented in Michael Wadleigh's film *Woodstock*, the soulful folk singer was climaxing his two-and-a-half-hour-plus set by transforming a traditional spiritual ("Motherless Children") into a historic anthem ("Freedom"). Melanie sensed terror in his voice. At least that was how she was feeling. Informed that she'd be performing next, she started obsessing about what she was going to sing and for how long. "I didn't have a time constraint," she said. "I don't remember anyone saying twenty minutes, forty minutes, nothing about time. I heaved and then again. Fortunately, I hadn't eaten or had anything to drink."[7]

Melanie stopped preparing after learning that a solo set by Country Joe McDonald, scheduled to appear the following day with Country Joe & the Fish, was on deck. It set the pattern for the day. Someone would tell Melanie to get ready and somebody else would tell her to forget about it. She had no idea when she was going to get her turn.

There was a large backstage tent, but it was for the "stars and VIPs." Melanie was ushered instead to a row of dirt-floor teepees. Tim Hardin, whom Dylan called "the greatest living songwriter," was in the next tent. Melanie knew his songs "If I Were a Carpenter," "Lady Came from Baltimore," and "Reason to Believe." Bobby Darin, Johnny Cash, and Rod Stewart covered them. Keith Emerson of the Nice (and later Emerson, Lake, and Palmer) arranged "How Can We Hang on to a Dream" as an organ-driven rocker. Melanie had recorded a demo of "If I Were a Carpenter" a year before. The promoters wanted him to go on first, but he refused.

John Sebastian, who had just left the Lovin' Spoonful, Hardin, and Bert Sommer followed Country Joe. An ex-member of the Left Banke ("Walk Away Renee"), and cowriter with Felix Pappalardi of songs played by Leslie West's pre-Mountain band the Vagrants, Sommer was managed by Kornfeld. His solo debut, *The Road to Travel*, had recently been released and he was working on a follow-up (*Inside Bert Sommer*). At the same time, he was appearing in the Broadway production of *Hair*. "Bert had a killer voice," remembered his guitarist/keyboard player Ira Stone.

5

"He liked to sit on the floor, cross-legged and barefoot, and accompany himself with his guitar. His songs were quite good."

Sommer's Woodstock experience would inspire him to pen the title track of his third album, *We're All Playing in the Same Band*, his only top-fifty hit. "I spent every penny I had trying to get it into the top thirty," said Kornfeld, who released it on his independent Eleuthera label.

A multiethnic folk-jazz-rock octet from Los Angeles, Sweetwater, was scheduled to kick off the festival but they arrived late. "We figured we'd jump in the car," explained lead singer Nancy DeJongh, "and just go out there to the stage. . . . The car stopped on this one-lane road, and anxiety set in. Just total gridlock."[8]

For Melanie, the whole experience was upsetting. She felt as though she was about to face a firing squad. She had never sung for more than a few hundred people at a time. Adding to alienation, she was "probably one of the only ones . . . not doing drugs. I had all those ideals—no war, no insanity, be kind, and be sharing. I stayed true to myself. I was a purist, a vegetarian, not a druggie."[9]

Sitting alone in her tent, Melanie had nothing but her guitar, not even a backstage pass. She feared that if she wandered too far, she'd be in trouble. Sure enough, she had barely taken a step into the fresh air when a husky security guard started pushing her into the crowd. "No, no, no," she insisted, "I'm a singer!"

"Sure, sure," replied her assailant. Melanie started singing "Beautiful People," her first single. It had been getting airplay on New York's WNEW-FM and would go on to be a turntable hit.

Allowed to return to her tent after a lot more convincing, Melanie avoided wandering from it again. Her problems, though, were just beginning. Scared to death, she developed a deep, bronchial cough that kept getting louder and LOUDER. Hearing her uncontrolled hacking, Joan Baez sent her assistant over with a pot of tea, honey, and a lemon. Baez's gesture had the desired effect. Since her teens, Melanie had considered the "Barefoot Madonna" a musical superhero, and she sang her songs.

The tea, honey, and lemon soothed Melanie's cough, but the hours continued to crawl. The gloom lifted briefly when it started to rain. Melanie figured everybody would pack up and go home. "I thought [the rain] was going to be my reprieve," she said, "and I was going to be saved.

Every ounce of me was praying that I didn't have to do this. I thought . . . if there is a God, prove it, I have to get out of here!"[10]

She wouldn't be so fortunate. George Harrison's sitar guru, Ravi Shankar, was finishing a long set of ragas, and Melanie's favorite group, the Incredible String Band, scheduled next, was refusing to play in the rain. A message arrived at Melanie's tent telling her to get ready. This time, there would be no turning back. The dread intensified. "Shankar got a standing ovation," Melanie told Phil Symes, the ex-Tamla/Motown director who would run Neighborhood Records in the United Kingdom and Europe in the early '70s, "and they didn't want to let him go. There's nothing like going on after the audience doesn't want the person before you to leave. . . . I started crying. . . . I was scared of being in such a place . . . with so many people."[11]

Standing in the rain, waiting to be announced, Melanie wished she could be anywhere else. Two weeks before activist/clown Hugh Romney was rechristened "Wavy Gravy" by B. B. King, he and his Hog Farm Collective passed candles out to the crowd. Production coordinator John Morris stepped to the mic and proclaimed, "This is the largest crowd of people ever assembled for a concert in history but it's so dark here, we can't see you and you can't see each other. So, when I say 'three,' I want every one of you to light a match."[12]

"I remember looking up the hill and seeing all these flickering candles," recalled Melanie's aunt, Jeanne Altomare Iarrobino, who made her own way to the festival. "It was as though people were in tiered seats."

In the thick of this candle-lighting ceremony, Melanie had what she remembered as "an out-of-body experience." After walking across what felt like a plank, she saw herself sitting as though she was watching from above her right shoulder. Everything got quiet. Lighting director-turned-master-of-ceremonies Edward Herbert Beresford "Chip" Monck stepped to the mic, said very simply, "Please welcome . . . Melanie," and she began.

Opening with "Close to It All," Melanie didn't have a set list; everything flowed naturally. It was just her guitar, her voice, and her spirit. She later recalled the candles when she wrote "Lay Down (Candles in the Rain)." Seeing the mountain of light, she thought the universe was lighting up. The whole hillside was lit by the time she finished.

Connecting with a half million people would have taken Melanie years of performing concerts.

Arlo Guthrie and Baez followed Melanie's set, but, by then, she was on her way to a Manhattan hotel for a much-deserved rest. The following day, she participated in a TV panel discussion about the festival's significance. In less than twenty-four hours, she had transformed into a spokesperson for an event that she had had little clue about before.

As history continued to unfold on Woodstock's second day, viewers at home watched Melanie sing "Baby Guitar" on Johnny Cash's previously taped ABC-TV show. She had written it after a particularly grueling press conference party. When a British record label executive inquired about her sex life, she was unsure of how to respond. Without saying a word, she gathered her guitar, left the party, and returned to her room. She spent the rest of the night writing the song. At one point, it had sixty-seven verses—some with imaginative images of mutilation. The anger didn't last, though. By morning, she had forgiven everyone, and the song was shortened to its not-so-traumatic state.

Melanie and Cash dueted on the Wanda Jackson–popularized "Silver Threads and Golden Needles," by Dick Reynolds and Jack Rhodes, but her shyness prevented her from having much interaction with the legendary country singer. She was uncomfortable with his flirting, but fascinated by his "reckless abandon," and, decades later, tried to capture that in her tribute song, "Working Legend."

Agreeing to the minimum $750 for performing at Woodstock, Melanie would go unpaid. She would be absent from the Warner Brothers–distributed film and its triple-album soundtrack, but *Woodstock II* would include "Beautiful People" and "Birthday of the Sun," written a day before the festival.

Part 2
FORMATIVE YEARS (1947–1967)

CHAPTER 2
"BORN TO BE"

A bustling neighborhood in Queens, New York's northwest corner, Astoria borders Long Island City, Sunnyside, Woodside, and the East River facing Manhattan. It was named after John Jacob Astor (1763–1848), a German-born furrier who could see it from his Manhattan mansion but never set foot in it. Tony Bennett, Ethel Merman, Patrick McGoohan, and Dee Snider (Twisted Sister) were born there. George Maharis and Christopher Walken grew up playing in its streets, as did New York Yankees Hall of Fame pitcher Edward "Whitey" Ford.

In its Steinway Place factory, Steinway & Sons has produced quality pianos since 1863. Long before Hollywood, Astoria was a hub for moviemaking with scores of films emanating from one of, at one time, many studios. Its film industry has been resurrecting. The original Paramount Studio on Thirty-Sixth Street (opened as the Famous Players–Lasky Studio in 1920) has been thriving since its revival as the Kaufman-Astoria Studio in the early '80s. Television shows (*Sesame Street* and *Law & Order*), movies (*Hair*, *The Wiz*, and *Goodfellas*), and Melanie's video, *Rock & Roll Heart* originated from there.

Melanie's journey began in Astoria's general hospital on Monday, February 3, 1947. She spent her early years sharing a fourth-floor walkup apartment with her parents, maternal grandmother Paolina "Pauline" Maffei, and Uncle George Altomare (1931–2023).

The three-bedroom apartment had a living room, dining room, and an eat-in kitchen but only one bathroom. It had a tub but no shower.

Melanie would sometimes lock the door and lose herself in thought until someone knocked. It was the only place she could be alone.

Melanie's domain was the living room, but her most cherished memories took place outdoors. On Saturday afternoons, neighborhood girls would congregate in an alley and compete over whose doll was the prettiest and whose doll had the best clothes. Sitting on blankets, they'd spend hours brushing their dolls' hair. The woman who owned the property grew roses. Melanie would forever remember the splendor of their fragrance and the joy that came when the woman let her pick roses or cut them for her.

Sent to the grocery store for ham, cheese, milk, or bread, Melanie would be paid a quarter. It was as though she had won the lottery. She'd go into the candy store and fill her pockets with penny candy. Sometimes, she'd fill a paper bag with potato chips scooped out of a barrel. She especially loved Sugar Daddies—trying to resist biting them.

Melanie shared a bedroom with her uncle, who was studying for a master's degree at City College of New York and often out late. Melanie would go to sleep in the bed, surrounded by "a nightstand, bureau, and armoire," and wake "magically" on a cot in the living room. "We didn't have enough room for everyone," remembered Uncle George. "When it came time for me to sleep or study, I'd roll a folding bed into the living room, unfold it, and put her to bed."

On nights that he was home, Uncle George regaled his niece with wondrous stories. "We had a Prince Albert tobacco can filled with little objects," he recalled, "like a piece of aluminum that the person who gave it to me said was a part from a plane that was shot down. When I put Melanie to bed, I'd tell her stories about these objects. I made them up as I went along. She still has that can. She's kept it because it reminds her of those stories."

"I remember things other people forget," Melanie said. "I had an uncle who was studying child psychology and he practiced on me. Details that other children would have forgotten remained in my mind because he gave them so much attention."[1]

A New York–born, second-generation, Russian/Ukrainian American, Melanie's father Frederick "Freddy" Safka (1924–2009) attended Long Island City High School. Her Chelsea, Massachusetts–born mother,

Pauline Agnes "Polly" Altomare (1926–2003), of Italian American descent, attended the specialized School of Industrial Arts (now the High School of Art and Design) in Manhattan. "They hit it off from day one," remembered Uncle George. "They went out as a steady couple until they got married. Freddy was very popular. He liked to dress sharp, and he could dance the jitterbug. Even at a young age, he made money by buying and selling things. He had a regular job, too, at his uncle's delicatessen."

As youngsters, Polly and her siblings "moved around a lot," recalled Aunt Jeanne, "from one apartment to another. Our father wasn't always around. He was extremely irresponsible."

"The Depression was a terrible time," said Uncle George. "If you were working, you were making money. If you were poor, that wasn't so bad either. You didn't have this or that, but you were living. The worst was being impoverished. That's where we were when we were kids. My father was gone by the time that I was nine or ten. We knew poverty and cold-water flats."

Melanie's grandmother was a firm supporter of workers' rights, serving as a shop steward for the Amalgamated Clothing Workers Union. Her ideals had a strong impact on Uncle George, who started the American Federation of Teachers (AFT) with Albert Shankar in 1959. After it merged with another union to become the United Federation of Teachers (UFT) a year later, he became vice president.

Wanting to live in the country, Melanie collected "pods, acorns, and other things that grew." Even in the city, she'd find natural things to fascinate her. She and her grandmother would stroll down a street, go to a park, or walk by the Triboro Bridge, and the older woman would point things out to her. When dandelions started to grow in the spring, she'd say, "They're green. You can eat them. You can cook them or put them in a salad."

Melanie's parents named her after her Ukrainian grandmother (her father's mother), Melania. "There was one (Melanie) in *Gone with the Wind*," she explained, "and that was it . . . and my grandmother. . . . I wanted to be Jane, Carol, Ann, [or] anything other than Melanie. . . . I just wanted to be like all the other girls with names like everybody else."[2]

Grandma Melania didn't speak much English. She lost her demolition expert husband (Melanie's grandfather) to a work-related accident shortly after they arrived in the United States as refugees. Afterward, she would stare out the window for hours talking to the sun. She managed, however, to raise three sons. Melanie's father, Freddy, was the youngest.

Uncle Johnny, the oldest, was a bit of a bully, but Freddy was his match. He'd put a paint bucket on the edge of a door so that, when Uncle Johnny opened it, the bucket fell, and the paint spilled over him.

Freddy was adventurous and sometimes did dangerous things. "He was playing with this hammer-like projectile," said Uncle George. "You'd insert a roll of caps—the kind used for cap guns—throw it into the air and wait for it to land on a hard surface and fire. He tried doing it and it shot off in his eye. As long as we knew him, he was blind in that one eye."

Melanie not only looked like her father, but she inherited many of his traits, especially his sense of humor. To her, he seemed to brighten everything. There would be weekly Sunday afternoon arguments in the apartment—the capitalists against the communists, the pagans against the Catholics—but no matter how dramatic things got, Freddy had a way of making them light.

Melanie's father taught her to ride her bicycle. She remembered riding for the first time. Thinking that her father was holding her, she was riding confidently until she asked if he was still there and heard his voice getting farther and farther away.

Polly was "the most generous person when it came to giving and providing," recalled Melanie's sister Stephanie (born November 4, 1953). "I remember an apple orchard in Lincroft, New Jersey, that employed migrant workers. They lived in shanties, tiny shacks. Our mother wanted us to understand how good we had it. She brought them food and clothing and gave them money. She made sure to bring us with her and instilled a sense in us of doing the right thing, but she had a short fuse too. She was full-blooded Italian, and she had a temper, though she would get over it quickly. She never hit us; she wasn't physical."

Polly sang "nearly all the time," on or off the stage. "She had a powerfully strong voice," remembered Stephanie, "whether she was singing or yelling. I remember vacationing in the Poconos. My sister and I would stay in the room at night, and Mom would go to sing in the club. I don't know if she was paid but she certainly ran with the jazz crowd. It was a tight little group."

Traditional jazz and big band swing were Polly's métier, but she was fascinated by avant-garde experimentation. She brought her daughters to concerts by free jazz pioneers Ornette Coleman, Sonny Rollins, and Sun Ra. "It was something she enjoyed immensely," said Stephanie.

An amateur saxophone player, Freddy occasionally joined family sing-alongs. Most of his focus, however, remained on retail business and restaurants. "I don't remember my dad living with us," said Stephanie, who was sixteen when her parents divorced. "He'd work somewhere during the week and come home on weekends. My sister was far more influenced by having him in the house; I didn't interact with him too much."

Between union organizing and attending school, Uncle George played guitar and sang Woody Guthrie songs and Depression-era tunes like "One Meat Ball" and "Brother, Can You Spare a Dime?" Visiting the Hopi Indian Reservation during a cross-country trip, he brought home pottery that Melanie found enchanting. He also brought back stories about the Hopi snake dance. Listening to his every word, Melanie pictured each movement in her mind. Before long, she couldn't resist attempting the tribal dance. Starting on the floor with her legs crossed, and head down, she slowly lifted her head and then her hands and arms. Rising to her feet, she swayed side to side like a snake. She loved doing this dance. Whenever they had company, Uncle George would play his ocarina or whistle and Melanie would do the Hopi snake dance.

Dreaming of Melanie becoming a star, Polly enrolled her in tap dancing lessons. Melanie learned the basic steps and liked the clicking sound of the dancing shoes, but music was her calling, not dancing. "My sister visited my office during lunch hour," remembered Aunt Jeanne, "and Melanie sang while we ate lunch. As soon as she could talk, she could sing."

"[Melanie's] voice has gotten much stronger," said Stephanie. "She controls it like an instrument. When she was younger, she just shouted it out. Then, she learned the technique. The theater background helps. There was never a question of whether or not she was going to be on a stage. That was her destiny."

Singing Nat King Cole's "Dance Ballerina Dance" before her second birthday, Melanie astonished listeners when she sang. She had a gift for memorizing lyrics. By the age of four, she had an extensive repertoire. People thought she was something special. Grandmother Pauline taught her Italian pop songs including "Viene Su (Say You Love Me, Too)," recorded by Dean Martin in 1949, and "Bola Colomba," a hit for Italian songstress Nilla Pizzi two years later.

Melanie began recording before her fifth birthday. Polly brought her to a studio "where anyone could make a record for fifty cents." Uncle George also documented his niece's singing. "My friend had a reel-to-reel tape recorder," he remembered. "We went to his house in Washington Heights and recorded Melanie singing some of my mother's songs, some of Polly's songs, some of Jeanne's songs, and some of the folk and labor songs that I taught her."

Certain that she was going to be the next Shirley Temple, Polly taught Melanie hand motions to go with the songs. She directed her to clasp her hands together each time she sang the word "jolly" during the children's song, "Playmate, Come Out and Play with Me." "No one gives Polly the credit that she deserves," said Uncle George. "She sang in weekly amateur shows and brought Melanie. She made her daughter's dresses and put her up on the stage."

Melanie and Polly appeared on *Live Like a Millionaire*, a General Mills–sponsored NBC radio contest based on *Arthur Godfrey's Talent Scouts*, in which parents and children competed together. Polly had the show recorded and a 78-rpm disc pressed. She sang a torch song and Melanie sang, "Gimme a Little Kiss, Will Ya, Huh" by Roy Turk and "Whispering" Jack Smith.

Poking fun at Melanie's childish naivete, the show's host, Jack McCoy, asked the four-year-old, "So, what are you going to sing?" When she innocently answered "Gimme a Little Kiss, Will Ya, Huh," he responded, "I'd be glad to." The audience howled but the youngster stared at him "like he was crazy."

Mother and daughter placed second behind an African American father and son. The winner received $1,000 but Melanie was fine as runner-up. She received a doll that "cried 'real' tears." She waited for "weeks for it to come in the mail."

Polly taught Melanie to play baritone ukulele. "Someone at the bank where Jeanne worked taught her a few chords," Uncle George explained, "and she taught the rest of us. Everyone in the family knew when to change a chord. It was instinctive. None of us had any lessons."

Melanie's first song had three chords. For the first, she placed a finger on the third fret of the top string. The second required placing her fingers on the first and second frets. The third added a third finger. One could play a multitude of songs with those three chords, and she did.

Moving to western Massachusetts in early 1951, Melanie and her parents settled into an apartment in Westfield. Freddy became the assistant manager of a discount store.

Melanie and her mother regularly participated in Moose Club events, sometimes traveling to perform. On April 25 and 26, 1951, they appeared in a minstrel show at the Moose Lodge in Seaside Heights, New Jersey. Melanie harmonized with a children's choir, Polly's Mistrelettes, and sang "Gimme a Little Kiss, Will Ya, Huh" by herself.

When Polly became pregnant in early 1953, Melanie and her parents returned to Astoria to be closer to her grandmother. Feeling more like she was coming back from a long vacation than returning after living somewhere else, she recognized the difference when her grandmother took her on a "real" vacation to Lake Winnipesaukee, New Hampshire. Rising with the sun, they started each day with a lavish breakfast of freshly baked bread and rolls, French toast, jam, relish, and maple syrup. To the six-year-old, this was heaven, the most unbelievable kind of life.

Melanie's grandmother taught her to swim. Her first memories of trusting someone came during these swimming lessons. She knew her grandmother would be there for her and not let her drown.

For her first six and a half years, Melanie was an only child. That never really changed. When her mother informed her that a baby was on its way, she couldn't have cared less. Then one day, Polly was hanging a curtain and Melanie heard her scream. BOOM! That was it. She was off to the hospital. When she came home, she had Stephanie with her. Melanie was convinced that the stork brought her. She knew all about storks from cards that had come to the house, and she bought into the image of a stork carrying a baby in its beak. She had little use for a baby sister, however. "I was left on my own," Stephanie remembered, "and I got into trouble. I had my fair share of incidents."

Concerned about her sister, Melanie brought her on the road as a backup singer. It didn't help. Becoming dependent on drugs, Stephanie entered a rehab clinic where she met and married another addict. The marriage quickly fell apart. She would endure a lot more before getting things together in her early twenties. "I suddenly grew up," she said. "I quit partying and hanging out with the wrong people and got serious about my life."

Stephanie eventually found her métier in antique jewelry, an interest that sparked when she purchased a vintage necklace at the age of eight. From the mid-'90s, she and auctioneer Nicholas Deutsch ran the Whitewater Antique Mall in Fort Anne, New Jersey, overseeing nearly three dozen antique dealers. "I love antique jewelry," she said, "and I'm surrounded by it. I get to see new stuff every day. The hard part is keeping from buying everything that I want."

As youngsters, Melanie and Stephanie spent a lot of time in Lake Carmel, New York, a little over an hour north of Astoria, where Aunt Jeanne and her husband, Sabato "Uncle Sonny" Iarrobino, moved New Year's Eve 1955. The son of New York's chief architect Vince Iarrobino, Uncle Sonny built it. "We had a dock that went out over the lake," remembered Aunt Jeanne. "When Melanie was eleven, she loved to go out there with her guitar, sit at the end of the dock, and sing. She liked the way her voice sounded over the water as if she was in a concert hall."

One weekend, the Safkas went to the lake with their neighbors, Betty and Buddy, and their daughter, Kathy. Polly never had anything nice to say about Betty and, to Melanie, everything she said seemed right. She couldn't remember seeing Betty crack a smile. After the adults brought a basket filled with salami, provolone, eggplant, Italian bread, cookies, and wine into the cabin, they went back outside. Melanie, Stephanie, and Kathy were waiting, anxious to change into their bathing suits, when they heard screaming and lots of crying. Melanie was petrified. Something was indeed dreadfully wrong. Her father and Betty had learned about Buddy and Polly's affair. It ruined plans for the weekend. The salami and provolone went uneaten, and nobody swam. Shortly afterward, Buddy, Betty, and Kathy moved, and Melanie never saw them again.

Fred and Polly wouldn't divorce until June 13, 1969 (finalized September 24) but they slept in separate bedrooms. Melanie shared a room with her mother. Her father and sister had rooms of their own. She would forever wish that her family stayed together but she knew that wasn't going to happen.

CHAPTER 3
"BOY NEXT DOOR"

The Safkas moved to Bayside, Queens, in 1959, shortly after Melanie's twelfth birthday. "All the other people seemed to have been there forever," she said. "I was a stranger, and I took the attitude for hostility. I wasted a lot of time putting on attitudes to protect myself."[1]

Melanie's alienation deepened after the family relocated to Long Branch, New Jersey, in early 1963. A beach town three hours south of Manhattan, between the Shrewsbury River and the Atlantic Ocean, Long Branch was America's first seaside resort. Presidents Chester Arthur, Ulysses S. Grant, Benjamin Harrison, Rutherford B. Hayes, William McKinley, and Woodrow Wilson vacationed there. President James Garfield and his wife Lucretia were waiting for a train to take them to Long Branch in July 1881 when a mentally unstable attorney and self-ordained preacher, Charles Guiteau, shot Garfield twice from behind. Despite his wounds, the president and his wife continued with their planned trip, hoping the ocean air would help his recuperation. It wouldn't. Eleven weeks after their arrival, Garfield succumbed to his wounds, impacted by unsterilized medical treatment.

At first, the Safkas lived in a red Cape Cod–style house at 228 Albert Place. Melanie loved houses; they had backyards. Her father agreed but her mother was partial to apartments, and they soon moved to a garden apartment. The beach was down the street and Melanie could walk to it. She loved to swim.

Opening an arts and crafts store in the Monmouth Mall, in Eatontown, ten minutes west of Long Branch, Polly based its name, Paint-N-Place, on *Peyton Place*, the best-selling novel, movie, and TV drama starring Mia Farrow and Ryan O'Neal. It was a small shop until she took

19

over the store next door. Stanley Tomczak, a frequent summertime visitor, "had family in Long Branch," he recalled, "and I'd visit for a week every summer. I'd borrow a bicycle and ride to the shopping center. Polly was always very nice. She'd give you things—a poster or a photo— whenever you came into the shop."

Tomczak found Polly similarly generous away from the store. "She was always giving," he said. "Whenever you left her house, your hands were never empty. She would give you something she made or something she cooked. I once mentioned that I liked her Pyrex coffeepot. It was the first time I had ever seen one. The next time I was there when I was leaving, she handed me one of those pots."

Being a New Yorker in a New Jersey beach town had little impact until school started, and Melanie found herself an outsider—the only beatnik oddball at Long Branch High School. "I couldn't classify myself in those days," she told *Scene*. "I didn't fit in with the cheerleaders; I didn't fit in with the brains or the tough kids. There were so many cliques . . . and I didn't belong to any of them."[2]

Melanie experienced Greenwich Village in its prime. She wasn't interested in politics but was drawn to the aesthetic sensitivity.

As a teen, Melanie would walk the streets of the Village, barefoot, with a guitar strapped across her back. Sometimes, she'd stop and sing. Crowds would gather around her, but she didn't feel comfortable collecting money for singing. Even in places where they passed a hat, she'd run away as soon as her song ended.

"Melanie would sing in coffeehouses," said Uncle George, "and Polly would be outside, in her Oldsmobile, waiting to take her home. She was the classic stage mother."

During the summer of 1963, sixteen-year-old Melanie and her mother drove cross-country on Route 66. Melanie was deeply depressed. She had broken up with her boyfriend the night before their departure and she continued to sulk until reaching the Southwest. Stopping at an American Indian gift shop, in Arizona, she pleaded with her mother to buy her a pair of suede, knee-high, black-fringed boots with molded white soles. She was so glad that her mother consented. She felt wonderful in these boots. They made her feel like an American Indian princess, but she found that wearing them to school was a mistake. Few high school students wore boots as fashion statements at the time; they hadn't become "hip" yet. The school's code of dress was simple—boys wore ties, girls wore dresses. Only troublemakers broke the dress code—and now Melanie. School administrators instituted a new "no boots" rule in her honor and sent her to see the school psychologist. "I was a victim of ridicule," she claimed, "because I would find these things that I would find beautiful, and I would wear them, not to cause a sensation, but it would. That made me very defiant in protecting my right to express myself the way I want to. . . . Why can't I wear my hair in pigtails with Indian moccasins?"[3]

The boots weren't the only problem. Melanie struggled to fit in with her classmates. She was convinced that the teachers hated her, misinterpreting her introversion to be belligerence. "She's just quiet," suggested Hall of Fame disc jockey Bruce "Cousin Brucie" Morrow, "introspective like George Harrison."

Melanie listened quietly as the school psychologist ranted for what seemed like "days and days." Shown an inkblot, she was asked what it was. "Two people making love," she responded without hesitation. The psychologist showed her another. Just as swiftly, the teen said that it was two more people making love. Shown another ink spot, she hesitated before telling him that it was two animals making love. Sure enough, her parents were summoned to the school. When they arrived, the psychiatrist told them, "She needs deep psychoanalysis."

Melanie's mother agreed but her father asked, "How much is it going to cost?" and "How long is going to take?" The psychologist became indignant. "You can't put a price on your daughter's mental health!"

Unperturbed, Melanie's father glared at the psychologist and asked, "Will she get better?" Melanie was appalled but deep down she realized that her father was saving her from possible danger. She was sure psychiatrists would uncover all kinds of things once they began to probe her. She knew she wasn't crazy. She didn't see things the way most other people did but that's all there was to it. "Melanie was precocious in a way," remembered Uncle George, "but she wasn't obnoxious. She was a sweet kid."

Music provided relief. Introduced to German composer Kurt Weill and Belgian songwriter Jacques Brel in a high school music class, Melanie was completely immersed in their songs. She adored the playfulness in French cabaret singer Édith Piaf's voice when she sang them. Her mother had little interest in Broadway musicals or cabaret, but they enchanted her.

Melanie's school days began with news being broadcast over loudspeakers in each classroom. One day, there was an announcement about a talent competition at a nearby school. Long Branch High School students could participate if they chose, and Melanie did. Her father drove her to the contest. When the emcee called her name, she walked to the mic and froze. The silence made her father uneasy. When the audience quieted and she finally began to sing, he took a deep breath and sighed in relief.

Melanie had heard two versions of the New Orleans classic, "The House of the Rising Sun." Joan Baez sang one and Nina Simone the other (Eric Burdon and the Animals hadn't covered it yet). Morphing both versions into her interpretation, Melanie caused the audience to go wild. It was no contest—she won easily, receiving a trophy "at least two feet high" inscribed with her name as the "Hootenanny Contest Winner." The next day, her victory was announced over the school's loudspeakers—"Melanie Safka won a contest . . . and today we're going to have a fire drill."

Melanie didn't have many friends at school. The Civil Rights Movement was in the news, and she was committed to combating social injustice. "One of the first books that I remember making a strong impact on me," she said, "was this graphic journal called *The Family of Man*. I was reading William Saroyan and Kurt Vonnegut, and it made so much sense that we do things that are unpleasant to each other, and we keep creating more and more insanity and there is enough of everything, but somehow we don't distribute it properly. All these thoughts were coming to me that the world had to change."[4]

Melanie forced herself to sing at school dances, despite intense stage fright. She'd blow everyone away with her powerful voice, but as soon as she hit the final note, she'd run off the stage and leave. She didn't wait for feedback.

As the only white member of an integrated R&B singing group, Melanie felt intimidated. She believed her bandmates took advantage of her progressive views and bossed her around. She was uncomfortable with the treatment but, incapable of articulating her objections, she didn't say anything and did whatever they asked. She wouldn't remember the group's name but could recall many evenings singing with them, mostly at pizza places. A local band, the Aztecs, occasionally backed them.

Long Branch's boardwalk had plenty of places to sing, especially during the summer. Melanie had a powerful voice, and people would stop and listen whenever she sang.

Securing a regular solo gig at a Monmouth University student café, the Inkwell Coffee House, Melanie sang every Monday for four or five hours without a break (her option). At the end of the night, she'd receive twenty dollars. Sometimes, she'd sing at the Quay, a smoky club on Ocean Boulevard, in Sea Bright, ten miles north of Long Branch. Polly sang there and encouraged the owner to book her. Because Melanie was underage, she had to be escorted by her mother, Uncle George, or another adult. "Melanie's audience," remembered Uncle George, "saw her as a young, independent hippie singing for her supper."[5]

By then, Melanie had graduated from ukulele to acoustic guitar, a gift from her father. He obtained the six-string from Goya's distributor to Two Guys from Harrison (later shortened to Two Guys), the New Jersey discount store chain he helped to start a year before she was born. When he handed her the instrument, she thought she had died and gone to heaven.

Uncle George had been the first in the family to play guitar. "I'd visit Melanie and her parents in Long Branch," he said, "and bring my guitar and records—Joan Baez and early folk music. I taught Melanie some basic chords. They were ukulele chords, only a little more complicated. A guitarist doesn't need to know many chords to sing a whole repertoire of songs, not just folk songs. With four chords, you could sing an entire series of 'Blue Moon' songs. They all have the same chord pattern, just different words, and different melodies."

Learning chords was difficult, but Melanie was dedicated. She realized that she'd never have as pure a voice, but she learned Joan Baez's songs off her records. She especially loved it when Baez sang folk songs like the British ballad, "John Riley," which Melanie would later record.

The late '50s/early '60s was a golden era for revivalist folk music. Inspired by the Weavers, Pete Seeger's quartet with Ronnie Gilbert, Fred Hellerman, and Lee Hays, folk groups proliferated. Some like the Kingston Trio and Peter, Paul & Mary made their presence felt on the hit parade. Melanie would tour with the Kingston Trio and Glenn Yarborough in the early 2000s, but she preferred broadside ballads, Library of Congress field recordings, and folk songs sung by "authentic" musicians like British balladeer Ewan MacColl and Pennsylvania-born Ed McCurdy. Accompanying herself on guitar, she found it easier to be a folk singer than a pop singer like Brenda Lee or a group like the Shirelles, but they lived very well together in her love of music.

On Sunday, February 9, 1964, seventy-three million people tuned in to the first of the Beatles' three appearances on CBS-TV's *Ed Sullivan Show*. Unimpressed, Melanie clumped the Liverpudlian Mop-tops in with the multitude of bands playing "glitzy pop music." She'd change her opinion within a few years. "When [the Beatles] did 'Revolution,' the *White Album*, and *Abbey Road*," she explained, "my spirituality was awakened, and I got very interested in the Beatles."[6]

Melanie would record Lennon and McCartney's "We Can Work It Out" and "Any Time at All." She sang "Rocky Raccoon" on a 1978 CBS-TV tribute show and would participate in a three-night concert, *America Celebrates the Beatles*, at New York's Town Hall, in February 2014. Celebrating the fiftieth anniversary of the Fab Four's arrival in the United States, the all-star concert also included Tommy James, Al Jardine (the Beach Boys), Melissa Manchester, Fred Schneider (the B52s), Gene Cornish (the Rascals), Greg Hawkes (the Cars), Marshall Crenshaw, and Ron Dante (the Archies). It climaxed with Melanie's reunion with pianist/arranger Roger Kellaway after more than three decades.

Encouraged by Melanie's enthusiasm and musical talent, Fred looked into having her recorded. He balked after being told that it would cost $5,000.

Making the rounds of New York–based record companies, Melanie sang for label presidents and A&R directors, who were unconvinced. One "especially condescending" record mogul suggested that she "go home, get married, and have a couple of kids."

During her junior year of high school, Melanie developed a crush on a thirty-five-year-old drama teacher. She wasn't in his class, but she'd see him in the hall. One day, she made eye contact. The flow was apparent, and he reciprocated. That was it. He was married, but it didn't matter. Dark and mysterious, he set her teenage heart aflame. They began to stay after school and talk. "It was the most comfortable relationship

I'd ever had," Melanie confided to *Cosmopolitan*. "It was much less of a nervous thing than thinking of really being open with somebody my own age because I didn't trust kids. I just didn't trust anybody my own age. The only people I ever felt comfortable with were people much older than me."[7]

Gossip about a young girl and a teacher spread quickly through Long Branch High School. Melanie hated being there. She knew that the end of the school year was approaching, and the following year would be her last, but she couldn't take it anymore. She considered dropping out, but her father was insistent that she go to college. She decided that running away would be the only solution. She wouldn't have to go to college. She could do something else. She didn't know what, but she was "ready to go on the road like Jack Kerouac, meet interesting people, and figure it out."

Melanie thought about volunteering for the Peace Corps but realized "there was no outlet in the Peace Corps for people who played guitar and sang. You had to know how to build bridges and purify water and stuff."[8]

Considering Mexico a destination, Melanie "read books all about the place and the people." "I wanted to help the natives," she said. "I was going to take things they needed like food, and I was going to tend the sick . . . but I didn't have the proper certificates. . . . They wouldn't let me in."[9]

California offered a better option; she wouldn't need a passport. Melanie began raising money for a plane ticket. A year before, her father had given her an expensive sunlamp acquired from one of his clients. She sold it, along with other items, and got enough money.

It wouldn't be clear sailing. The person helping her sell her things told Melanie that he had friends in Los Angeles and gave her a phone number. He assured her that she could stay with them.

Leaving for the airport, Melanie didn't take her guitar, believing that "it would be too much of a giveaway."

Before walking to the ticket counter, Melanie put on a blonde wig. She told the airline attendant that her name was Eve Dane. She wouldn't remember where she got the name, but it was before airlines required identification, and she had no problem getting a boarding pass.

Once aboard the plane, Melanie introduced herself to the passenger in the next seat. They began to talk. He told her that his name was Robert Ridgely (1931–1997). A well-traveled character actor, he would become a regular in Jonathan Demme and Mel Brooks films and appear on *Get Smart, Sea Hunt*, and *Coach*. His deep, resonant voice made him a natural for voice-over work. At the time, he was appearing as Lieutenant Kimbro in the short-lived ABC-TV World War II series *The Gallant Men*. Melanie hadn't seen the show and didn't recognize him. The actor asked the young runaway about her destination and inquired about her age. She made up all kinds of stories. He knew she was lying but he didn't let on. Before long, the conversation turned to music. Ridgely had a guitar in the overhead bin. He took it down and they started singing. Melanie told him she wrote songs.

After the plane landed, Melanie and the actor went their separate ways. Melanie walked to a phone booth outside the luggage check and called the number given to her before she left New Jersey. She let it ring for a while but there was no answer. She was starting to panic when Ridgely walked by with a man helping him with his luggage. They stopped and the actor asked, "Are you all right?" Melanie explained how the people she was supposed to be staying with weren't answering their telephone. She didn't know their address. The actor listened to her sad tale and then said, "Don't worry, I know the woman who runs the Hollywood Studio Club for Girls."

Operated by the Young Women's Christian Association (YWCA), the Hollywood Studio Club for Girls provided inexpensive housing for women in the motion picture business between 1916 and 1976. More than ten thousand women called it home during its fifty-nine-year run, including Marilyn Monroe, Donna Reed, Kim Novak, Maureen O'Sullivan, Rita Moreno, Barbara Eden, and Sharon Tate. Residents were required not only to be actors but also had to be recommended by a working actor. Ridgely assured Melanie he could get her a room. Bolstered by his kindness, she walked confidently out of the terminal with him and his assistant. A limousine was waiting. She got in the back seat, and they drove to the Hollywood Studio Club for Girls. When they arrived, Ridgely walked inside. It was obvious that he knew the woman who ran it. "Hi, Jane, how're you doing?"

"Oh, Robert, it's so good to see you."

"This is Eve Dane. She's going to be here for a while. She's a musician and she sings."

Provided with a room with a bathroom and a bed for a dollar a day, Melanie felt "truly landed." Bidding farewell to Ridgely, she said, "Thank you very much," and that was it. They would never see each other again.

Melanie stayed at the Hollywood Studio Club for weeks. As her savings dwindled, she thought of finding work. She figured that she'd walk into a restaurant or a retail shop, announce that she wanted a job, and that would be that. She would quickly learn otherwise. Job seekers were required to list previous employees and places of residence on their applications. It put her out of the running.

Strolling around downtown Los Angeles, contemplating her next move, Melanie came upon a street musician. They started talking about music and it escalated into a variety of subjects. The street musician invited her to a party. "All kinds of interesting people will be coming," he promised. "It'll be fun."

Melanie said that she'd love to go. Later that night, the street musician picked her up at the Hollywood Studio Club and drove her to a rundown house in an unfamiliar part of the city. It felt creepy. Nobody was there other than the street musician and one of his friends. Melanie grew increasingly uncomfortable when no one else arrived. Excusing herself to go the bathroom, she instead ran out the front door and continued running, certain that she was in "real danger." She kept running, running, running right onto the LA Freeway. It wasn't long before highway patrol arrived. "Who are you? What are you doing here?"

"I'm Eve Dane. I'm going to the Hollywood Studio Club for Girls."

An officer demanded her to "Get in!" as he opened the back door. Melanie thought the police were offering her a ride home. They weren't. Instead, they brought her to a newsstand that had a phone booth. They wrote her name down, and noted where she was staying, but left her stranded.

Hailing a cab, Melanie finally made it back to the Hollywood Studio Club. It was the middle of the night. She knew it was past curfew, but she walked quietly to her room. It wasn't long before her intercom rang. She heard a voice say, "Melanie, is that you?" Instinctively, she answered, "Yes," and, then thought, "Uh-oh! She just called me Melanie!"

"Melanie," the voice continued, "there are two people here to see you."

Melanie thought it had to be her mother and father, but it wasn't. It was two police officers. They had heard that police in New Jersey were seeking her. They didn't say a word other than to inform her that they were taking her to the Girls' Detention Home. She had no choice but to pack her belongings and go with them.

Turmoil ensued as soon as Melanie arrived at the Girls' Detention Home. The warden demanded that she remove the makeup from her face. Melanie explained that she had already taken her makeup off, but the warden snapped, "I want your face scrubbed now!" and gave her soap. Melanie scrubbed her face, but the warden kept insisting that the makeup wasn't off. The teen continued to scrub until her face was raw.

Melanie's cell had a bed, sink, and toilet. Anyone could look through the window and see her going to the bathroom. The loneliness eased after a blonde pickpocket, Mary, befriended her. Taking her under her wing, Mary taught her "the ropes of jail existence."

One day, Mary asked the young runaway what she had done. Melanie explained that she hadn't done anything but run away from home. Mary asked why she was in jail. The teen confessed that she didn't know. Police hadn't charged her with any crime. Mary suggested that she inform the authorities. Melanie followed her friend's advice, but the warden refused to release her until one of her parents came to claim her.

Freddy flew to Los Angeles soon afterward. Melanie was alone in her cell when a guard arrived to escort her to the administrator's office. Seeing her father, she "thanked God." She hadn't meant to cause any problems, but her father had to now know how serious she was about not going to college. She hated the idea of school. She was tired of other students poking fun at her and fed up with being the subject of gossip. She didn't have any friends and she didn't want to go through the torment again.

On the flight back to New Jersey, Melanie and her father discussed her future. "College will be different," Freddy promised. "I can't, I can't," Melanie argued. The debate went back and forth until Freddy asked, "What about another kind of school?" Melanie agreed to consider it. She and her father would investigate music schools but, at the time, music education was geared to symphonic music. There were no classes in pop or folk music. Melanie hadn't studied music theory, so she didn't even meet the prerequisites. She wasn't qualified to audition.

Acting school would be a final resort. Melanie had seen a stock company production of *Othello* and thought that acting could be fun. She hadn't participated in a school play, but she successfully auditioned for entry into the American Academy of Dramatic Arts (AADA) in Manhattan. Founded in 1884, it's the oldest acting school in the English-speaking world. Lauren Bacall, Cecil B. DeMille, Kirk Douglas, Agnes Moorehead, Robert Redford, Don Rickles, Edward G. Robinson, and Spencer Tracy were alumni. Danny DeVito was in Melanie's class. "It was hard for me to get up in class," Melanie confessed, "but, whenever I did, I felt that I was good, and that people were somehow interested."[10]

Before her first acting class, Melanie had to make up the high school classes she missed while she was away. She refused to return to Long Branch High School. Her father arranged for her to transfer to a school in a nearby town, Red Bank—paying $800 for her to attend—but it was no better. Melanie's reputation as a "communist instigator" preceded her arrival, and administrators gave her trouble.

During her senior year, Melanie borrowed books from the school's library. One was overdue; she had admittedly lost it. A week before her June 1964 graduation, the school informed her that she wouldn't be allowed to attend the ceremony with the rest of the senior class. Her father went to plead with the principal. Defending her passionately, he offered to replace the book. The principal turned him down. He looked at Melanie as representing everything that was wrong with America.

Melanie didn't care about the graduation ceremony, but she felt bad for her father. He had business clients and friends whose children were graduating. Melanie got her diploma in the mail.

In April 2015, the school (now Red Bank Regional High School) inducted Melanie into its Distinguished Alumni Hall of Fame. Jazz great William "Count" Basie, a student more than eighty years before, was a previous inductee. At her induction, Melanie reunited with John "Mr. Bro" Brzostoski (Bro-STOW-skee) (1926–2023), the only faculty member she connected with as a student. Still feisty, the long-retired arts teacher told me about the atmosphere of the school when Melanie attended. "It was totalistic and paternal," he said, "and they were so used to being the boss that they couldn't even think of anybody not listening to them."

Brzostoski, who also taught Oriental Art and Buddhism at the New School for Social Research in Greenwich Village, became faculty adviser of Red Bank High School's folk song club. "Nobody else wanted to sponsor them," he said. "Once a week after school, students came to my room with their guitars and played for each other. At first, I sat at my desk and ignored them. They kept plucking away. Finally, I couldn't take it anymore and said, 'This is terrible.' They said, 'What can we do?' and I said, 'We're going to put on a show. You're going to play on stage and other people are going to read poetry. We'll raise money for Tibetan refugees.'"[11]

This student group played concerts as the Nothing Strums. Melanie was too much of a loner to be an official member, but she performed at many of the same informal gatherings. "The first show Melanie became involved with," remembered Brzostoski, "was at the Old Mill in Tinton Falls. I thought we were going to have a lot of poetry because I didn't think we had any folk singers worth a hoot. I can remember where I was standing when Melanie asked if she could play. I said, 'Sure.' She was really good."

Soon after missing her graduation, Melanie accompanied Brzostoski and members of the Nothing Strums to the beach. "Melanie was gallivanting in the water," remembered Brzostoski. "She was up to her waist, splashing, and trying to get us to do the same thing. Eventually, everyone else faded away until it was just the two of us. I said, 'I want to congratulate you on your graduation.' I kissed her as a graduation present and I kissed her again. She said, 'What's that one for?' I said, 'That one was for me.' The administration imagined that all kinds of hanky-panky went on with the Nothing Strums but there was nothing but true affection."[12]

During the time she had been on the West Coast, Melanie's teacher "friend" spoke with her parents. He was truly concerned. Now that she was no longer attending the school where he taught, they were free to be together (he was separating from his wife). They continued seeing each other after Melanie's graduation but "it didn't answer [her] inner calling" and they went their separate ways.

Melanie often thought of Robert Ridgely. He had gone out of his way to help her, but a reunion never materialized. They reconnected, however, when the soundtrack of *Boogie Nights* (1997), starring Mark Wahlberg and Burt Reynolds, included "Brand New Key." Shortly after the film's release, Melanie took her then seventeen-year-old son, Beau, and his friends to see it. During one pivotal scene, the camera zoomed in on a woman wearing nothing but a pair of roller skates. That's when Melanie's song played. As she slipped under her seat, she didn't know what to do. After the movie was over, she warned Beau's friends not to tell their mothers or anyone—ever!

Melanie thought that she recognized one of the actors in the film. Sure enough, Ridgely had portrayed the morally despicable Colonel James. Watching the closing credits, Melanie read, "In memory of Robert Ridgely." The actor succumbed to cancer immediately after completing the movie. It seemed a bizarre way to meet again but Melanie believed it wasn't an accident; their paths were destined to cross once more.

CHAPTER 4
"JAMMING ALONE"

M elanie didn't have a summer vacation after high school. She went directly to the American Academy of Dramatic Arts (AADA), commuting over an hour each way by bus and train. She briefly shared a room in a hotel but found it a tense experience. "I always felt that I was so easy to get along with," she told *Seventeen*, "but I think I kept to myself too much. . . . I wasn't used to . . . girlfriends. The most frightening thing is to argue with your own sex. I really thought I was sick because I couldn't adjust until I found some girls the complete opposite of me, and we got along fine."

Melanie wound up sharing an apartment with three women attending the drama academy. "We'd go into the small bathroom," remembered Ruthie Dytches, who opened an acting school in Tel Aviv following graduation, "light candles, and sit around the tub listening to Melanie sing. We would all wear long hippie-style dresses. Melanie, with flowers in her hair, would sit on the toilet singing to us."

"Melanie and I spent a lot of time together at school," added Annie McGreevey, who became an illustrious film director, writer, and acting teacher, "but she wasn't around the apartment too much during the evening. She was already plugged into the folk scene and playing in the Village."

Not everyone in the apartment was so accommodating. "We had a roommate, Jackie," said McGreevey, "a little older, in her mid-twenties. Melanie was into lighting candles, but Jackie would go right through the roof. She thought we were going to burn the place down. Ruthie and I could listen to Melanie all night, but Jackie would go nuts. She wanted to sleep; she had to go to work in the morning. The rest of us plugged into the arts and didn't worry about sleep."

Once a week, Melanie's mother brought her "a chicken, a bottle of Wishbone Italian dressing, and a head of lettuce." She'd throw the chicken into a pan, drench the lettuce in dressing, and eat it with the chicken. McGreevey remembered the "care packages" that Melanie would receive from her mother. "There would be lasagna, and all kinds of wonderful delicacies, which Melanie very generously shared with us. Everybody was starving. We had no money. We were young artists who had come to New York to get a start."

Mime instructor Paul Curtis led Melanie and her classmates through emotion-stirring activities. During one, a student stood silently while the rest of the class watched. Giggling at first, the student would work his or her way through the laughter and begin to cry. It was a way of getting students in touch with their deepest emotions.

Melanie appeared as the Cheshire cat in *Alice in Wonderland* and Laura Wingfield in Tennessee Williams's *The Glass Menagerie*. She spent most of the summer at the Penland School of Crafts, in Asheville, North Carolina, studying pottery under Bruce Bangert. She learned to center clay on a wheel, glaze with things from nature, make different-colored dyes, and put chemicals into dyes to achieve different effects. She spent hours shaping clay, firing it in the kiln, and glazing. She considered becoming a potter but wasn't sure if she had "enough dedication to master the craft."

Sitting around the campfire, playing her guitar, Melanie realized she was a better singer than a potter. Back to school for her sophomore year, she sang between classes. Afterward, she'd go to Greenwich Village with her guitar and sing. She thought nothing about walking New York streets, carrying a black-handled riding crop with tassels and wearing a black leather trench coat and boots. "I write songs to say things to people I couldn't tell them otherwise," she explained. "If someone upsets me or annoys me I won't say anything to them, I'll write it down."[1]

After graduating with an Associate of Occupational Studies degree, Melanie worked with a children's theater group in Massachusetts. At the end of the summer, she found herself adrift. "I was absolutely nowhere," she recalled. "I wasn't one of those people with a résumé and photo."[2]

Returning to her parents' Long Branch apartment, Melanie commuted each day to New York. She'd pick up the day's entertainment trade papers, head to Matera's Café in the West Village, and purchase "a cup of coffee and a slice of Mother Matera's amazing apple pie." Meticulously going through the papers, she'd take notes and circle audition announcements. "I never answered any," she admitted. "They asked for a young, pretty girl and I instantly disqualified myself."[3]

"I wandered around New York City . . . getting nowhere," Melanie told BBC Radio 1. "I didn't care what I ate, where I slept, who I slept with. The police would pick me up in the worst sections of town at four in the morning. I didn't want to impose myself on anyone because I felt so low. . . . I think the only thing that kept me going was thinking what a tragic figure I was."[4]

Skimming the trade papers one day, Melanie came across an announcement for auditions for *Fiddler on the Roof.* Set in a Jewish settlement in czarist Russia in 1905, the musical was based on Yiddish author Sholem Aleichem's stories about a dairyman (Tevye) and his five daughters. Premiering at Broadway's Imperial Theater, in September 1964, with music by Jerry Bock, lyrics by Sheldon Harrick, and libretto by Joseph Stein, it would become the first musical to surpass three thousand performances.

Melanie auditioned to be one of Tevye's daughters. Women going to auditions at the time customarily dressed in black gowns and wore pearls; they didn't express individuality. Breaking tradition, Melanie wore a flowing peasant dress with a scarf over her hair. She wanted to look like the character in the play.

The audition was beyond belief. Hundreds of women were reading for one role or another. It didn't take long before Melanie realized that her choice of regalia set her apart. The way people glared at her should have been enough to drive her from the room. When she walked onto the stage to audition, the people doing the audition laughed. She fudged her way through it as best as she could, but the experience was horrifying.

It wasn't, however, enough to keep her from trying. Soon afterward, a friend phoned with news about a revival of *Dark of the Moon.* Howard Richardson and William Berney's musical dramatization of a seventeenth-century Scottish folk song, "The Ballad of Barbara Allen," *Dark of the Moon* spent ten months on Broadway in 1945. The saga of a "wolf boy in the Appalachian Mountains" was definitely not in the mainstream. Producers were seeking "a girl who could play guitar and sing."

Riding the train from New Jersey, Melanie brought her six-string. She didn't have a trained voice, but she knew this was the part for her; she was Barbara Allen.

The audition was at 1619 Broadway, an eleven-story monolith in the heart of New York's theater district north of Times Square. Popularly known as the Brill Building, it housed almost two hundred music businesses. Melanie breezed past the formally attired door attendant as she entered the building. Scrutinizing the massive directory on the lobby wall, she was overwhelmed. She didn't know the office number or any detail about the audition other than that a girl was needed to play Barbara Allen.

Melanie watched the attendant greet people, unsure of whether to ask for his help or not. Sometimes, he'd acknowledge them by name. Other times, he'd just say "How do you do?" while opening the door. In between, he'd mutter under his breath and curse. Summoning enough courage, she asked if he knew where they were holding auditions for *Dark of the Moon*. Without hesitation, he pointed to the building and directed her to suite 511, telling her that they were always doing unusual things. Thanking him, Melanie took the elevator to the fifth floor.

The audition, however, wasn't in suite 511. That was the office of Hugo & Luigi Publishing. Cousins Luigi Creatore and Hugo Peretti had parlayed a partnership that began with recordings by Peretti's wife, a children's author, in the 1940s, into a powerhouse of popular music. As co-owners of the mob-connected Roulette Records in the '50s, Creatore, the son of a renowned Naples-born immigrant bandleader, and Peretti, a trumpet player, scored hits with Georgia Gibbs ("Dance with Me Henry") and Jimmie Rodgers ("Honeycomb"). Moving to RCA in 1960, they produced smooth-voiced Perry Como, Little Peggy March ("I Will Follow Him"), the Isley Brothers ("Twist and Shout"), and Sam Cooke ("Chain Gang," "Twistin' the Night Away," and "Wonderful World"). Accomplished songwriters, they often wrote with George David Weiss, a Juilliard graduate who played violin, piano, saxophone, and clarinet. Penning the title track of Elvis Presley's 1960 film, *Wild in the Country*, they scored a chart-topper when Presley sang "Can't Help Falling in Love" in his 1962 film, *Blue Hawaii*. It was their second number-one hit in two years. A year before, they topped the charts in more than three dozen countries, and sold more than fifteen million records, when Brooklyn-based doo-wop group the Tokens sang

"The Lion Sleeps Tonight." The song featured English-language verses Weiss had written for a song that originated with high-pitched, South African vocalist Solomon Linda and the Evening Birds in 1938. Pete Seeger and the Weavers covered it as "Wimoweh" in 1957, mishearing the original "Uyimbube" (Zulu for "You Are the Lion."). As "The Lion Sleeps Tonight," the Tokens' single topped the charts. It made a comeback in the 1994 Disney film *The Lion King*. Linda had died nearly penniless more than three decades before, but his family sued Disney for copyright infringement and settled for an undisclosed but substantial amount.

When Melanie stumbled into their office, Hugo and Luigi were branching out to musical theater. *Maggie Flynn*, about the 1863 New York Draft Riots, starring Shirley Jones (*The Partridge Family*) and her husband Jack Cassidy (*The Mary Tyler Moore Show*), would premiere on Broadway, at the American National Theater Academy (ANTA) Playhouse, in October 1968. It would close after ten weeks.

Melanie was nearly out of breath when she reached Hugo and Luigi's office. Their receptionist, Joyce, interrupted what she was doing, took a perplexed look at her, and said, "Can I help you?"

"Are you auditioning for *Dark of the Moon*?"

"No, I'm sorry; this is a music publishing company."

It wasn't what Melanie wanted to hear. She started talking a mile a minute, becoming more and more hysterical as she spoke. She had no choice; she had to get to this audition. Her life depended on it. "Wait a second, wait a second," Joyce broke in, "I'll look in the building directory and see if I can help you. Calm down. It'll be all right."

Phoning the Actors Guild, Joyce managed to track down the audition. Wishing the young actor luck, she sent her on her way. Melanie headed to the audition. Her instincts proved right. Over the next few hours, she'd read for someone, sit for a while, and then read for someone else. She knew she had the part (though the musical would go unproduced due to insufficient funding).

Returning to Hugo and Luigi's office to thank the receptionist, Melanie was telling Joyce how well the audition had gone when Hugo and Luigi walked into their office. Seeing her holding a guitar, they assumed she was one more aspiring artist hoping for an audition and said, "Set her up for Thursday."

Joyce looked at them and said, "I don't think you've got the right girl." Then she turned to Melanie and asked if she could come back on Thursday. Melanie was confused. To her, music publishers meant sheet music. Her mother had "stacks and stacks of sheet music and their covers always listed the publishers." Nevertheless, she agreed to return.

Though she had given up any thought of becoming a professional potter, Melanie continued to dabble in ceramics. She'd mold clay into circular or oval shapes that she'd paint, put sticks in the bottoms, bake in a kiln, and call "moonflowers." She would later make them of papier-mâché. Returning for her appointment with Hugo and Luigi, she brought Joyce a moonflower.

Entering suite 511, one could easily be deceived. Its institutional-green outer office contained gray filing cabinets and Joyce's desk. The inner office where the cousins worked, however, was a different story. Gilt lined everything, an extremely expensive decor with plush carpeting, ornate decorations, and matching Louis XIV desks. Hugo sat behind the desk on the left and Luigi behind the desk on the right. Sitting between them, Melanie felt as though she was in a museum. "Sing us something," requested the cousins. Melanie opted for original songs, thinking that was what they, as publishers, wanted to hear. She sang the soon-to-be-forgotten "There Should Have Been a Rainbow by Now" and a heart-breaker ("Momma Momma") that would appear on her debut album. One of her first compositions, she wrote it when she was fifteen. Addressed to her mother, the song gave a voice to "someone unable to fit in, someone constantly laughed at, made fun of, and made to feel out of place."

As Melanie sang, Hugo and Luigi eyed one another. They asked her about songwriting but barely gave her time to answer before Luigi interrupted and said, "We've just hired Peter Schekeryk to run our production company. He'll be coming in next week, come back and sing for him."

A week later, Melanie was ushered into Schekeryk's office. It had a window looking out onto the street and was barely large enough to squeeze in a singer and a piano. As soon as she started singing, she could sense her music moving him. Then, he abruptly got up and went into Hugo and Luigi's office. He was gone for what felt like an eternity. She was sure that he was telling them to forget about her. Instead, he had gone to see if they had signed her yet. "They said to Peter," Melanie recalled, "'she sounds like someone singing underwater . . . but maybe you have something you could do with her.'"⁵

When Peter returned, Melanie sang a few more songs. "I had the feeling that I was hearing something I had never heard before," Peter would tell *DISCoveries*. "Her sound was unique, and it just gave me chills. I knew I was onto something good. The aura in the room, everything felt right. Things like that come only once in a lifetime. I was lucky to be there. I was just the person who grabbed it."⁶

Scheduled to go to Atlantic City to record a band, Peter invited Melanie to join him. She agreed, giving no thought as to how she'd get home. She figured she'd be in New Jersey; she could always take a cab.

Sitting in the back seat of a chauffeur-driven car that she would recall as "more modest than a limousine," Melanie and Peter sang along with the radio and talked about music. When they arrived at their destination, Peter prepared to work with the band. He asked Melanie where she was planning to stay. By then, it was obvious that they were going to spend the night together. They booked a room in a hotel and that was it. They would be together for the next forty-four years and have two daughters, Leilah Schekeryk Hayman and Jeordie Schekeryk, a son, Beau Jarred Schekeryk, two granddaughters, Christiana and Analisa (or Analiese, as Melanie named her), and a grandson, Kingston. It would be a historic partnership.

CHAPTER 5
"DO YOU BELIEVE"

Peter Schekeryk was born on June 24, 1942, in Zhabie ("Highland Place"), a Ukrainian town along the Chorni Cheremosh River in the Carpathian Mountains. His mother listed February 23 on his birth certificate so he could qualify for milk rations longer during wartime.

Zhabie was alternately governed by Austria and Poland for many centuries. Absorbed into the Ukrainian States of the Soviet Republic after World War II, it was renamed Verkovyna in 1962. Along with thousands of Ukrainians, its populace endured great sorrow. Tortured and murdered by Stalin's Marxist-Leninist forces during "the Great Purge," they sustained severe famine in 1946 and 1947.

Peter's mother, Paraska (whom Melanie lovingly called Baba) was a dancer in a Ukrainian dance troupe and his father, Dmytro Schekeryk, was a singer and storyteller. Dmytro played the bandura, a plucked, triangular stringed instrument that produces a gentle harpsichord-like sound. He also played a wooden alpine horn (trimbita) so huge he had to place it on the ground when he played it.

Departing from Bremerhaven, Germany aboard the steamship General W. M. Black, in October 1949, seven-year-old Peter accompanied his parents when they came to the United States with the dance troupe. Their days in show business ended when members of the troupe took jobs constructing Long Island's planned community of Levittown and made the most money they had ever made. Settling in Philadelphia, Peter's mother returned to Ukraine to retrieve his older sister Katrina.

Peter's father lost his job maintaining Atlantic City's boardwalk when a storm destroyed most of the boardwalk. He tried a variety of other

41

jobs but contracted pneumonia and died at the age of forty-two. Peter believed his dad died of a broken heart.

Working in a Philadelphia shoe store by day, Peter haunted music clubs at night. Fascinated by the recording process, he apprenticed under songwriter, arranger, pianist, producer, and founder of Cameo Records, Bernard "Bernie Lowe" Lowenthal.

Producer/studio owner Bill Jerome was one of Peter's first connections in New York. "My brother [Steve] and I started recording in 1958 when I was fourteen," Jerome remembered from his South Florida condominium. "We bought a record cutter, a couple of mics, and an Apex mono tape recorder and advertised that we did wedding recordings at churches, synagogues, anywhere. We did a lot of business. We used the money to build a studio in Brooklyn. After we had a little luck with a local group (the Chance) in 1959, we moved to a larger location. We put a record shop in the front and a recording studio in the back. Peter came into the record store one day. I wasn't there. My brother called me later and told me that some lunatic had come into the store raving about how he could connect us with major labels. That's how we met Peter. He was a wild man, but we loved him."

Crossing into Manhattan, the Jerome brothers brought their production and engineering skills to violinist/producer/arranger Harry Lookofsky's World United Studio at 1595 Broadway. Peter "finagled his way" into a position as a talent scout and coproducer. One of his first projects was helping to form a garage rock band, the Magic Plants. After studio musicians backed him on their debut single, "I'm a Nothing" b/w "I Know She's Waiting There," lead singer/guitarist Michael "Mick" Wexler needed accompanists to tour. "Peter came to see my band in Greenwich Village," remembered bassist Tom Finn, who would play for the Magic Plants and later for the Left Banke. "He told us to come to the studio and see Harry."

Verve Records released the Magic Plants' next single, but it didn't chart, and the group broke up. The musicians Peter brought to the studio, however, hooked up with Lookofsky's fifteen-year-old son. "When we went to World United to audition for Harry," said Finn, "we met Michael (Brown). He was a nerdy kid working for his father, but he wanted to be like us. We were miles ahead of him; we had girlfriends. He really wanted to hang out with us. He made the studio available late at night when his father wasn't around, and we'd have an all-night party. We'd sing, play instruments, and beat drums. Michael would play piano. That's how the Left Banke formed. Michael wrote 'Walk Away Renee' about my girlfriend (he also wrote 'Pretty Ballerina' and 'She May Call You Up Tonight' about her). She was in the studio when we recorded it. He was so nervous, he left and recorded his part later."

Bill Jerome recalled another project. "The four of us—Harry, Peter, my brother, and I—produced a Four Seasons–like version of Bruce Chanel's 'Hey Baby.' Peter brought it to Bang Records (the label started in 1965 by ex–Atlantic Records staff producer Bert Berns with backing from Atlantic owners Ahmet and Nesuhi Ertegun and Jerry Wexler) but we didn't want to go with Bang Records. We wanted to go with a major label. We had just had a major hit with 'Walk Away Renee' and we were extremely hot. We could get it placed with RCA or Columbia. When Peter told us that he committed the master to Bang Records, we said 'Forget it, tell them that the deal is off.' When Peter came back, he wasn't in such good shape. We said, 'Okay, we don't want trouble. Let's go with Bang Records.'"

Peter's first success as a producer came in February 1968, when "A Question of Temperature," by a New Jersey–based psychedelic band, the Balloon Farm, broke into *Billboard*'s Top 40, peaking at number thirty-seven. On the single released by Laurie Records, the song's title was incorrectly listed as "A Question of Tempature" and Peter's name was misspelled "Shekeryk." Brownsville Station, the Lords of the Church, Mindflux, and Human Sexual Response would cover the song. The Balloon Farm's lead singer/guitarist Mike Appel would become Bruce Springsteen's first manager. A couple of years after the Balloon Farm sessions, Melanie and Peter were recording at 914 Studio, in Blauvelt, New York, about twenty minutes north of New York City. Springsteen and the E Street Band were working on demos of songs that would appear on their 1973 debut album, *Greetings from Asbury Park, N.J.* when they ran out of money. Peter provided free studio time. After Melanie finished for the night, Springsteen and the E Street Band took over. Peter had first seen the Boss when he fronted Steel Mill, which included future E Street Band members, and had come home raving about this incredible performer. He wanted to sign Springsteen to a management deal, but Melanie objected. She had met him previously in Long Branch and remembered him hanging out at an antique shop. She considered him "scroungy and not the kind of person [she] would want for a friend."

Peter almost worked with Billy Joel, as well. The piano player's first manager (Irving Mazur) came to see him in his office. He wasn't there but record producer Arthur Marcus "Artie" Ripp was. Ripp signed Joel to a production deal that stripped him of his songwriting royalties for the next ten years.

With Peter's endorsement, Melanie was offered a contract by Hugo & Luigi. The first line read, "Melanie Safka, herein referred to as artist." "It was the first time anybody ever called me an artist."[1]

Having to obtain her mother's signature on the contract, Melanie threatened to not talk to her mother if she didn't sign.

Polly signed and "[Hugo & Luigi] had me for everything— songwriting, singing, [and] going to the bathroom."[2]

Writing songs and singing demos, Melanie "hardly made enough money to pay for bus fare into New York," she remembered, "so to appease me . . . the bosses gave me an office, a writing room. I had a bathroom key. It was my big thing—to have a key to a ladies' room in New York City."[3]

Melanie's first songwriting credits came for writing both sides of a single—"Sad Song" b/w "Love in My Mind," produced by Peter. The single, released by United Artists, was credited to "Mommy." The group's actual name was Mother, but the label thought they'd get confused with Frank Zappa's Mothers of Invention and changed their name. Melanie sang background vocals and helped Peter produce the single, but she wasn't thrilled with the name Mommy; she liked Mother.

The single's arranger/conductor, John Abbott, previously arranged Dion's "Abraham, Martin, and John" and the Left Banke's "Walk Away Renee." "[Abbott] was able to do anything," remembered Tom Finn. "He could write for strings, rhythm sections, or vocals. He was incredible . . . somebody who always had plenty of ideas and contributed greatly to our sound. When it came to recording, he was in charge. He knew what all of the studio musicians and singers were supposed to be doing."

Peter wasn't given a huge budget to record his future wife. That didn't stop him. Scheduled to produce a record by the Marshmallows for CBS/Columbia, he switched their session and put Melanie in the studio instead. He loved taking those kinds of chances. Melanie didn't know anything about it until much later, but "Peter completely bamboozled the record company."

There was a full orchestra in the studio. Peter and Melanie met with Abbott before the session, and he prepared the arrangements. Melanie recorded "Beautiful People," and "Why Did Not My Mother Tell Me (All the Things I Should Have Known Today)." She liked "Beautiful People" but was unhappy about the other song. To her, it came off as pompous. She was uncomfortable molding a song to an arrangement as Peter forced her to do. It would be their first disagreement.

Abbott's string arrangement brought "Beautiful People" to life. Recorded in a single take, with Peter feverously conducting the musicians, and Melanie singing with a power that few white women ever achieve, it would become a hit single in the Netherlands, Germany, and the United Kingdom.

From the outset, Melanie defied categorization. "Melanie's songs are composites," said Paris-based *Folk and Blues*. "She uses in turn blues, traditional ballads, and children's songs. She has a beautiful mellow-sounding guitar, which she plays easily. Her voice and her enthusiasm could raise mountains on the condition that those who need it open their ears."[4]

"Her voice lurches, creaks, croaks, and very often slips out of key," added *New Musical Express*, "and, yet, there is an unquestioned magic in the drama, emotion, and pathos of her delivery—the voice of experience—yet the look of an innocent child."[5]

Melanie found Peter an enigma. She knew he was a producer who liked her music but little else. Hoping to get to know him better, she invited him for dinner with her and her mother. Peter took a bus to New Jersey. Arriving in Long Branch, he tried to hail a cab but was unsuccessful. Polly had to pick him up. When they got back to the house, they enjoyed a home-cooked lemon chicken dinner. Peter was extremely gracious.

Part 3

STARDOM (1967–1969)

CHAPTER 6
"BABE RAINBOW"

Hugo and Luigi were unsure of Melanie's potential, so Peter suggested a trade. In exchange for her contract, he offered the Marshmallows, who had a record climbing the charts. They agreed. Taking over Melanie's career, Peter secured a deal with CBS-owned Columbia Records, one of the oldest and most respected labels.

Columbia released Melanie's first single, on Christmas Day 1967, as "My Beautiful People," to differentiate it from a soon-to-be-forgotten pop tune by Kenny O'Dell. WNEW-FM's William "Rosko" Mercer was the first DJ to play it. Melanie was shopping for shoes in Greenwich Village when she heard the smoky-voiced announcer say, "Now, here's a new girl singer who's got something very important to say and I really think you should listen to her."

"I started shaking," Melanie remembered, "[and the salesman] looked up at me and said, 'What's the matter, honey, aren't these your size?'"[1]

At the time, CBS/Columbia was going through corporate turnover. Brooklyn born attorney Clive Davis had been offered the presidency of CBS's music instrument division (which included Fender), but he turned it down. Instead, CBS president Goddard Lieberson handed him the reins of CBS's record labels, including Columbia. Davis became the first attorney to run a record label. Aligned with Ahmet Ertegun, Mo Austin, Joe Smith, Irv Azoff, and *Rolling Stone* publisher Jan Wenner, he would rule over the music industry.

Summoned to Davis's office, Melanie thought she was going to get a chance to record an album. She quickly found out how wrong she was. The great John Hammond, who signed her to Columbia, had been supportive and easy to speak to, but Davis projected an entirely different vibe.

He let her ramble for a few minutes before holding his hand up and say-ing, "Ahem. . . . We just signed Michelle Lee."

"Uh . . . okay."

"And . . . Michelle Lee," Davis continued, "just got the Colgate commercial."

"That's nice," said Melanie, unsure of how to interpret what she was hearing. Then, Davis said, "And . . . you . . . uh, Melanie . . . what's your last name?"

Melanie got a red-hot feeling in her neck. Self-doubt ran through her head. What had she done wrong? Davis opened a drawer, took a Michelle Lee photograph out of his desk, held it up for her to see, and sneered, "She's recording an album. You have the presumption to assume we're going to do an album with you."

Melanie was mortified. She was about to release what would be a moderately successful single and she thought an album would be the next logical step. She began to question what she was doing in Davis's office without Peter. She expected encouragement but, instead, the label chief was communicating that it didn't matter how many songs she had, she wasn't singing in a toothpaste commercial. She started to cry, and Davis wasted no time chastising her for it. That was the breaking point. Leaping up, Melanie ran out of the office. When she told Peter what happened, he assured her, "It's all right. We've got a deal with Buddah Records."

"Peter came to see me at Capitol," recalled Artie Kornfeld, "but I wasn't in a position to sign Melanie. We had Linda Ronstadt, and that's where we were putting our money, but I said, 'Let me introduce you to Artie Ripp and get you a deal at Buddah.'"

Melanie would maintain possession of her songs when she signed with Buddah, but the label would own her recordings.

Buddah traced back to Ripp's MGM-distributed Kama Sutra label, which scored mid-'60s hits with the Critters, the Shangri-Las, and John Sebastian's Lovin' Spoonful. As a member of the Four Temptations, a decade earlier, he had sung on a couple of forgettable singles for ABC/Paramount. His forte, however, was production. An apprentice to George Goldner, producer/founder of Tico, Roulette, and Red Bird Records, in the late '50s and early '60s, he cut his teeth with Frankie Lymon & the Teenagers and Little Anthony & the Imperials. Stepping out as an independent producer, in 1964 he launched Kama Sutra with financial backing from Hy Mizrahi and Phil Steinberg. Accountant Art Kass came aboard shortly afterward. After three years of nonstop hits, they severed ties with MGM and launched Buddah Records in late 1967.

One of Buddah's first administrative recruits, Brooklyn-born Neil Bogart (Bogatz) had danced on Alan Freed's late-'50s TV show *The Big Beat*. Reinventing himself as pop singer Neil Scott, he scored a minor hit, in 1961, with "Bobby" (number 58). Business was more his calling. After a brief stint selling ads for *Cashbox*, Bogart became a promotion man/ general manager for MGM Records and then rose to vice president/sales manager/artist relations director for Cameo-Parkway. When Allen Klein acquired Cameo-Parkway in early 1967 (renaming it ABKCO), twenty-five-year-old Bogart led its promotion staff and Bob Reno, ex-head of Kama Sutra Publishing, to Buddah. He summed up his philosophy when he told an interviewer, "Hype—what a marvelous, misused word. If you hype something and it succeeds, you're a genius, it wasn't hype."[2]

"Neil was the biggest impresario type that ever hit the music business," claimed Fredric Dannen in *Hit Men, Power Brokers, and Fast Money Inside the Music Business*. "Spend, parties, promotion, fly jocks in, [and] hire twenty-five promotion men, whatever it took. He was a mover and shaker. There was nobody like Neil . . . the type that shoots for the moon and hits the stars."[3]

Bogart adored Melanie. He told her they had a spiritual connection—both being born on February 3—but she strongly disagreed with his style of promotion. He would say or do anything, including promoting her as a "flower child" with long hair and Bedouin wedding dresses. He spread word that she was a Jewish girl from Brooklyn. It ingrained her with record distributors; it was just what they wanted to hear. For years, a Jewish newspaper published an annual interview with her. Nobody asked if she was Jewish. Finally, one reporter inquired, "How did your Jewish upbringing affect your life?" and she admitted that she wasn't Jewish. The newspaper never interviewed her again.

Bogart's promotion went beyond standard practices. "Buddah paid off radio stations and deejays all over the eastern seaboard. Many of the guys working at Buddah Records were promo men who had an extensive network of contacts. They had wined and dined the radio jocks for years."[4]

Buddah's roster included the Edwin Hawkins Singers, Curtis Mayfield, the Isley Brothers, and Captain Beefheart, but its reputation was built on Don Kirshner's animated rock band, the Archies, and Jeff Katz and Jerry Kasenetz's bubblegum groups the Ohio Express, 1910 Fruit- gum Company, and the Lemon Pipers. "We are giving kids something to identify with," Bogart told *Time*, "clean, fresh, and happy."[5]

Melanie was unconcerned with the label's reputation. She believed that, if a company knew how to sell records, it didn't matter whose records it was selling. It was another miscalculation. "*Rolling Stone* waged war against Buddah Records," Melanie recalled, "[and] absolutely mas- sacred me."[6]

"[The underground press] threw mud at me," she continued, "and anything else they could do to say things about me that made me feel like I wanted to die. They would put me together with Bobby Sherman in the same article. It was insulting. It just wasn't the time to be who I was. Even though everybody thinks of me as the perfect Woodstock child, it just wasn't my time."[7]

Peter, Paul, and Mary's arranger/producer Milt Okun, and Lou Christie's manager Stan Polley proposed taking over Melanie's manage- ment, but they were insistent that she rehearse between-song patter. To her, that was appalling. Despite her theater background, she couldn't fathom reciting rehearsed lines and making them sound spontaneous. Her music was about baring her soul and communicating with people. The last thing that she was going to do was pretend. That school of entertainment left her completely cold.

Peter saw Melanie as a complete package onstage by herself. When it came to recording, however, he employed skilled session players to back her. "[In the studio], you don't have a living sound but a recorded sound," Melanie said, "and, as you know, there's quite a difference. Fun- nily enough, if I record in front of an audience, I don't feel like I've made a record because I don't do anything different—I just sing and play my songs."[8]

As a producer, Peter was into experimentation—employing everything from an orchestra to a Bulgarian choir—at a time when record companies gave artists carte blanche. He and Melanie spent a lot of time searching for unique musical instruments. Expense was no object. A string section might cost more than bass, drums, and guitar, but that didn't prohibit it. Peter was totally about the "feel" and there was nothing as important.

Melanie adored working with Roger Kellaway (1939–), the Waban, Massachusetts–born pianist and composer of "Remembering You," the closing theme of CBS-TV's *All in the Family*. A graduate of the New England Conservatory of Music, Kellaway was a former sideman for J. J. Johnson, Kai Winding, Oliver Nelson, Sonny Rollins, Sonny Stitt, Clark Terry, Ben Webster, and Jimmy Witherspoon. A seasoned bandleader, he had been Bobby Darin's music director for years. He would score a Best Instrumental Arrangement Grammy for the Eddie Daniel Band's *Memos from Paradise* in 1988.

Inspired by experimental composer John Cage, Kellaway stuck nuts, bolts, bubble gum, and pieces of paper between the strings of his piano, coaxing all kinds of interesting sounds from his keyboard. "[A piano] has a multitude of colors depending on how you prepare it," he explained. "You use a normal grand piano . . . and depending on where you put the nuts and bolts in the strings . . . you'll get a different overtone."[9]

Melanie wasn't trained musically in any way, shape, or form. Kellaway brought the musical expertise she lacked. "I got a phone call from Artie Ripp," he remembered,

about an artist he wanted me to arrange. She was into the Incredible String Band and really liked using instrumental colors, which was lovely for me. I could go in different directions in terms of the arrangements. She's always had great pipes with a lot of power and directness. She's one of the best singers of standards that I've ever heard. We would take ten minutes out during a session and do something like Gershwin's "Someone to Watch Over Me." I was amazed by her phrasing until she told me that she had grown up listening to her mother's Billie Holiday and Bessie Smith records. Many pop singers try to sing standards but she's one of the only ones who could really do it. We shared that passion, but Peter had no idea about that kind of music. He was very much a hands-in-the-dirt kind of person. He was in love with R&B. One track that he let us do, "Here I Am," showed that relationship with standards. I used string players and saxophonist Al Cohn.

Peter took a drawn-out approach to recording. "I know no other producer who would do this," said Kellaway, but I never thought of Peter as very musical. When I worked with Bobby Darin, I'd go up to his suite before we recorded. He'd tell me who was in the band and let me know that we would be recording in three weeks. We hardly had any rehearsals except for discussing keys. I would just go off by myself and write a "Bobby Darin" album. When we went into the studio, we would have a double session booked. He didn't want any overtime. We had to do six songs in three hours with a thirty-five-piece orchestra. We were moving. With Peter, it was a stretched-out process. We would record for a week with three guitars, keyboards, drums, and percussion. The following week, he and I would listen to all of these recordings, and he'd pick out the licks that he liked. Then, we would record again with the same musicians except now they were reading from charts. We did every album that way.

There was no concern about money, and nobody cared about expenses. I would have a session booked for two in the afternoon but sometimes they wouldn't be ready to record the orchestration until at least four in the morning. By ten o'clock, people would be falling asleep, but we'd keep going.

Orchestrating charts during the summer, Kellaway worked without air-conditioning. "Peter loved the string parts so much," he recalled, "he hired the Cadillacs to put their voices on the same notes. We did one track with three trap drummers. When we recorded *Madrugada*, Peter wanted to have a bassoon play a Slavic melody. I thought it was a great idea, so I recorded four bassoons. He put them on the track four times each. Another time, I used a twenty-four-piece orchestra. Peter put them on the track twice. I laughed when the critics called it over-produced."

Melanie typically recorded three songs per session. "I would prepare as I would for a stage performance," she said, "with more emphasis on my voice—vocal exercises, teas, and elixirs."[10]

Recording didn't take long but mixing, splicing, and editing did. Bruce Staple engineered the early sessions at Allegro Sound Studio in the basement of 1650 Broadway.

Peter hadn't yet started drinking alcohol (he preferred buttermilk) but, between his impulsive whims and ideas and Staple's altered consciousness, hours and hours would be spent splicing tape. Two-inch reel-to-reel tape covered the floor of the control room. Melanie occasionally came to the studio to help but she hated dissecting and putting things together.

Released in November 1968, *Born to Be* was reissued a year later as *My First Album*. "As a songwriter, [Melanie] is superb," said *Hi-Fi* in its review, "tackling with ease topics as diverse as prostitution ("Bo Bo's Party"), promiscuity ("I Really Loved Harold"), and commitment ("Close to It All" and "Animal Crackers"). She composes forceful, personal lyrics and houses them perfectly in simple, often hummable melodies. . . . Melanie is more of an actor than . . . a singer. She is in turn sorrowful, jaded, gaily ironic, and childishly appealing as she renders ten vignettes."[11]

"The voice is that of a young girl," suggested *Billboard*, "but the way [Melanie] conveys musical thought is that of one wise beyond her years."

"Her voice may not be anything fancy on a stick," said *Melody Maker*, "her guitar may indeed need tuning, but she has her own songs to sing—her own lifestyle to work out."[12]

"[Melanie] makes great play of the fact that she was born under Aquarius," said BBC-2's *Late Night Tune Up*, "the sign of many great inventors and writers. Aquarius, it seems, is the sign of the stars. It is also the sign of about 800,000,000 others who didn't make it. Melanie, however, shows every prospect of improving the ratio."[13]

Not all reviews were positive. The London-based *Evening Standard* derided Melanie for being "another of those super-intense, trill-voiced girls who sings as though she's crusading to put the world right."

The *Sunday Mirror* questioned whether Melanie was "as thousands of her followers swear, the new Pied Piper, whose vocal personality induces something approaching mass hypnosis, or is she, as a booing minority in the Paris Opera House recently proclaimed, a fake who is fooling even the intelligentsia?"[14]

"*Born to Be* was very self-conscious," Melanie told journalist Margie English. "I was told that I had a very unusual voice. I started listening to myself and I thought, 'Wow, it is pretty weird.' I figured that was what people liked about me, so I grabbed on to all those mannerisms—the quiver and the little kid voice—and hung onto them. I was terribly nervous in the recording sessions. I was terrified of the musicians. I was sure they'd think I wasn't anything and had a hell of a nerve taking up their time."[15]

The emotionally foreboding opening track, "In the Hour," set the stage for what was to come. It's not a happy song. Melanie didn't feel responsible for anyone else's happiness. She needed to communicate about the universe in which she lived, and songs were her medium for doing so.

Kurt Weill influenced "I'm Back in Town" with its oom-pah-pah rhythm, minor chords, discordance, and dark twist at the end. The first single released in the United Kingdom, it inspired the London-based *Daily Star* to proclaim Melanie "the next Streisand."

Peter repeatedly told Melanie that she had a European sensibility. He and Bogart arranged with French producer Eddie Barclay to release the album in France on Barclay Records. "Bo Bo's Party" was an obscure song in the United States, but Barclay released it as a single, with "Mr. Tambourine Man" on the B-side, and it shot to the top of the French pop charts. Its success inspired French vocalist and impresario Gilbert "Monsieur 10,000 Volts" Becaud, the "Frank Sinatra of France," to add Melanie to his annual revue at Paris's Olympia Palace.

Bernard DeBosson, director of Barclay's international department, arranged for Melanie to tour France, Belgium, and Holland. Artie Ripp promoted her in Paris at MIDEM (Marché International du Disque Et de L'edition Musicale), an annual international music exhibition, conference, and festival. "In one week," Rapp told the French-language *Journal of Show Business*, "you can see all the foreign representatives. . . . It allows me to introduce artists like Melanie into France."[16]

The album's next tune, "I Really Loved Harold." questioned morality. Melanie had gone to a high school where girls wore pleated skirts, crewneck sweaters, and knee socks. They didn't sleep with anyone unless they were married. The song was her reaction to that kind of life.

Remembering her grandmother telling her that "the children in Europe are starving, eat, eat, eat," Melanie proposed eradicating world hunger with "Animal Crackers." "We all get our little boxes of animal crackers," she said. "We name the animals and eat them in several ways. Decapitate a crunchy head or amputate them. Or soggy, eat them whole in your mouth soaked with milk, when we only knew milk was good for you and didn't find out till later, the dairy industry, with the blessings of the FDA, spent big-time promoting this in the age of science."[17]

The song included a nod to Alice's Restaurant for serving "animal cracker pizza" and a salute to its proprietor for knowing that "animal crackers are in this year." There's a line in the song, "Some people think that fatties are nice." Melanie had always felt overweight. The standard was "extremely thin British model Twiggy." Melanie was convinced she was "the wrong body type."

The words of "Christopher Robin (Is Saying His Prayers)" and "Alexander Beetle" were written by British author Alan Alexander "A. A." Milne (1882–1956). When she left for acting school, Melanie brought Milne's compendium, *The World of Christopher Robin: The Complete When We Were Young and Now We Are Six (Winnie the Pooh)* with her. As soon as she read "Christopher Robin (Is Saying His Prayers)" and "Alexander Beetle," she put music to Milne's words. Both songs were well sung out before she recorded them. It rarely occurred to anyone that they were children's songs. She didn't think of them that way; it was just the child in her. The Milne estate felt differently, sending a letter refusing permission to use Milne's words. Buddah removed "Christopher Robin" from the album's second printing but restored it to subsequent reissues. Nobody could do anything about it now; it's become a folk song.

Melanie loved the lyrics of Dylan's "Mr. Tambourine Man." "Jingle jangle" was the perfect description of an early morning. She felt obliged to sing it as soon she heard it. She played the "wrong" chords but made the song her own. Melanie's introduction to the Minstrel Boy had come via Joan Baez, who promoted him heavily at the start of his career. Melanie didn't consider Dylan much of a singer at first, thinking he sounded too much like Woody Guthrie.

Phil Ochs had a stronger influence, and Melanie covered two songs— "Outside of a Small Circle of Friends" and "Miranda"—from his *Pleasures of the Harbor* album. She met the Ohio-born protest singer at Kent State University during his rock and roll glitter phase in the early 1970s. She encountered him again on May 9, 1974, when he organized an Evening with Salvador Allende: Friends for Chile benefit concert in Madison Square Garden's Felt Forum. "Chile, of course, was a country in peril, one that badly needed friends after their democratically-elected president . . . was [assassinated] by the military (with an assist from our very good friends of the Central Intelligence Agency) in Santiago on September 11, 1973."[18]

The concert featured Dylan, Dave Van Ronk, Arlo Guthrie, Pete Seeger, and the Beach Boys' Dennis Wilson and Mike Love. When she came onto the stage, Melanie was so deep in thought she didn't notice Ochs, Dylan, and Van Ronk escorting her. She started singing, "Ring the Living Bell," and, all of a sudden, there were three people singing with her. They continued to harmonize as she followed with Pete Seeger's "My Rainbow Race."

Backstage, as Dylan berated Ochs for wearing an "ice-cream man's suit," the woman escorting him went around pickpocketing people. "I was so angry at everybody," recalled Ochs's sister, Sonny. "Melanie brought her pet ferret, and her daughter was running around with it backstage."

Melanie's longtime photographer, Maddy Miller, thought it crazy. It seemed like everyone, but Pete Seeger and Melanie, was drunk and stoned.

Melanie was surprised that Ochs (who would commit suicide two years later) surrounded himself with militant and political people, not musicians or artists. She felt bad for him, especially after hearing him tell a group of people, "I'm just a singer, what effect do I have? I could be doing better things."

The pinnacle of *Born to Be* came with "Close to It All," the opening song of Melanie's Woodstock set. Doo-wopper-turned-bluesman Dion would cover it in 1971. Forty-one years later, it would provide a rousing finale for the musical adaptation of Melanie's journal, *Melanie and the Record Man*. Melanie was feeling in tune with nature when she wrote the song. She had decided that she and Peter would go camping. Peter had grown up on city sidewalks and definitely wasn't a camper, but he willingly consented to his wife's desire. Melanie borrowed a tent from Uncle George. He tried to show her how to put it up, but when she and Peter arrived at the campground, they couldn't figure out how to do it. Fortunately, other campers came to their rescue. It turned into a communal experience. It was starting to rain, and they had to get the tent up fast. During the night, Melanie heard sounds she had never heard before and had a hard time falling asleep. When she woke in the morning, she stayed in her sleeping bag watching spiders walking across the ceiling of the tent. She had always assumed that, because her mother was afraid of bugs, she would be too. But, gazing at the spiders, she realized that she wasn't frightened. Spiders were just little creatures. It made her feel close to it all. She loved being in the woods so much she proposed camping every other week or, at least, once a month. She thought it would keep them grounded—they would never go camping again.

Born to Be concluded with a freshly composed holiday treat, "Merry Christmas." Melanie would rerecord it for her Christmas album, *Antlers*, in 1997. "We lived on the top floor," she recalled of her childhood, "and someone would go up with jingle bells or make prancing noises on the roof and I would think it was the reindeer. I was told to go to bed or Santa wouldn't come."[19]

CHAPTER 7
"I TRIED TO DIE YOUNG"

Peter and Melanie officially tied the knot before going to Paris. They had been living together for a year, but Peter worried that they would have difficulty sharing a room unless they were legally married. A few days before New Year's Eve 1968, a limousine brought them to a justice of the peace in Yonkers, New York. They had already taken blood tests and completed the necessary paperwork. They celebrated afterward with pizza.

Opposed to the legal rigmarole of marriage, Melanie had no desire to become a wife. She came from a broken household, and she hated the government's intrusion into people's lives. She knew she could get a divorce if it didn't work out, but it was quite a concession. The wedding day was somber. Melanie wore a beautiful black suit that she bought in England. It buttoned down the front of the blouse and came with a skirt. She felt pretty in it, but it was black.

Peter was still married to his first wife, Marian, when he met Melanie. Their son, Peter Jr., was born in 1963. It was obvious, however, that the marriage was over. Peter would stay at his mother's house or in the basement of the Safka home. He never brought up his marriage and Melanie let it pass. "Peter took the first royalty check that Melanie got," claimed Uncle George, "went to Mexico, and got divorced."

Melanie and Peter announced their nuptials during a New Year's party, in Cousin Brucie's Manhattan loft, broadcast by WABC-AM. "[The station] received hundreds of phone calls of congratulations," remembered Morrow from his home in New York's Hudson Valley. "I couldn't repeat too many of them. It would have taken up the whole show. People reacted very favorably and very quickly."

Sometime in the mid-1980s, Morrow and his wife, Jodie, ran into Melanie and Peter in a Morristown, New Jersey restaurant. "They just happened to come in," recalled the legendary DJ. "We invited them to our place the following evening. Melanie brought her guitar. I loved her serenading me. She has such a powerful voice. She could hold her own with anybody."

The Morrows' new home had "a large, cavernous living room with a high ceiling that was perfect for acoustics. Melanie took out her guitar and started singing. My cat got so scared she screamed and ran out of the room. We couldn't find her for a day."

On September 5, 2020, then-eighty-five-year-old Morrow returned to WABC with *Cousin Brucie's Saturday Night Rock & Roll Party*. He continued to advocate for Melanie's music. "I've never stopped playing her records," he said. "I talk about seeing her at Woodstock with the candles in the rain and about her [being] one of the original folk-rock singers. I credit her for bringing that kind of music to the forefront."

Peter and Melanie considered New Year's Eve as their wedding anniversary but, once they had kids, their anniversary got lost in the shuffle.

Melanie never adopted the Schekeryk surname. "I'm not ashamed of it," she told *Biography*, "but very few know how to pronounce it. When I began to sing, I used my maiden name [Safka]. For some unknown reason, when my first album came out, it only carried my first name . . . and that's the way it has been ever since."[1]

Excited to be going to Paris, Melanie grew frustrated once the plane landed. She had studied the language in high school, but she didn't know any conversational French and had a hard time communicating. She'd go into a shop, ask for something, and storekeepers would stare at her as if she came from another planet. They had no idea what she was saying.

A more welcoming reception waited at the 1,772-seat Olympia Palace. Audiences embraced Melanie wholeheartedly. Listening intently to her songs, they applauded enthusiastically when she was done. "Melanie represents a special trend in modern American folk music," proclaimed the *Journal of Show Business*. "Influenced (whether voluntary or not) by Bob Dylan, she belongs to the post-Dylan group, of which she is in the process of becoming one of the best members. Her voice is mellower than that of Joan Baez, and above all more natural and firm, and it allows her to get the most from her interpretation of songs. She composes songs of a remarkable quality."[2]

The Olympia Palace revue included dancers, fire-eaters, Arabian acrobats, and the New York City Ballet, a burlesque troupe comprised of "women who had never been to New York City and certainly weren't doing ballet." Melanie shared a dressing room with twelve camels belonging to the Arabian acrobats. She would joke that her dresses still had the faint smell of camel urine.

Second on the bill, Melanie performed a sixteen-minute set between Algerian jugglers and an illusionist from Lyon, France. Smooth-voiced Parisian crooner Julien Clerc was also in the revue. His recording of "La Cavalerie," with lyrics by Etienne Roda-Gil, would top the French pop charts in May 1968, and become an anthem of the French student rebellion.

Olympia Palace owner/manager Bruno Coquatrix attended the first rehearsal. He had presented every important artist in France, including Édith Piaf. It was quite intimidating. A Piaf enthusiast since high school, Melanie read several books about her. Coquatrix's name appeared in them, so she knew who he was. She began to sing "Beautiful People" but only made it halfway through before Coquatrix ran onto the stage waving his hands and shouting "No, no, no, no!" Gilbert Becaud ran over quickly. He and Coquatrix said something to each other in French. Then, he turned to Melanie and, with his hands flailing, warned that the audience would never stand for anyone standing on stage with their guitar; they were going to hate her. They had to do something quick. Coquatrix devised a new entry for the young songstress. Where Melanie had originally walked onto the stage, holding her guitar, slumped down into a straight-backed chair, and started to sing, she would now start at the top of an elaborate staircase with the New York City Ballet lining both sides and slowly walk to the bottom, where the last girl on her left would hand her a guitar. Glitzy orchestrated music would be playing but it would suddenly get silent. Melanie would take her guitar, walk to a chair, sit down, and play. It didn't blend in with the rest of the show, however, and she ended up coming out in silence alone. The simplicity was such a jolt it worked. Becaud told Melanie she had something that reached into people's souls.

On opening night, Melanie was terrified. Becaud came into her dressing room and gave her a pep talk. Coming inches from her face, he told her to "take the audience and fuck them."

Melanie did what she had always done, pouring her heart into her performance. The audience responded with a standing ovation. *Variety* described her as "a teenage Yank folk and protest singer with a neat beat, a big and penetrating dramatic voice, and professional presence that keep her potent songs piercing, taking, and revealing. Whether lamenting man's wartime inhumanities, family misunderstandings, or youthful hang-ups, she has a vibration and poise that clicks even with the lingo barrier."[3]

European DJs had the freedom to play anything they wanted. It could be a folk song or a schmaltzy pop tune. They'd follow a record by a jazz quartet, pop singer, or the Beatles with Joan Baez, Judy Collins, or Melanie. Alan Freed, the "godfather" of rock and roll radio, used to gear his show and concert revues for teenagers in the 1950s, but AM radio had eased into market-dominated, lowest-common-denominator programming. "There was a hungry audience looking for something else," remembered Morrow. "They wanted to break away from their parents and the old guard. . . . The audience became very sophisticated. They demanded more from radio."

Peter and Melanie remained in Paris for six months. Returning to New York, they met with Bogart, who had wild plans. Proposing that they stage a wedding in Central Park, he described a headline-grabbing gala with a "hippie" theme. Pop artist Peter Max would be commissioned to design the stage and beautiful women would bounce on pastel-colored balloons. Melanie looked at Bogart in horror. Paying her no mind, he continued to rave about how wonderful this extravaganza was going to be. Hundreds of thousands of people would be coming with love beads around their necks and flowers in their hair. Finally, Melanie interrupted, "No! I can't do that!" The office became silent. Bogart remained motionless for a moment and then said, "What! What do you mean?"

"It doesn't feel real," replied Melanie.

Everyone turned in her direction. It was inconceivable that their artist was turning down this opportunity for mega-publicity. Peter tried convincing her to change her mind, but it was no use. Peter apologized but Melanie's decision was firm. Buddah was promoting her as the ultimate flower child, and she was going along with that, but she refused to turn her marriage into a public spectacle. After all, she had worn black to her wedding.

In a July 1969 profile of women songwriters that included Joni Mitchell and Laura Nyro, *Newsweek*'s Hubert Saal claimed that Melanie "usually carries the throbbing, plaintive courage of Lotte Lenye and the bittersweet sound . . . is reminiscent of Kurt Weill."[4]

Admitting that she preferred public transportation, Melanie told Saal that "the bus is the most public contact I have, and I love it. . . . I feel responsible for the people riding next to me on the bus. If everyone felt responsible and wanted to be nice, it could even stop wars—don't you think?"[5]

Former Hugo & Luigi employee Michael Hugo arranged for Melanie to participate in the Stanley Kramer–produced film *R.P.M.* (revolutions per minute). She wrote two songs ("Stop! I Don't Wanna Hear It Anymore" and "We Don't Know Where We're Going") with Perry Botkin Jr. and Barry DeVorzon. The former had arranged songs for Bobby Darin, Harry Nilsson, the Lettermen, Ed Ames, and Harpers Bizarre. His father played guitar for Hoagy Carmichael, Glenn Miller, Benny Goodman, Bob Hope, Fred Astaire, Spike Jones, and the Dorsey Brothers and served as Bing Crosby's music director. A New York–born songwriter, and founder of Valiant Records, DeVorzon penned a number-one country hit ("Just Married") for Marty Robbins in 1958 and a pop chart-topper ("Dreamin'") for rockabilly pioneer Johnny Burnett two years later. Botkin Jr. and DeVorzon would continue to supply songs for Kramer's films.

Erich Segal, who would author *Love Story*, wrote the script. Anthony Quinn portrayed a liberal college professor. Ann-Margret played his graduate student mistress. "[*R.P.M.* is] a woefully inept 1960's student rad pic," railed movie critic Dennis Schwartz. "[It] even makes *The Strawberry Statement* seem hip."[6]

"It's a horrible film," Melanie complained, "not properly acted. The people who play the college students are a bunch of brats."[7]

Melanie did her best to disconnect from *R.P.M.* She was slated to appear on BBC-TV's *Top of the Pops*, but producers canceled her appearance when she refused to sing "Stop! I Don't Wanna Hear It Anymore." "It's an insane song," she told Symes, "and I hate it . . . and I hate the movie it came from."[8]

Slightly more satisfaction was derived from writing the complete score and singing in a British film, *All the Right Noises*, coproduced by Si Litvinoff, a high-level entertainment attorney whose clients included artists (Andy Warhol), writers (Terry Southern), and actors (Joel Grey, Beatrice Arthur, Rip Torn, and Orson Bean). Written and directed by Gerry O'Hara, the movie told the heartbreaking tale of an ill-fated affair between a married stage/film electrician (British actor Tom Bell) and a fifteen-year-old West End chorus girl (Buenos Aires–born Olivia Hussey, fresh from wowing the world in Franco Zeffirelli's Academy Award– winning *Romeo and Juliet*). *Laugh-In*'s "Sock it to me" girl, Judy Carne, played the electrician's wife.

The placement of her songs in the film startled Melanie. "Just as . . . Carne takes off her clothes and gets into bed with Tom Bell," she told *Melody Maker*, "my voice comes over with a poignant song in the middle of their lovemaking."[9]

Recording the soundtrack with the London Symphony Orchestra (with the Rolling Stones in the adjacent studio), Melanie and Peter had a lot of control over the music. Melanie loved being behind the scenes and fantasized about becoming strictly a writer rather than a performer ridiculed by magazines like *Rolling Stone*. Perhaps, people would leave her alone.

"BEAUTIFUL PEOPLE"

There have been annual reunions of the Woodstock Festival since 1969. Organized or not, people congregate at the historic site each year between August 15 and August 17. Some years have been especially memorable. On the eighteenth anniversary, in 1987, Melanie performed in front of a five-and-a-half-ton monument at the southeast corner of Hurd and West Shore Roads in Bethel. "As a crowd of several dozen Woodstockers sat or stood nearby," the Middletown *Times-Herald Record* reported, "[Melanie] played her old favorites on an acoustic guitar. . . . She may be one of the only original Woodstock musicians to make it to the site this year. Peter Schekeryk, her husband and manager, beamed as his wife played, 'Look how much fun they're having,' he said. 'You can't buy that. We didn't want to miss it. We wanted to be here—we're here every year.'"[1]

Nineteen eighty-nine was Woodstock's twentieth anniversary. Melanie participated in a reunion tour with Richie Havens, John Sebastian, Country Joe McDonald, Ten Years After, Blood, Sweat & Tears, Sha Na Na, and Canned Heat. The "official" anniversary show in Silver Lake, New York, with Timothy Leary emceeing, also featured non-Woodstock acts including Leon Russell & Edgar Winter and the Chambers Brothers. Jim Katz filmed it as *20 Years After: A Woodstock Reunion*. Prohibited from holding it on the original field, they set up a stage at a hotel.

Meanwhile, Melanie got word that more than forty thousand people were gathering at Yasgur's farm two hours away. "I started playing at 5:07," said Rich Pell, the singer-songwriter who secured permission from Charles and June Gelish, then-owners of the property, to stage the celebration, "the same time Richie Havens started at the original festival."

Pell ran the weekend like an open mic. "Anyone who wanted to play," he said, "could sign up. There were no auditions. It wasn't an elitist show. The best acts were the unpolished ones. It didn't matter. The spirit was great."

When the promoter of the official reunion heard that this ragtag festival was going on, he warned musicians he had hired that he wouldn't pay anyone who went to this clandestine show. Melanie went anyway. Jimi Hendrix's father, James "Al" Hendrix, introduced her. Standing on a makeshift stage, singing one song after another, she "felt like Santa Claus."

The reunion promoter ended up reneging on most of his contracts. Performers went unpaid whether they heeded his edict or not. Melanie certainly wasn't paid. She had gone to the original site and played. She assured herself that it had been well worth it.

Woodstock's twenty-fifth anniversary in August 1994 was again marred by competing reunions. Sid Bernstein planned to hold an event on the original site but Woodstock Ventures, producers of the 1969 festival, filed an $80,000,000 lawsuit for various claims including trademark infringement. They planned to stage their own "Summer of Love" festival in Saugerties, New York. Reaching a compromise, Bernstein agreed to omit the word "Woodstock" from his festival. Bethel refused to issue permits, however, and he canceled his event. Twelve thousand people showed up anyway. Issuing an official "Declaration of Civility and Kindness to Promote Bethel '94," Richie Havens and Melanie went to play.

Returning to the former Yasgur Farm three years later, Melanie again defied opposition. "They dug a six-foot trench around the field," she told the *Boston Herald*. "They had tow-trucks there to haul away parked cars and they had armed guards but I . . . snuck in anyway. I sang to the people . . . paid to keep people like me out. They didn't know what to do with me."[2]

On Woodstock's twenty-ninth anniversary, a year later, the farm staged a three-day festival, A Day in the Garden, produced by Alan Gerry, the billionaire founder of Cablevision. Gerry purchased the thirty-seven-acre hillside and surrounding acreage a year before, envisioning a "permanent international attraction." Pavilion Amphitheater at Bethel Woods presented its first concert on July 4, 2006. A Woodstock museum followed two years later. A Day in the Garden included performances by Ziggy Marley, Don Henley, Stevie Nicks, and Lou Reed. Ten Years After, Richie Havens, Pete Townshend, David Crosby, Johnny Winter, Arlo Guthrie, and The Band's Rick Danko and Garth Hudson represented the 1969 festival.

Melanie opened the festival's second day. "There was lots of singing along with Melanie and her son and daughters," reported festival attendee Fredrik King, "Quite a few of the younger people, as well as us supposedly more dignified older folks, were standing and dancing."[3]

"The long hair was flowing," added the *Orange County Times Herald-Record*. "[Melanie's] tent dress was billowing. Her strong voice was working."[4]

As usual, not everything went well. Melanie learned that she wasn't going to receive the agreed-upon compensation. Pete Townshend came into her dressing room, and they talked about it. The Associated Press reported, "Townshend and Joni Mitchell were paid six figures to play the Woodstock event; Melanie performed for free."[5]

CHAPTER 9
"CLOSE TO IT ALL"

here was great anticipation for the festival at the Powder Ridge Ski Area, in Middlefield, Connecticut, scheduled for Friday, July 31, to Sunday, August 2, 1970. A half-page ad on the back cover of *Rolling Stone* promised a lineup rivaling Woodstock's. A last-minute injunction, however, resulted in its cancellation. "The promoters did not meet the specifications in the town ordinance," reported the *Record-Journal.*[1]

Melanie was in an apartment owned by her mother, in Long Branch, with Peter and Maddy Miller, when she heard a radio announcement about the cancellation. She wanted to go anyway; people were there. The *New York Times* reported more than thirty thousand.

At the time, America was going through a period of great tension. Anyone in a uniform hated anyone with long hair, and vice versa. A concertgoer was murdered during the Rolling Stones' free Altamont show less than half a year after Woodstock and four students were shot by the National Guard during an anti-war demonstration at Kent State University five months after that. Melanie felt that she was taking her life in her hands by going to Powder Ridge. Everybody on the field felt that they were taking their lives in their hands. Who knew if they were going to send in the National Guard or not?

Arriving at Powder Ridge, Melanie went to the ski lodge, where a press conference was going on. Reporters were asking such goofy questions she had to get away. Connecting with radio station WINS-AM's news team, she put her guitar in the trunk of their car and crouched down in the back seat. Police threatened to arrest anyone defying the injunction. As soon as the car drove onto the field, Bill Hanley's sound crew hooked a public address system to a generator from a Mister Softee truck. After a few tunes, Melanie made her getaway with the same news team. Police arrested Hanley and Powder Ridge owners Louis and Herman Zemel for violating the injunction.

A couple of days later (August 5), Melanie appeared on the summer replacement ABC-TV show, *Johnny Cash Presents the Everly Brothers*. She sang "Lay Down (Candles in the Rain)" on a stage filled with helium balloons, and "Ruby Tuesday" in a two-seat, vintage airplane with Don Everly. During the show's finale, Melanie joined Tina Turner, teen idol Bobby Sherman, and the Everly Brothers for the civil rights anthem "This Little Light of Mine." Turner gave Melanie her tambourine.

Combining gospel music and rock felt natural. Most people labeled her a folk singer because of her acoustic guitar, flowing hair, and Bedouin dresses, but Melanie never considered herself a folkie. She knew that what she was doing wasn't rock and roll, but she also knew it wasn't folk music. She told people that she played songs and Peter would interject, "It's Melanie's music."

John Bower's Strawberry Fields Festival took place at Mosport Park Raceway, in Bowmanville, Ontario (about seventy miles east of Toronto), from Friday, August 7, to Sunday, August 10, 1970. Bower's Rock and Roll Festival, the previous September, included a once-in-a-lifetime performance by the Plastic Ono Band (John Lennon, Yoko Ono, Eric Clapton, Klaus Voorman, and Alan White). Attempting to circumvent growing opposition to a mass musical gathering, Bower billed his 1970 event as "The First Annual Strawberry Cup Trophy (Motorcycle) Race." Promising some contemporary entertainment, he quietly assembled a star-studded lineup that included Procol Harum, Jose Feliciano, Alice Cooper, and Sly & the Family Stone, along with Melanie. Led Zeppelin and Leonard Cohen failed to show. Arthur Wishart of Ontario's legislative assembly applied for an injunction to stop the festival. The Supreme Court denied Wishart's claim and the festival went on, though thousands from the United States were turned back at the border for having less than forty dollars. For Melanie, it was another horrible experience. It rained torrentially, there was mud everywhere, but she inexplicably dressed in white.

The Isle of Wight Festival (August 26–31, 1970) on the 160-square-mile island off the coast of Hampshire, England, was first held in 1968, when Jefferson Airplane was its only major act. The festival came into its own the following year, when Dylan (making his first appearance since his motorcycle accident a year and a half before) performed with the Band. By 1970, the word had spread. An estimated six hundred thousand people gathered, surpassing the number at Woodstock.

Melanie arrived on a four-seat plane at 5:00 a.m. on Friday. Scheduled to sing that night, she wouldn't perform until two days later. The plane wouldn't start. The pilot had to get out and spin the propeller by hand. Melanie and Maddy Miller thought they were going to be killed.

The weather was bitterly cold and festival attendees tried keeping warm by huddling around coal fires. Melanie choked on the fumes. Scottish folk-rocker Donovan lent her his caravan, complete with a wood-burning stove, and she waited it out. It was a very long wait.

On Sunday night, Melanie received word that she would be going on after the Who. The promoters wanted the Doors to do it, but Jim Morrison refused.

Earlier that day, Melanie was alone in Donovan's caravan when the door burst open. The Who's drummer, Keith Moon, and British comic Murray Roman stormed in and launched into a hilarious routine. Melanie didn't recognize them, but they cheered her up immensely. Moon volunteered to introduce her.

Melanie had no idea that the Who planned to perform its rock opera *Tommy* for the first time in Europe. No wonder nobody wanted to follow them. It was a massive production. By the time that they got all of their equipment off the stage, it was the crack of dawn. "It was so late," Melanie recalled, "that even the guy who was filming me was keeling over with sleep in his eyes."

As she walked onto the stage, Moon handed Melanie one of his drumsticks. It was only then that she realized who he was. "I nearly died when I found out," she said, "but I didn't let on to the fact that I hadn't recognized him. . . . He really extended his warmth to me, knowing that I'd had such a hard weekend."[2]

Melanie understood the obstacles she faced. "There was a friendly atmosphere," she recalled, "but [the audience] was finished. They had just seen *Tommy*—Roger Daltrey, Pete Townshend, John Entwistle, and

Keith Moon in [their] prime. Here I was with just my guitar and my voice."[3]

Despite the late hour, Melanie won the crowd over. "I started to sing," she said. "The dawn was coming, and the sun was rising. Little by little, I see heads popping up. I woke everybody up. I played one of my best concerts."[4]

The crowd responded with four standing ovations. It was a very powerful experience. Melanie sang "Mr. Tambourine Man" as the sun was coming up.

The Isle of Wight Festival would mark the final festival appearance by Hendrix. He and Melanie flew back to the United States on the same plane, a nine-hour flight. At first, she didn't say a word. A group of intoxicated men began harassing the left-handed guitarist and making snide remarks. She was ready to defend him, but Hendrix settled her down and told her not to worry. They started to talk. Hendrix was extremely cool, but Melanie's shyness prevented her from saying much beyond a few things here and there. She explained how she had started out by singing Appalachian folk music and he told her that that kind of music also inspired him. She could hear it in the chord progressions he played. When they got off the plane, they walked together to the terminal. The guitarist warned her against going through customs with him. Sure enough, customs agents kept him long after she had gone.

Melanie sometimes found customs a hassle. On a flight to England, she brought a container filled with nuts and dried fruit to eat. A security guard found the container and asked her what it was. She tried to explain but a second security guard sneered, "Don't you know? That's what 'they' eat."

There would be no Isle of Wight festivals for the next thirty-three years. Shortly after the 1970 festival, Parliament prohibited the gathering of more than five thousand people without a special license. Returning for the June 2002 resurrection, Melanie was backed by the Medina High Community Choir under the direction of Hannah Brear (in her eighth month of pregnancy), and the Medina High School Choir under Richard Williams.

Nothing like the last Isle of Wight Festival, the 2002 revival "was more like a big carnival," said Melanie. "They had a Ferris wheel and amusement rides. All of the acts arrived with a great flourish; P!nk came flying out of a cannon."

Melanie wanted to say hello to Paul McCartney, but security was incredibly tight. There was no mingling between performers. Artists were shuttled back and forth from the stage to the dressing rooms in golf carts. Melanie was disappointed when promoters put her on during the day; she preferred the dark.

Melanie found Glastonbury Fayre, on Worthy Farm, near Pilton, Somerset, England (Thursday, June 20–Sunday, June 24, 1971), incredibly magical. Nicolas Roeg and Peter Neil filmed the five-day event and released a documentary film. Melanie performed along with David Bowie, Traffic, and Fairport Convention. Celebrating the summer solstice, it took place close to Stonehenge and there were many Wiccans and wizards among attendees. Melanie hung out at a farmhouse during the day and performed at night. She felt like she was singing to "more than the people who were there," like she was singing for "people who had passed on and people yet to come." She found the Fayre's fortieth anniversary, in 2011, much different. There were six stages, and, like the Isle of Wight Festival, it had become "much more of a carnival." It rained for days and days. Melanie was ankle-deep in mud and not having fun.

Garden Party III at the two-hundred-acre Crystal Garden Park, in a southeastern suburb of London, was the setting for Harry Goldsmith's twice-annual concert series. Melanie appeared at the June 3, 1972, concert, the first show of the second season. NBC filmed the nine-hour concert and broadcast an edited sampling in the United States titled *Good Vibrations '72 from London*. It was one of the first stereo simulcast TV shows. Viewers watched it on TV while listening to FM stations. Melanie sang "Beautiful People," "Someday I'll be a Farmer," and "Ring the Living Bell." It threatened to thunderstorm all day. Melanie was in the middle of "Look What They've Done to My Song, Ma" when power to the stage was cut off as a precaution. Unfazed, Melanie sang "Bitter Bad," "Peace Will Come," "Psychotherapy," and "Together Alone" without electricity. Her voice was so powerful she had no problem. "I really wish it had been a nice day," she told *New Musical Express*. "It would have been really pretty. I didn't like being that far away from people . . . and with all the umbrellas, there was really a surrealistic look. . . . All the people looked like they were at the funeral, and I was being buried or drowned."[5]

Returning to Glastonbury in June 1983, Melanie headlined a three-day festival organized by the British Campaign for Nuclear Disarmament. It was a very tense time. The proximity of nuclear weapons unnerved Europeans and they were expressing their dislike for it. Melanie wanted to play music, not be political. "I never liked preaching," she said. "There are so many agendas going on, and people have to be really naive to believe that we can only be represented by two parties. It's ludicrous. It's a trick with mirrors. It's a diversionary tactic to keep people believing that one side is for the good and the other side is for the bad, that one is for the rich, and that one is for the poor. I've always been very suspicious of politics."[6]

Melanie performed at numerous "protest" festivals—they were happening everywhere but the United States—but, to her, Woodstock was about peace, not protesting. "I worry about music being manipulated to suit somebody's political goals," she told the *St. Petersburg Times*. "My heart would be into an anti-war demonstration, then, I would find that the organization I was supporting couldn't care less about ending the war. They had another agenda, and the anti-war thing was just a way of attracting attention."[7]

Melanie's only August 1989 appearance came at the Sidmouth Folk Festival. "There's much more humanitarian spirit in festivals like Sidmouth," she said. "They're not as hyped up, as promoted, or as corporate. People are pulled in by their love of music and, in England, people listen more. . . . You know people are getting everything."[8]

Traveling to England was another horrifying experience. The flight from the United States was delayed and Melanie had to wait for hours before departing. Arriving in England, amid scorching summer heat, she stayed at a hotel without air-conditioning. Sweating profusely, Melanie was unable to sleep. "Seagulls made unbelievably unearthly noises right outside my window," she told *Express and Echo Exeter*. "At 3 a.m., these seagulls [were] having some kind of celebration or pagan ritual and it [sounded] like the suffering of all humanity for all eternity. I have never heard noise like it."[9]

On August 13, 1989—two days shy of Woodstock's twentieth anniversary—Melanie headlined the International Music Peace Festival in Moscow's hundred-thousand-seat Lenin Stadium. It was her first trip to Russia. Peter didn't come. He had a green card, but he wasn't a citizen of the United States, and he feared not being able to return.

It was a critical time. Communist Party General Secretary Mikhail Gorbachev's policy reform was leading to a period of "perestroika" that would restructure the Soviet political and economic system and factor in the dissolution of the USSR two years later. Young people behind the Iron Curtain were becoming part of the whole world. It was a very jubilant occasion. Bon Jovi, Ozzy Osbourne, Mötley Crüe, and the Scorpions performed, but most of the music was Italian-style punk rock. Melanie felt out of her element.

Stas Namin, leader of the Soviet rock band Gorky Park, and a promoter of large-scale concerts, arranged for her appearance. He and Peter were friends, but Melanie considered him "a real elitist." Namin's grandfather, Anastas Mikoyan, was a former president of the Soviet Union.

Attendance surpassed the stadium's official capacity, and the mood was intense. Melanie started singing "Peace Will Come (According to Plan)" but it was the wrong choice. The crowd showed their disapproval immediately. She transitioned to "Beautiful People," thinking it would be meaningful, but people weren't looking for meaning. They were looking for ROCK AND ROLL!!!!

Fearing that the crowd would kick her off the stage, Melanie lay her guitar aside and got down on all fours. Pounding a beat on the stage with her fists, she started chanting, "All we are saying is give peace a chance." Namin and his band joined, and the chant spread through the arena. It was electrifying and it won the crowd over.

Jarvis Cocker, a national treasure in the United Kingdom, spearheaded the Britpop movement as frontman of the alt-rock band Pulp in the '80s and '90s. Host of *Jarvis Cocker's Sunday Service* on BBC Radio 6, he composed soundtracks for Harry Potter films. Nancy Sinatra and Marianne Faithfull covered his songs. In April 2007, the Sheffield-born singer-songwriter served as celebrity host of the fourteenth Meltdown Festival in Southbank Centre, London's twenty-one-acre arts complex. Like previous Meltdown hosts Elvis Costello, David Bowie, and Patti Smith, he chose that year's performers and visual artists. He assembled an eclectic lineup that not only included Melanie but also Devo (their first European tour in seventeen years), the Jesus & Mary Chain (reuniting after eight years), Iggy and the Stooges, and Motörhead. The legendary founder of the 13th Floor Elevators and originator of the term "psychedelic rock," Roger Kynard "Roky" Erickson, made his long-overdue debut UK appearance. "It's not just who you book," Cocker explained. "It's how you're going to combine things . . . that you wouldn't necessarily think go together."[10]

A DVD of Melanie's Meltdown performance, *Melanie: For One Night Only* was released in September 2007. Her show in the nine-hundred-seat Queen Elizabeth Hall, where Marc Bolan and T-Rex once opened for her, sold out. This time, her opening act was British visual artist and idiosyncratic singer-songwriter Mathew Sawyer and the Ghosts. "[Melanie] ambled on looking greyer and wider than she used to," observed one attendee, "but that big voice hadn't changed. Dressed like a Sun Ra refugee and accompanied by her genius guitarist son Beau, she gave us a two-hour mix of old and new material, interspersed with chat that got more rambling and bizarre as the night went on."[11]

The dressing room had a couch, a couple of chairs, and a small table with a mirror. Melanie was alone in the room when a white feather floated down in front of her. She had no idea where it came from—there were no adornments or throw pillows—but she picked it up and put it on a table. The director's wife, who was a metaphysical psychic, came backstage after her performance and told her that, when she had been onstage, there had been an angel with her. Melanie agreed.

Part 4
CHORDS OF FAME (1969–1973)

CHAPTER 10

"NICKEL SONG"

Released in October 1969, Melanie's self-titled second album was renamed *Affectionately Melanie* when it was reissued. It was more introspective than her first. She knew there was a buzz around her and her music, but she could sense people's "shallow motivation" and she despised it. Preferring solitude, she was feeling "like a human campfire" surrounded by people. "[Audiences] were reacting to the aura that was built around me," she told *Rolling Stone*, "what they had read in the magazines and what was being promoted."[1]

Melanie and Peter used a variety of studios to record *Affectionately Melanie*. Tommy Kaye's "Soul Sister Annie" was recorded at Sound Recording Studios in Los Angeles, "Johnny Boy" at C.B.E. Studios in Paris, and "Tuning My Guitar," "Deep Down Low," and Joni Mitchell's "For My Father" at Wessex Studio in London, England. The remaining tracks—"I'm Back in Town," "Any Guy," "Uptown Down," "Again," and "Beautiful People"—were done at Allegro Sound Studio in New York.

A thirteen-second reprise of "I'm Back in Town," from *Born to Be*, opened *Affectionately Melanie*. "Uptown Down" followed, reflecting on the disillusionment of fame. "I never wanted to be a celebrity," Melanie explained. "I've gotten pretty good at doing interviews, and I've gotten a certain amount of professionalism, but, as far as my natural instincts as a person, I'm the type who's not even a bit comfortable walking through a crowded room."[2]

Kurt Weill inspired the surprise twist at the end of the next tune, "Any Guy." "I don't regret any of the songs I've written," Melanie told *Melody Maker*. "I like a lot of them more than I used to, like 'Any Guy.' . . . I didn't like anything about it. . . . Now, I do. It's a funny song. It's nice to be able to take an old song and find new life in it."[3]

Set in her dressing room as she prepares to perform, Melanie responded to her mother's discouragement with "Tuning My Guitar." Pondering about the people who hoped some of her "stardom" would rub off on them, she recalled the days when she played music for fun. Commercial success wasn't her aim; she was singing to ease the pain.

"Beautiful People" was rerecorded for the album. Dutch singer Mathilde Santing would score a top-ten hit with it in 1997. Hamburg-based punk band Die Goldenen Zitronen would cover it on their 2009 album, *Die Entstehung der Nacht*. Sandra Bernhard would sing it on her live album *I Love Being Me, Don't You?* two years later.

Whenever she thought of "Lay Down (Candles in the Rain)," Melanie heard a gospel choir in her head. She knew which one. Buddah had the Oakland, California–based Edwin Hawkins Singers on its roster. Originating in 1967 as the Northern California State Youth Choir of the Church of God in Christ (COGIC), its forty-eight members, aged seventeen to twenty-five, flourished under Hawkins, pianist at the Ephesian Church of God in Christ in Berkeley. Their arrangement of an eighteenth-century hymn, "Oh Happy Day," became a major hit in 1969. Selling more than two million copies, it crossed over to the pop charts, peaking at number four, and scored a "Best Soul Gospel Performance" Grammy.

Melanie shared her vision with Peter, who persuaded Bogart to connect her with the group's leader. When they spoke by phone, Melanie told Hawkins her plan. His response startled her. "We only do songs if the Lord, Jesus, or God are mentioned," insisted the choir director. "Are any of those references in your song?"

"Not exactly but they're in there."

Hawkins hemmed and hawed. "I don't know."

Melanie tried to reassure him. "If you could hear it, you'd get where I'm coming from."

"Sorry, we only do non-secular songs."

Hawkins ended the call.

Refusing to take no for an answer, Peter and Melanie headed to the high school auditorium where the Edwin Hawkins Singers rehearsed. Believing that Peter had arranged their visit (which he hadn't), Melanie walked into the auditorium, took her guitar from its case, and started to sing. Somewhere in the middle of the second verse, the chorus joined in. Hawkins threw his hands up and said, "Okay, I guess we're doing it."

Melanie, Peter, and the Edwin Hawkins Singers went into the studio with Freddie Catero, who had engineered records by Barbra Streisand, Bob Dylan, Janis Joplin, and Santana. Santana's percussionist, Rico Reyes, played congas. It was an exceptionally intense session; nobody wanted to stop. Peter kept circling his finger in the air signaling them to keep going. It just went on and on, an incredibly spontaneous creative explosion. They recorded the song once and that was it. Buddah edited it to nearly half of its seven-minute-plus length when they released the single in the United States, but the full recording came out in England. That was the record business. American radio needed records to be a maximum of two minutes and forty-five seconds. It was an unspoken rule.

When she recorded "Lay Down (Candles in the Rain)," Melanie sang "Meher Baba Lives Again" in tribute to the Indian mystic who had "dropped his physical body" eight months before Woodstock. The son of Irani Zoroastrians, Merwan Sheriar "Meher Baba" Irani (1894–1969) maintained a vow of silence beginning in 1925. He communicated via an alphabet board and hand gestures interpreted by his disciples. Pete Townshend and Bobby McFerrin were devotees. Melanie attended a few of his workshops in New York but she found him failing to satisfy her spiritual quest. She would substitute "men can live as brothers" when she performed the song.

Most critics overlooked the significance of a white woman scoring a chart-topping hit with a Black gospel group. *Rolling Stone* called "Lay Down (Candles in the Rain)" "a damnation of any ability that I had," Melanie said. "They didn't mention that I wrote the song and . . . [they] said that my voice was like a pencil scratch across the record."

In the album's liner notes, Melanie wrote, "Dear Edwin Hawkins Singers, I was so afraid I would always have to sing alone. Thanks to all of you, I got a chance to sing with the whole world."[4]

Released as the first single, the title track of Melanie's third album, "Lay Down (Candles in the Rain)" reached number one in Canada, Denmark, and the Netherlands, number two in Australia, and number four in France and the United States. The album sold more than a million copies in six months.

Sometime during the late 1980s, a ticket buyer bought out the first two rows for a Melanie concert and brought members of his family and people close to him to the show. Afterward, he came backstage and told his tale. Nearly two decades before, he had been the commander of a helicopter platoon in Vietnam. They were behind enemy lines. They were completely lost, but they could hear the faint sound of a radio playing "Lay Down (Candles in the Rain)" in the distance and followed the signal to safety. All these years later, he has a daughter named Melanie. Members of his platoon still get together for reunions. They listen to the song and cry.

It became customary to light candles during Melanie's concerts, but fire marshals often gave her and promoters a rough time. At one show, uniformed firemen linked their arms and stood in front of the stage. "If anybody dared light a candle," Melanie said, "they were going to mace them."[5]

The album included one of the earliest covers of a James Taylor song. Peter had brought home a copy of Taylor's debut album, on the Beatles' Apple Records, in December 1968. When Melanie appeared as a guest DJ on a local radio station, she played some of the songs. "Carolina in My Mind" was her favorite and she recorded it.

Melanie loved the Rolling Stones' "Ruby Tuesday," especially Keith Richard's lyrics. Unsure of the chords, Melanie played what worked with her voice. In the studio, her accompanists tried to get her to play the right chords. "Don't you know there's a D minor there? That's where the F-sharp minor goes."

Insisting that she liked it the way that it was, Melanie stuck to her guns and Peter backed her up. It became her song. She would record it multiple times, including a hip-hop version.

Melanie's spiritual journey led to Scientology, the controversial system of beliefs and practices developed by science fiction author L. Ron Hubbard in 1954 and governed by his successor, David Miscavige, since 1987. Repeatedly partaking in its dieting and physical cleansing programs, Melanie and Peter frequented the religion's headquarters in Clearwater, Florida. When they briefly separated, Melanie found shelter in a Southern California cabana owned by then-Scientologist Karen Black.

When Melanie and Beau returned to the West Coast to videotape a pair of duets with Miley Cyrus in 2015, they visited the heavily guarded

Scientology headquarters (about one hundred miles from Los Angeles). Six months later, the Nashville Church of Scientology presented Melanie with its Peaceful Revolution Award.

A foundation of Scientology is a belief in "theta" or what other religions call "self," "spirit," or "soul." According to its founder's teachings, this immortal energy is the essence of a living being, not one's body, name, physical universe, or mind. Through public performance, Melanie believed that she came closer to the theta within her. When things were going well, there were no barriers between the theta in her and the audience. That symbiotic connection lifted everyone's spirit but, just as it would be established, the show would end. The audience would go home, leaving Melanie alone with unspent energy. The title track on her live album, "Leftover Wine," reflected this post-concert experience.

"What Have They Done to My Song Ma" (also "Look What They've Done to My Song, Ma") was deceptively playful. But its message was literal. Melanie and Peter were constantly disagreeing when they were recording. "I would try to communicate what I wanted in nontechnical terms," Melanie said, "like I want it to be more airy here or have a more solid beat. Sometimes they got it but sometimes it was a battle."[6]

Ray Charles's rendition of "Look What They've Done to My Song, Ma" broke into the charts in 1971. It would peak at number twenty-five on the R&B charts and number sixty-seven on the pop charts in the United States and mark the first time that Melanie truly considered herself a songwriter; someone she admired was singing her song. She was thrilled when the "Genius of Soul" sang it on British TV with Barbra Streisand. She was less amused when General Mills Raisin Crisp Oatmeal used it in a TV commercial and changed the words to "Look what they've done to my oatmeal."

Melanie also wasn't ecstatic when the New Seekers scored a top-twenty hit with a carbon copy of "Look What They've Done to My Song, Ma" in 1970. The London-based folk-pop group, led by Keith Potger of the original Australia-based group the Seekers ("Georgy Girl" and "I'll Never Find Another You"), followed with an album, titled after a cloned version of "Beautiful People," that included a duplicate of "The Nickel Song."

Miley Cyrus recorded "Look What They've Done to My Song, Ma," during a backyard acoustic session in 2012, but made it her own, even changing some of it. Melanie was so exhilarated that she fused Cyrus's approach with her own. Cyrus's full-band version was featured in Lina Esco's Sundance-winning film, *Free the Nipple* (2014).

Connecting via social media, Melanie and Cyrus developed a strong bond. "I really like her," Melanie said. "She has a total sense of the absurd and a great comedic sense."

Melanie believed that Cyrus's recordings harkened back to when pop singers "interpreted songs the way they heard them." "That was the art of a singer," she said, "to make a song their own."

Despite their forty-six-year difference, they were "two people sharing songs and inspiring each other. Athletes pass torches, not musicians. Musicians continue to create."

CHAPTER 11

"YOU CALL YOURSELF A WRITER"

S eated on a high-backed chair, with her guitar balanced on her knee, Melanie didn't seem to be dancing when she played. Under her long dress, however, her feet would be tapping away at a hundred miles per hour. She emitted so much energy she could have lit a stadium by herself. Beatles biographer Philip Norman described her June 1969 London show for *Sunday Times* readers: "Alone under a spotlight, long hair falling down, mandarin trousers concealing who knows what kind of legs, guitar accompaniment mainly the key of E, and the occasional ending in tears. The difference is in power. Her voice rises like Havana smoke and batters like a cannonade and sometimes makes the heart stand still."[1]

Other writers agreed. "[Melanie] is a real singer," proclaimed the *Houston Chronicle*, "capable of generating enormous excitement just sitting, picking, patting her foot, and singing. No sound mix or echo chamber required. Strumming a pounding, swinging guitar, and modulating her voice from a raw blast to a fragile croak, she can be pert and cheeky; as in 'Animal Crackers,' hurt but defiant as in 'Steppin,' or lyrically touching as in ballads like 'Baby Day,' and she raps with her fans—and even takes requests—like the humblest troubadour."[2]

When Melanie made her first appearance on the *Ed Sullivan Show*, on October 14, 1970, Peter invited the audience to sit on the stage surrounding her. The show's dour host hadn't seen fans as dedicated to an artist since Elvis Presley. The connection was real. For the first time, Melanie felt that she had friends. One of the first musicians to schedule after-show meet-and-greets, she'd spend hours talking to fans, posing for pictures, and signing albums.

Having grown up watching NBC-TV's *The Tonight Show*, Melanie was terrified when she appeared on the show on October 8, 1969, less than two months after Woodstock. She didn't utter a word. Preparing for the show, she fretted over what she was going to wear. Producers told her that whatever she wore, it had to be blue. She was known for wearing long Bedouin wedding dresses, but she decided to have an outfit created for her. Picturing a "peasant blouse with bell bottoms," she purchased blue fabric and hand-embroidered trimming in an East Village Ukrainian shop and brought them to a tailor who made her a one-piece jumpsuit with a zippered back. She felt "completely silly in it," but it was blue.

Returning to *The Tonight Show* on December 5, 1972, Melanie was much more relaxed. In addition to singing "Together Alone" and "Do You Believe," she joined a guest panel with Sammy Davis Jr. and Sandy Duncan and spoke with the show's host, Johnny Carson.

When Melanie played her first major solo concert, at New York's 1,500-seat Town Hall, on November 21, 1970, "Beautiful People" buttons were stuck to the back of chairs. Ticket holders took them home as souvenirs.

Other than a few words about her guitar, Melanie didn't say anything. Segueing from one song to the next, she was unsure if she was connecting with the audience until people rose from their seats, approached the stage, and sat down surrounding her. "Listeners drift toward the stage like hesitant butterflies," reported *Seventeen*, "moving always closer to the source of the sound. Down the aisles and up the steps, slipping onto the stage in successive waves, tenderly they closed in to crouch, kneel, [and] sit around her."[3]

Peter recorded Melanie's June 1970 show at Carnegie Hall. A live album, *Leftover Wine*, was released three months later. It would chart at thirty-three in the United States, twenty-two in the United Kingdom and Canada, and eight in Australia. Melanie had little input into the recording. She didn't mind if Peter recorded her, but she was "much too terrified to think about it."

Headlining at Carnegie Hall was the pinnacle of making it in show business, but it coincided with a depressing time in Melanie's life. She had been close to her mother. They shared a passion for music, but her mother never had the "real" singing career she dreamed of having. Melanie was becoming the person her mother wanted to be. It caused a great schism between them. Peter would bounce into a room with exciting news and Melanie would sense her mother becoming livid. She remembered kicking Peter under the table more than once and telling him to be quiet. As the Carnegie Hall show drew closer, the conflict intensified. Polly lobbied to be the opening act, but Melanie and Peter didn't think jazz standards would resonate with her fans and they turned her down.

Leftover Wine was unofficially subtitled "Margie's Birthday Party," referring to Margaret "Margie" English, the journalist *Look* magazine assigned to interview Melanie, accompanied by photographer Maddy Miller. English would pen several articles about Melanie. In the first, published in *Look*'s May 19, 1970, issue, she told readers, "[Melanie] sings of her mistakes, people she shouldn't have loved, [and] gifts she shouldn't have given without being semi-tragic."[4]

Melanie felt an affinity for the journalist—intellectually and spiritually. When they spoke, she could feel their conversation lifting her to a higher level. Their discussions provided a deeper perception. Melanie's lifelong friendship, however, wound up being with Miller, who initiated the article. "I was working at *Look* magazine as a photo researcher," Miller remembered from her Manhattan apartment. "I had already shot one or two things for the magazine, but I'd go off and give myself additional projects. There was a DJ on WNEW-FM, Rosko, who I really loved. I got in touch with him and asked if I could photograph him. He said, 'Yes.'"

At the WNEW-FM studio, Miller photographed Rosko spinning records.

"He kept playing Melanie's 'Beautiful People,'" she recalled,

and I asked him, "Who's that? She's got a great voice." He said, "That's Melanie." I asked if she played concerts, and he told me that she was going to do a show at Long Island University in Brooklyn. I went with my camera. I was standing at the foot of the stage taking pictures. Peter was standing next to me. I told him that I worked for *Look*, and he suggested that I pitch a story. Soon afterward, I got in touch with him and Melanie and said, "Guess what, they said 'Yes.'"

The journalist and photographer met Melanie and Peter at their Long Branch apartment. "We went to the beach," Miller remembered, "and shot some photos. Melanie made lunch—a dandelion and orange salad. It was the first time that I'd had a salad without iceberg lettuce."

Melanie had barely begun her Carnegie Hall performance when the audience rose from their seats and approached the stage. "I was standing with Melanie's mother," recalled Miller, "when, all of a sudden, everybody started running toward the stage. Polly was going, 'Oh my God, they're going to kill her,' but I rushed forward too. I didn't want to miss photographing this event."

The loyalty of Melanie's audience struck English. "They leave gifts by the microphone for her," she wrote in the January 12, 1971, issue of *Look*. "They shout 'We love you' from the balcony. While she's singing, the kids leave their seats, climb onto the stage, and snuggle around her. It's a very sweet, dramatic gesture."[5]

"[Melanie] drew strength from [the audience]," English wrote in her liner notes for *Leftover Wine*, "and sang on until she had no more songs. When she rose to leave, some of them embraced her, and tears were exchanged."[6]

Studio versions of most songs on *Leftover Wine*—"Close to It All," "Uptown Down," "Momma Momma," "The Saddest Thing," "Animal Crackers," "Tuning My Guitar," and the title track—appeared on Melanie's first three albums. One of three new tunes, "Psychotherapy" was set to the melody of "Battle Hymn of the Republic" or "John Brown's Body." The origin of its lyrics is unknown, but Berkeley, California–based folk song collector/chorus leader Miriam Berg remembered David "Charlie Brown" Altman singing them in the early 1960s. "He used to be a regular at the Teton Tea Parties," Berg told me, "the all-night folk song sessions we began in Jackson Hole, Wyoming, in 1960, and continued in Berkeley and Oakland, California, from 1961 until 1977."

Melanie recorded the closing track, "Peace Will Come (According to Plan)," in the studio before the Carnegie Hall shows with Ron Frangipane (keyboards), Al Gorgoni (guitar), George Devans (percussion), Joseph Macho (fretless bass), Sal DiTroia (guitar), Art Kaplan (woodwinds), and Greg Diamond (drums). She had been inspired to write it while driving on a California highway with Peter. It was new geography to her. When she ran away as a teenager, she flew to Los Angeles and didn't see the mountains. Gazing out of the car's window, she saw a hill and imagined that she was the kind of enormous creature that could lie across it, with the hill in the small of her back, and her hands reaching out. She felt part of the Earth, part of nature, part of a great plan.

During the chorus, Melanie sang "There's a chance peace will come in your life, please buy one," referring to raffle tickets as "chances." Few people caught the reference. It was a bit obscure, but it was one of many in-jokes Melanie implanted into her songs. John Lennon sang "Give peace a chance" and she sang, "There's a chance peace will come." She wasn't anti-war but pro-peace—an entirely different stance.

"PSYCHOTHERAPY"

Touring could be incredibly brutal. In the wake of Jim Morrison's March 1, 1969, arrest for allegedly exposing himself during a Doors concert, Melanie and her band experienced harsh treatment in a Miami Beach hotel. Before leaving for the concert, she ordered hot tea with lemon and honey for her throat. It took a long time for room service to deliver it—nearly an hour. By the time it finally arrived, served in a metal water bottle, it was time to leave for the concert. The waiter watched Melanie prepare the tea and start to walk out the door. He immediately stopped her. "Ahem. . . . What are you doing?" "I'm taking this tea with me to the concert. I'll bring the bottle back when I finish." "You can't leave the hotel with that," he insisted. "It's hotel property." "I'll bring it back," she promised. "I have a show."

The waiter was adamant that Melanie couldn't take the pot of tea with her. Her mother looked in bewilderment and asked, "Do you think we're going to steal the bottle?" The waiter stared coldly and snarled, "That's exactly what I think."

The situation continued to escalate. Polly slapped the waiter across his face, and he called security. Frantically, Melanie said, "We've got to go," as she marched past the yelling and out of the room. Her band followed. They were walking through the lobby when, suddenly, out of nowhere, hotel security sprayed them with mace. It was horrible—all over a bottle. Melanie would forever blame Jim Morrison.

Reviewing Melanie's September 5, 1971, show at the Performing Arts Center in Saratoga Springs, *Record World* proclaimed, "One of the most charismatic performers around charmed the audience once again."[1]

Melanie's performance was "enchanting for its style, simplicity, and taste," added *Billboard*'s Robert Sobel. "Her self-composed songs are filled with deep feelings and melodic architecture . . . far above the hollow wastelands and surface noise produced by most other youthful artists. All her attributes, the haunting wails, the inner storm she creates with her strong strumming on acoustic guitar, the powerful lyrics, which are full of fantasy/reality and hold out pertinent messages and meanings to youth, enraptured the audience with one outpouring after another."[2]

Not all critics agreed. When she appeared before a sold-out audience at Toronto's Massey Hall, for the second time in six months, in October 1971, Jim Smith at *New Musical Express* found Melanie's "sugar-sweet" songs disappointing. "There is no questioning Miss Safka's talent," he said, "or the sincerity of her gushing enthusiasm for the audience, but a hardened critic can find the show sweet to the point of sickly."[3]

Melanie was experiencing a wonderfully creative time. She brought a women's singing group, the Pennywhistlers, directed by folklorist, singer, ex–*Sing Out!* editor, and artistic director of the Center for Traditional Music and Dance in New York, Ethel Raim, to the studio to sing background vocals. Formed as a Yiddish folk song group in 1962, the Pennywhistlers expanded their repertoire to include tunes from Eastern Europe and the Balkans. A quarter of a century before the Bulgarian State Radio & Television Female Vocal Choir became an international sensation, they mesmerized audiences with their singing.

The Pennywhistlers joined Melanie on "What Wondrous Love," a Southern Baptist hymn she learned while she was studying pottery in North Carolina. "I wrote it down from memory," she said, "and I'm pretty sure I messed up the middle verse. I left out a part about Christ."

"None of it was written beforehand," remembered Raim. "We arranged things a few different ways before coming up with something that worked."

Multi-instrumentalist Eric Weisberg (1939–2020) played fiddle on the album. A graduate of Greenwich Village's Little Red School House and New York's High School of Music and Art, he was a founding member of the folk revivalist group the Tarriers and replaced Ralph Rinzler in the Greenbrier Boys, the first urban bluegrass band in the early '60s.

When he connected with Melanie, he was on the verge of scoring a million-selling, Grammy-winning hit with Arthur "Guitar Boogie" Smith's 1955 instrumental, "Feudin' Banjos." Renamed "Dueling Banjos," and recorded with Steve Mandell, it featured in the 1972 film *Deliverance*. "There was a procession of guitar players going in and out of the studio," Weisberg recalled. "Peter was so picky. He constantly wanted to try different players. Every guitar player in New York was there at one time or another."

Nylon-string guitarist Hugh McCracken (1942–2013) played on the Left Banke's "Walk Away Renee" and recorded with Steely Dan, Billy Joel, Rahsaan Roland Kirk, Bob Dylan, John Lennon, and Yoko Ono. His schedule was so full he turned down an invitation to join Paul McCartney's Wings. McCracken "was one of the most laidback characters ever," said trumpet player Randy Brecker, who played with him later. "He knew how to get the best out of the sidemen and Melanie without saying too much. He played that way, too. He never played a lot of notes, but he played the right ones in the right place."

Classically trained Sal DiTroia (1941–2007) played guitar on several of Melanie's albums as well as records by Simon & Garfunkel, Dionne Warwick, and Burt Bacharach's soundtracks of *The Godfather*, *Butch Cassidy and the Sundance Kid*, and *Midnight Cowboy*. He recorded seven albums with Janis Ian, soloing on her chart-topping 1975 hit, "At Seventeen." His riffs kicked off Simon & Garfunkel's "The Boxer" and the Monkees' "I'm a Believer." Jeff Berry dubbed him "Sal the Hook." Melanie first played with him on her Columbia Records single, "My Beautiful People." "I think we did about fifty takes to get it," she said. "By the time the fiftieth take came, I was so exasperated. I knew what I wanted out of myself. . . . Sal was really patient."

Returning to Allegro Sound, Melanie recorded *The Good Book*, her sixth album in less than two and a half years. "I didn't think it would turn out too well," she admitted, "because I was rushed into it, but, now, listening to it, I think it's as good as *Candles in the Rain*."[4]

There were three cover tunes on *The Good Book*—"Sign on the Window" by Dylan, "My Father" by Judy Collins, and "Chords of Fame" by Phil Ochs. Melanie first heard the latter when he and his band opened for her during his rock and roll period and she fell in love with it. She asked Ochs to sing it for her backstage and he did. She wished she had written it.

When she heard Collins's "My Father," it rang true. She was sure that Collins's father was a different person than hers, but the lyrics hit her personally and she put passion into her rendition.

With harmonies by the Pennywhistlers, the title song was Melanie's way of "warning people to get things together before it was too late." Most people consider the Bible to be the "Good Book," but she questioned that assumption. The Earth was going through tumultuous times, and she could sense manipulation and intrusion. "When I wrote it," she told *New Musical Express*, "I actually started crying. . . . [I had a] feeling that the song was coming through me without any effort."[5]

Melanie often wrote from a perspective older than her chronological age. She couldn't yet comprehend songs like "The Saddest Thing," which reflected on the loss of loved ones, but she could express it through words. British DJ Fliptrix sampled the song and interpolated it into his 2010 rap tune, "Deep Sea Thought."

Reaching number thirty-five in *Billboard*, and number twenty-five in *Cashbox*, "The Nickel Song" was another tune about artistic exploitation. Like many of her best songs, Melanie "wrote it at an alarmingly fast pace, as if it already existed." She shaped words the way a sculptor chiseled an image from a rock.

Celebrating Melanie's perseverance despite being "afraid to walk down the street alone," "Babe Rainbow" was inspired by a black-and-white photograph in a London shop window of a woman "wearing nothing but the holster around her hips." "I imagined a whole life about her," Melanie told the *New Ingénue*, "other than the one the artist had made up about her. He had written that her parents were both champion fighters, but I imagined her to be me. I looked like that to myself, and I felt my essence was in that picture. I knew she was a [trouper] in whatever she was doing and there was something about her that made me sad."[6]

Buddah's art director Soozin Kaik chose Catherine Siracusa, whose work appeared regularly in *Bazaar*, *Glamour*, *Seventeen*, and the *New York Times*, to design *The Good Book*'s trifold, deep-blue-with-gold-lettering cover. "I knew the songs from the records," Siracusa told Melanie's biographer, John Lambo, "but I never knew what an incredible performer [Melanie] is."[7]

The centerfold sported a colorful montage of Maddy Miller's photographs of Melanie. One of the photos not taken during a weekend in Lake George, New York, captured Melanie kissing a cow in Virginia. She was a vegetarian and into communicating with animals and trees. She felt part of a new generation of progressive-minded people. It was apparent in her music and in how she was living.

CHAPTER 13
"FREEDOM KNOWS MY NAME"

P articipating in the UN General Assembly's Staff Day celebration, in October 1971, Melanie was "the best choice anyone could have made for the event, performing her songs of love and peace (gratis, at that) seemed at least an embodiment of the spirit of the UN as any staffers who were present for her concert. . . . She sang with so much appeal in her voice there seemed no doubt she should be the ultimate secret weapon in the cause of world peace."[1]

At a reception following her performance, Melanie spoke with UN staff members and their families. Secretary-General U Thant asked her to tour for the United Nations International Children's Emergency Fund (UNICEF) and she agreed. "I really can't believe that they wanted me," she confessed. "I remember collecting pennies on Halloween with a milk carton with a picture of Danny Kaye on it. I was waiting for some opportunity to do it. I think it is one of the only organizations definitely helping children. I'd really like to do a Christmas concert for UNICEF somewhere. I'll probably cry my way around the world on this tour. I can't wait."[2]

Melanie's first major decision without Peter, the UNICEF tour would result in serious financial loss. She was at her commercial peak, earning $20,000 per concert. Performing for charity instead of her usual fee meant a loss of at least a half-million dollars. "You don't go to Yugo-slavia," she later realized, "when you should've been doing TV specials and press in New York and dates at Madison Square Garden. You don't get a whole lot of press coverage, but I wanted to feel like I was giving . . . and being of some kind of service in this world."[3]

99

The UNICEF tour was rough—fifteen concerts in ten countries. The troupe went from one Eastern bloc country to another (Romania, East Germany, Austria, Belgium, and Yugoslavia) as well as Denmark, Holland, England, and Canada. "Romania was pretty strange," Melanie said. "I didn't know what to expect. They couldn't get my records, of course, but they heard my songs on the radio. There was an ominous feeling. Everything seemed drab—the clothes, people's expressions, just the whole vibration."

Peter couldn't go on the UNICEF tour because he wasn't a citizen of the United States and lacked immigration papers. He was afraid that, if he left, he wouldn't be able to get back. In his place, Ed Kelleher accompanied Melanie. A screenwriter, playwright, film/music critic, and Fordham University graduate, Kelleher would pen half a dozen horror novels with [Prince's publicist] Henrietta Vida, and the screenplays of *Invasion of the Blood Farmers* (1972), *Shriek of the Mutilated* (1974), *Lurkies* (1988), and *Prime Evil* (1988). Starting out by reviewing drive-in movie theaters as Edouard Dauphin for Detroit-based *Creem* magazine, he became a *Billboard* and *Cashbox* staff writer and CBS Records publicist. He would oversee Schekeryk Productions' publicity from 1979 until 1986.

Enjoying a close relationship with audiences outside the United States, Melanie made numerous television appearances, between concerts, in the Netherlands in July 1969. Melanie Appreciation Society founder Dia Huizinga was watching TV in her home near Amsterdam when she tuned in to a local variety show. Melanie was performing and Dia "was blown away by her songs," she remembered, "especially 'Beautiful People.' I had been feeling lonely and her words really hit me—they translated them into Dutch. She wasn't singing the way beautiful girls were supposed to sing and she wasn't screaming or slamming her guitar. I had never seen anything like it."

Huizinga made sure to be in the audience, a few days later, when Melanie appeared on another show. "I felt like I knew her," she said. "She was someone I might meet in the subway."

When Melanie returned to the Netherlands with the Edwin Hawkins Singers in 1970, Huizinga attended their concert in Amsterdam's prestigious Concertgebouw. "It was sold out," she remembered, "and I didn't have much money. I ended up in a terrible seat on the stage. I couldn't see anything but her head. I walked down to get a better look. Melanie turned away from the microphone, and I stormed forward. She welcomed me and said, 'I'm so happy you came.' The whole stage filled with people."

Huizinga would assist Melanie and Beau during subsequent tours of Belgium, Germany, and the Netherlands. Driving them from show to show and handling pre-concert preparations, she was "happy to be taking care of them," she said, "and letting them have no worries other than singing. I took care of everything else. It was so rewarding. I used to sit with the fans. Now, I was backstage, the first person she saw when she got off the stage. I was bursting with happiness; I felt like I was serving the muse."

On the road, Huizinga heard from Peter often. "He would call five, six, or seven times a day," she recalled, "and always be really enthusiastic. He would say, 'Tell me something good,' and ask me about the weather."

Once the UNICEF troupe crossed into the Iron Bloc, things changed. During a press conference, a reporter accused Melanie of being a capitalist propagandist. Insisting that she lived extravagantly in a huge mansion, he accused her of using the UNICEF tour for publicity. It was a brutal attack. Melanie was shocked that anyone would question her motivation. She was getting no compensation and "certainly wasn't doing the tour as a promotional stunt."

Melanie acquired a traveling companion in a Romanian restaurant. Asked by her translator where she wanted to eat dinner, she said that she "wanted to go where working Romanian people ate—not a touristy place," so the translator took her to a crowded, brightly lit restaurant. As they ate, a man came into the restaurant holding a rabbit by its ears and showing it to people. Melanie asked, "What's he doing with that rabbit?" The translator explained that the rabbit was going to be somebody's dinner. Melanie was shocked. "You mean that rabbit's going to be sold to someone to eat?" "Yes," answered the translator. "They're going to kill it, roast it, and eat it." Horrified, Melanie rose from her seat and announced that she was going to buy the rabbit. Paying the seller, and taking possession of the hare, she walked out of the restaurant. Bringing it back to the hotel, she placed it in a cardboard box. She hoped it would poop in the box, but it preferred "walking around dropping little round balls every-where." Melanie brought the rabbit all over Romania. When she left, the translator brought it to her brother's farm.

With a rare day off in Vienna, Melanie got to choose the day's activities. She could either go to a museum or Prater Amusement Park, where Joseph Cotten, Alida Valli, Orson Welles, and Trevor Howard filmed *The Third Man* in 1949. She opted for the amusement park, prodded by Ed Kelleher. It was a cold, gray day, and there weren't many people in the park. Melanie and her companions decided to ride bumper cars. She was "desperately trying to stay away from everybody in the driving pit" when she saw, from the corner of her eye, "a kid who looked like Dennis the Menace with glasses and a snarling face." Melanie tried frantically to get away, but he kept coming toward her—head-on. She moved the steering wheel to the right, to the left, and then to the right again, but her car wasn't going anywhere. Suddenly, BOOM! He smashed right into her. Melanie's face hit the steering wheel and a tooth broke in half. She was rushed to the dentist. It was Sunday but the dentist came to his office to see her. Deadening the pain with slivovitz, a distilled plum brandy, he hacked at her tooth for a minute before telling her that she would need a root canal. He put in a temporary filling so she wouldn't look toothless, but she was in severe pain. As soon as the troupe arrived in Romania, the following day, she rushed to a state-run dental office. After waiting for hours, she was ushered into a room where a woman dentist waited. The dentist banged on her tooth with a hammer, and she screamed. The dentist gave her an injection and it made her feel a lot better. After the procedure, she received three boxes with twelve vials in each box. There were words on the boxes, but they were in Russian, and she had no idea what they said. For the rest of the tour, she'd crack the top of one of the vials, score a line with a razor blade, pop it open, and drink the liquid. She felt fine. She liked this stuff, whatever it was. All through Eastern Europe, she was happy and without pain. After the tour, she told Peter about this magical elixir. He informed her that she had been drinking morphine.

The second half of the tour brought the UNICEF troupe to Japan and Korea. The differences with Eastern Europe were enormous. For Melanie, Japan was "the hardest country." She wasn't used to the sec-ond-class treatment she received as a woman and she felt ignored, which was to her much worse. It didn't help that she was reading "a heartbreaking book" by *Zorba the Greek* author Niko Kazantzakis. Everything about Japan depressed her. Audiences flocked to her concerts but, immediately after the show, she was kept isolated from fans and prevented from signing anything for anybody. She would be rushed to the hotel's presidential suite. Her road crew would go out after a show, but they never invited her.

CHAPTER 14
"SOME SAY (I GOT DEVIL)"

Melanie's relationship with Buddah grew increasingly strained. "I have this contract which says they can call for as many albums as they like," she complained. "In fact, they've been calling [for] so much they've started inventing albums. They've repackaged my first album and put out another one called *The Best of Melanie*, which I hope no one buys."[1]

Bogart's ideas for promotion were upsetting. "[They were] geared up to make me look like a bliss ninny," Melanie said. "I'd meet people and they would think they would have to talk to me in one-syllable words."[2]

As Melanie's three-year contract with Buddah approached renewal, Peter began to explore options. Paramount Pictures, a division of Gulf and Western Industries, Inc. (since 1989, Paramount Communications), offered $3,000,000 and the launching of Melanie's own label— Neighborhood Records—with distribution through its Famous Music Group. The Beatles had been the only other contemporary artist to own a record label (Apple Records).

Neighborhood Records occupied the sixty-eighth floor of the Gulf and Western Building (currently Trump Tower) on midtown Manhattan's Columbus Circle. Paramount Pictures had several floors and Gulf and Western had the rest. "It is hard to overstate the effect of the building on your sense of dimension and place," said *Rolling Stone*. "You walk into a lobby that is half-Vegas, half-Vatican, a vaulting altar of brass and obsidian that soars halfway to heaven."[3]

Owning a record label represented creative freedom for Melanie, but Buddah was furious when it learned she was defecting. Claiming it enticed her to renege on her contract, it sued Paramount for $25,000,000.

The case was settled out of court, but the jilted label wasn't done. It couldn't wait to exploit what Melanie left in its archives and released *Garden in the City*, a poorly mixed mishmash of covers of songs by Dylan ("Lay Lady Lay"), the Rolling Stones ("Jigsaw Puzzle"), and George Gershwin ("Somebody Loves Me"), two songs from *R.P.M.*, and an unfinished recording of "People in the Front Row." Buddah followed with an even worse double album, *The Four Sides of Melanie*. Its illustrated cover sported all kinds of cynical images including Peter with devil horns. Buddah's goal of sabotaging Melanie's career worked. Three albums of poorly recorded tracks left many bewildered.

Bogart was the "darling of the music industry." Distributors called him by his first name and knew his kids. As far as they were concerned, Melanie had done him wrong, and they had the power to retaliate. Without distribution, an artist was doomed. A new recording could get airplay but stagnate in a warehouse. Customers wouldn't be able to buy it, and interest would fade.

Melanie had high hopes for Neighborhood Records. She named it, chose its logo, and designed its office. She was especially proud of the mini-refrigerator/stove that was her most extravagant purchase. The top of it was a bar. It was beautifully compact. She could heat water for tea or cook soup. She planned to bring healthy food to the office and keep vegetables in the refrigerator. She had a purely aesthetic desire to make the office less stuffy and corporate-looking. She thought it was going to be their New York office forever.

A week or so before Melanie played a concert, her arrival would be preceded by Maddy Miller, who began working for her when she was still with Buddah, and graphic designer Ron Levine. Affectionately known as the Neighborhood Kids, they'd plaster posters all over town and make sure the record store was stocked with the recordings.

Despite rumors, Neighborhood Records/Schekeryk Productions' office was never the drug den some envisioned. There were, however, people hired by Peter whose intentions weren't to make the company thrive but to benefit themselves. They had no loyalty. One executive made a pass at Melanie in her dressing room, confessing how much he loved her.

Bridging out to other artists, Peter and Melanie signed Woodstock co-promoter Artie Kornfeld (his Neighborhood album, *At the Edge*, would go unreleased) and Melanie's favorite group, the Incredible String Band. She loved their archaic sound and the way they did unexpected things like changing tempos in the middle of songs. Their shows were loose and spontaneous. Dogs would be on the stage, not doing dog tricks, but just wandering around. She wished her shows could be more like theirs.

The Incredible String Band, however, was in the early stages of breaking up and its leaders Mike Heron and Robin Williamson were quarreling. Heron was determined to have a hit record, while Williamson preferred medieval instruments and approached music academically. Melanie got along better with him than she did with Heron, whom she didn't get to know very well despite touring together.

The Incredible String Band lived in Melanie and Peter's Central Park South apartment for a year. Neighborhood paid their expenses. Heartbroken when they disbanded, Melanie worked with Heron on his solo album, *Mike Heron's Reputation*, singing background on a song, "Evie," produced by Peter (who also produced "Meanwhile the Rain"). The label promoted Heron's album as much as possible, but it wasn't the Incredible String Band, and it sold poorly. Heron didn't honor his contract and released his next album (*Diamond of Dreams*) on his own label, Casablanca (no connection to Bogart's '70s disco label).

Melanie championed Janey & Dennis's song "Jason." She performed it during shows and recorded it, thinking that, if she liked it, other people would too. She promoted the duo every chance she got. During interviews, she raved about how much she liked the Queens, New York–based duo's writing. "When Dennis and I started writing together," Janey Street (nee Schramm) told me from her Nashville home, "we had known each other for a while. I had been singing with a blues band (Operation Blues) and Dennis had been playing keyboards in a Beatles cover band, the Shadows. He begged us to let him join because we were the 'cool ones.'

"When we started harmonizing, we became a whole other thing. It was amazing. Janis Ian encouraged me to write more with Dennis. She had gotten me into music. We met at summer camp when we were eleven. Dennis and I got our deal with Warner Brothers through Janis's people. Ironically, I was seventeen."

Booked by the William Morris Agency, Janey & Dennis opened for Melanie in "a large airplane hangar" in New Jersey. "There were ten thousand people," remembered Street. "We didn't get to meet her that day. She didn't get there until we finished our set. Then, we did WNEW-FM's Christmas show at the Fillmore East. Peter came up to us backstage and introduced himself."

As the opening act for Melanie's Central Park concert, on July 10, 1971, Janey & Dennis "got a standing ovation," remembered Dennis Pereca, now a New York–based piano technician/owner of the Pianotek Company, "and it changed our lives. Peter told us that he wanted us to open for Melanie regularly and we agreed. It was a good combination. We were playing for ten thousand people or more every night."

"They paid us an advance and a monthly salary," added Street, "and paid our expenses. It worked out fine. Melanie enjoyed audiences after we warmed them up and we had a house in Woodstock and were living nicely."

Janey & Dennis toured with Melanie for two years before the relationship soured. "Peter had great intentions for us," Pereca reflected, "and, under his supervision, we recorded our third album in Nyack, New York. It was a great album, so much more 'grown-up' than our previous album. We spent two years recording it. We had the best musicians in New York. We had country, reggae, blues, a little of this, a little of that, but Peter sold the rights to Capitol Records and the album never came out. We never forgave him."

Capitol released "Jason" b/w "Catskill Days" as a single in August 1974. "We got an opening spot with the Bee Gees' tour," said Street, "playing for twenty thousand people a night all over Canada. We put a great band together but nobody from the label came to the shows."

"That was our demise," added Pereca. "We were playing large venues like the Montreal Forum and getting great responses from audiences but there was no album for people to buy. We broke up shortly afterward. I went from opening for Melanie, touring with the Bee Gees, and living the high life, to cruising down Second Avenue driving a cab."

Street later "got a million-dollar deal with Arista," and released a solo album, *Heroes, Angels, and Friends* in 1984. "I had a video in the top ten," she said, "but Clive Davis refused to pick up my option. That was the end of that—another disappointment."

Peter produced a ten-track album for Five Dollar Shoes, an "Allman Brothers-meet-the-New-York-Dolls-with-a-touch-of-Pink-Floyd"[4] rock band featuring drummer Gregg Diamond, keyboard player Tom Graves, bassist Jim Gregory, harmonica player Mike Millius, and guitarist Scott Woody. Diamond and Millius shared lead vocals. One of the first glam rock bands, they wore platform shoes, brightly colored spandex, and flashy jewelry. The New York Dolls may have been there earlier, but Five Dollar Shoes took it to the next level. Melanie named them after a line in a traditional folk song—"Ain't Gonna Be Treated This Way" also known as "Goin' Down the Road Feeling Bad."

It's rumored that pre-Kiss Gene Simmons and Paul Stanley sang on Five Dollar Shoes' album, but Melanie wasn't sure. She didn't have a lot to do with what happened in the studio, preferring to record her vocals and get out of the way. She didn't have to hear her vocals back to make sure they were perfect. She knew when they were right. Peter, on the other hand, was obsessive. He'd stay in the studio until five in the morning. If anything needed fixing, he'd splice something in from another take.

"ANIMAL CRACKERS"

Melanie's appearance and lifestyle attracted considerable attention. "I always feel that I look my best," she said, "when I'm eating well and getting enough sleep. I try not to wear any skin makeup because I feel it's bad for you. I use mostly natural cosmetics and I wash my hair with herbal shampoo. I take vitamins every day and sometimes I break open a Vitamin E capsule and rub the oil over my face. That really helps my complexion."[1]

Melanie acquired her interest in nutrition from her mother, who suffered from arthritis. The doctor prescribed cortisone but Polly resisted. "[She] discovered that if she changed her diet, stopped eating bread . . . [and] stopped smoking," Melanie said, "she wouldn't have arthritis anymore."[2]

Going to extremes to maintain her diet, Melanie grew "alfalfa sprouts in hotel bathrooms," she told the *West Australian*. "They're the freshest vegetables you can get when you're traveling . . . and so nutritious."[3]

Regularly taking three dozen pills to supplement her daily vitamin intake, Melanie shifted to an organic diet. "I started to rebel a little bit," she explained, "and thought I was going to do without vitamins. . . . I got involved in a vegetarian diet, I was a 'fruitarian' for a while, then I was just a raw food person."[4]

Limiting her intake to five hundred calories a day, Melanie got "all her meals delivered from a doctor," the author of *Lillian Roxon's Rock Encyclopedia* told readers of London's *Sunday Times*, "foil-wrapped and deep-frozen TV dinners . . . kind of sparse but worth it if it makes the Bedouin gown cling so prettily. I take it the chicken and sprouts have the full approval of Melanie's Italian astrologer who calmed her down and changed her life by teaching her meditation and a Hindu chant or mantra. George Harrison goes in for mantras and look at what good shape he's in these days—thin and rich and very together."[5]

"Meditation helps the things inside of me to surface in my work," Melanie explained. "It has made me believe that the best I can do is to have a healing effect on other people. I just meditate every day on a series of symbols that tend to balance me. . . . You must be careful about meditating and chanting because there are certain chants that are harmful. . . . It has a tendency to make you withdraw. It's the sound of a recluse."[6]

Constant demands on her time and energy plagued Melanie. "Between not getting enough sleep, the wrong diet, and not having any time to myself," she said, "I was slowly becoming a physical and emotional wreck. With all the traveling I had to do, my body wasn't getting what it needed."[7]

Taking a respite from the spotlight, Melanie went by herself to the Hidden Valley Health Ranch, a holistic, alternative medicine clinic, in Escondido, California, run by Dr. Jorgen Bernard Jensen. A graduate of the West Coast Chiropractic College and the son of a chiropractor, Dr. Jensen authored more than three dozen books on natural healing before his death, at the age of ninety-three, in 2001. He turned to natural healing after contracting an incurable lung disease in the 1940s. Introduced to nutritious foods by a Seventh-Day Adventist physician, he regained his health. For the next sixty years, he traveled the world studying healing techniques in sixty-six countries including the United States and developing a holistic approach of his own. Considered "the father of iridology," a technique that uses the human eye, or iris, as a key to understanding a person's weaknesses and strengths, Dr. Jensen combined hydrotherapy, fasting, reflexology, color therapy, polarity, glandular balancing, homeopathy, herbology, diet, acupuncture, craniopathy, and personology.

The largest of four sanitariums, Dr. Jensen's Hidden Valley Health Ranch opened in 1955. People suffering from arthritis, cancer, weight disorders, and other chronic and degenerative diseases came from all over the world seeking relief.

Melanie's privacy dissipated as soon as someone noticed the guitar in her room. "I was asked to sing at this little communal gathering they held each night," she told Kelleher. "I started doing my material, but they weren't familiar with it. Then I got a request for 'Tell Me Why.' I had never heard it, so they taught it to me. I said, 'I'll put that on an album' and I did."

Taking a personal interest in his celebrity patient, Dr. Jensen suggested that Melanie eat meat a couple of times a week. She needed the protein. "It appalled me," she said, "because I was such a militant vegetarian, the obnoxious kind. I would go to Thanksgiving dinner and say, 'I'm not eating carcasses.'"[8]

"I was a vegetarian for over two years," she continued, "but I got sick. I wasn't really doing it right you know. I was just not getting the right things, and I was run down, and I just had a complete breakdown, physically and mentally."[9]

Against the doctor's advice, Melanie embarked on a forty-day fast. She didn't want to eat anymore. "You take so much impurity into your body every day," she said, "you have to let it out. People weren't meant to eat all the time."[10]

Nestled among the Escondido hills, Hidden Valley was set amid a natural wonderland. Melanie loved to walk the trails of the hills. She was awed by the sagebrush, fascinated by trees that curved and twirled, and all kinds of plants and vegetation. There was, however, a cougar looming in these hills. People warned Melanie to be careful, but she paid them little mind as she headed out on a hike. She had been fasting for more than twenty days, and her pace had slowed dramatically. She was shuffling along, singing to herself, when the mountain lion suddenly appeared, perched on a rock above her. Melanie was barely fazed. Looking at the tan-colored feline, she admired its beauty and kept walking as if it were nothing. The mountain lion roared and walked away.

Melanie loved being at Hidden Valley. She didn't feel ready to face the outside world. She was dealing with life—emotionally and spiritually—as well as her ongoing conflict with her mother, and she was desperately seeking answers to her spiritual quest. The absence of nourishment, however, was making her so hypersensitive that she couldn't watch television without breaking into tears. She went with a group of people to see a movie but could hardly sit through it. When the assemblage went to a restaurant after the film, she had a glass of water. She could see other people eating but eating seemed to be "what other species did." As the conversation around the table shifted from one topic to another, it became too much. Melanie broke down crying.

113

On her twenty-seventh day of fasting, Dr. Jensen ordered Melanie to eat. She protested, "No, no, no, I'm just getting used to this." The doctor insisted and Melanie reluctantly agreed. Breaking her fast with citrus juice (Dr. Jensen grew organic oranges), she swallowed a tablespoon, and her mouth "turned inside out." It was an intense sensation.

Dr. Jensen advised her to reintroduce herself to food in very small amounts—things like partially cooked, grated vegetables, a carrot, or a zucchini. He told her that she'd know instinctively what she should or shouldn't eat.

Soon after returning to New Jersey, Melanie went to a flea market in Englishtown. "On the way back home, I smelled something . . . wonderful coming from this McDonalds," she recalled, "and thought, 'A diet has occurred to me.' I ordered the whole package: a Big Mac, fries, and a milkshake. . . . No sooner did I finish that last bite than the song occurred to me. It was just a magical, biochemical reaction. I don't know whether the aroma reminded me of learning how to roller skate in Astoria. It was this whole 'whoosh' memory thing."[11]

Initially setting "Brand New Key" to "a slow, Cajun groove," Melanie imagined herself "sitting on a porch somewhere in the south with a couple of black women and a guy playing the harmonica or maybe a tuba . . . and we were just rocking away and stomping our feet."[12]

When she played the song for him, Peter proposed speeding it up. Melanie wasn't sure she agreed but Peter's vision as usual prevailed.

After recording her vocal track, Melanie returned to Dr. Jensen's ranch for a ten-day fast. Peter resumed work on the recording and over-dubbed "Oom-pa-ha, oom-pa-ha" harmonies sung by Sammy Turner, best known for his top-three 1959 hit, "Lavender-Blue (Dilly Dilly)," and J. R. Bailey, Mel Kent, and Kenny Williams of doo-wop singing group the Cadillacs. He also released an R&B version, credited to Four of a Kind, on his Toy Records label. *Record & Radio Mirror* described it as "Sammy dilly-dillying the squeaky lead over the others' chanting and plopping congas backup. . . . The result is really nice with some mellow gospel harmonies that show up, especially on the wordless flipside backing-track version."[13]

"Brand New Key" made an immediate impact. Elton John was riding his bicycle near his Middlesex, England, home when he heard it for the first time. He laughed so hard he fell off his bike. He would tell

Peter that the song permitted him to write novelty tunes like "Crocodile Rock."

An international smash, "Brand New Key" topped the charts in Canada, New Zealand, Australia, and the United States. "I never thought it would be a hit record," Melanie confessed. "It was the equivalent of a doodle."[14]

"[It] was a real one-off song. It wasn't typical. So much is marketing, the look, the package. That has so much to do with what people will read into. Even being a woman . . . there were certainly cute things other female [artists] did, but they weren't perceived like [I was] . . . a 'beatific flower child.' That kind of put a little bit of fluff on it—too cuddly and fluffy. Nothing could have been further from any of [the songs on my] other albums."[15]

Misinterpreting its lyrics, some radio stations banned "Brand New Key" for referring to wife-swapping key clubs, some for referring to a kilo of drugs, and some for being "too cute." "Because the song is light-hearted and bouncy," Melanie told *Cosmopolitan*, "and I recorded it in a high voice, I got criticized by underground FM heavies."[16]

Released in December 1971, Melanie's fifth album, *Gather Me*, reached number fifteen in the United States and number fourteen in Canada and the United Kingdom and broke into the top ten in Australia. *Billboard, Cash Box, Record World, Melody Maker*, and *Bravo* named Melanie the year's "Top Female Vocalist." "*Gather Me* is the best album I have ever done," she boasted to *New Musical Express*. "I wish it was the first album because everything else just didn't count. It's not so much the material as the attitude. It was a lot simpler and less tense."[17]

"I wasn't thinking about anything else," she added. "It's really the freest album I've ever made. I wasn't worried about the time limit and there wasn't any pressure to get a product out."[18]

Critics noticed immediately. "The cuts are rich with electric piano, woodwinds, congas, and harmonica," said Cameron Crowe. "The beat remains bouncy but for once fails to cross the line into sickeningly commercial ditties."[19]

"[Melanie] has done pretty good by herself," agreed *Fusion*, "hit tune after hit tune."[20]

In a poll conducted by *Melody Maker*, readers named Melanie the year's top female artist ahead of Diana Ross, Joni Mitchell, Cilla Black,

Mary Hopkin, Dusty Springfield, Aretha Franklin, Lulu, Shirley Bassey, and Dionne Warwick.

The success was tempered, however, by Melanie's personal struggles. She was finding it difficult to maintain balance. Everybody was always saying "Yes" to her, no matter what she asked. She couldn't do anything wrong, and it made her extremely distressed. She yearned for someone to stand up to her and tell her when her ideas weren't good, but there were very few people willing to do that. Insulated from reality, she found it impossible to live anything resembling a "normal" life. It left her with scars. "I never imagined anything would happen to me," she said. "I thought to get an agent you had to send him a glossy eight-by-ten picture of yourself smiling. I didn't reckon it was worth the postage."[21]

"Brand New Key" marked the apex of Melanie's ascent. The slide would be rough. The second single from *Gather Me*, "Ring the Living Bell" b/w "Railroad" stalled at number twenty-seven on the *Billboard* charts. Ed Kelleher described the A-side, which incorporated Gregorian chant verses and Middle Eastern influences, as "a song which begins as a chant—many voices, one aim—a split second of silence then Melanie, rhythmic and assured, leading the service. The other voices dart in and out like joyful shadows. The drums are right where you want them like friends. The song is there. It runs like clear water and Melanie runs with it. It's exciting. It's real. It's painfully beautiful. . . . She is about being positive. She is about 'Sing, give, and make a new beginning.'"[22]

"Ring the Living Bell" had all the markings of a chart-topper. Melanie was amazed that it didn't do better than it did. Radio programming and tastes in popular music were changing but people wanted her to stay in the same mold. Gulf and Western president Jim Judelson told her to write another song like "Brand New Key." It was like somebody speaking a foreign language. She wasn't a made-to-order songwriter. She couldn't force herself to write another song like "Brand New Key," or anything else. She couldn't duplicate something she had already done. "I had to battle several times in my career," she told the *Sun Sentinel*, "to express [myself] and create new things."[23]

Tactful to Judelson, Melanie was highly annoyed. "I'm not sure if I sing because I write songs," she said, "or I write songs because I sing. . . . Unfortunately, the songwriting business has become so corporate. . . . There are people teaching how to write pop songs and they have a formula. . . . Of course, eighty percent of the time, they are right, [but] the biggest hits are always the ones that don't follow a formula and just come from left field."[24]

The slide continued with the third single from *Gather Me*—"Some Day I'll Be a Farmer" b/w a cover of Dylan's "Lay Lady Lay." Stalling at 109 on the *Billboard* charts, the A side had been inspired by a visit to an acting school friend who experienced a mental breakdown and got electric shock treatment. She lived in a house, surrounded by rolling hills, in Darien, Connecticut. As they walked through the woods, the ex-classmates stopped by a rock and sat for hours and hours talking. Melanie imagined having a place where she could grow tomatoes. She could dig in the dirt, grow things, pick flowers, and collect berries and nuts. The idea of land fascinated her, but Peter was the absolute opposite. The last thing he wanted was to be on a farm. He grew up on a farm. His mother pickled her own food. In reality, Melanie was much too busy to be a farmer. She was constantly on the go, getting in and out of limousines, and on and off airplanes, though traveling was the last thing she wanted to do. She preferred staying at home and living the life she dreamed.

Part 5
AGAINST THE TIDE (1973–1978)

"SMILE"

‘‘There is a gingerbread house hidden by pines at the end of a long driveway in Lincroft (about twenty minutes northwest of Long Branch)," reported the *Asbury Park Sunday Press* in January 1973, "but there is no wicked witch for miles. Only a young couple lives there—with their six cats, two dogs, and a goat. It's called the Rag House. . . . The house is trimmed in red and its sprawling, log-cabin appearance and the quiet of the sheltered landscape inspire thoughts of somewhere high in the Swiss Alps."[1]

A rustic log cabin built in 1940, the Rag House originated as a retreat for priests. Melanie and Peter paid $40,000 for it (Zillow valued it in December 2023 at $2,202,492). Starting with a single bedroom, living room, and bathroom, Melanie and Peter expanded it with an additional twenty-seven rooms. It was the kind of place only a kid or someone with a lot of money could imagine. There were always celebrations of one thing or another. Musicians were always hanging out. Melanie and Peter lived on one side of the house with the kids on other, watched by their nanny, Dorothy Godfrey, from a small village near Cambridge, England.

The Rag House was large enough to accommodate Melanie's dreams. It became her creative outlet. She put everything she could into it. She used wood from an old barn, logs, old shingles, and hundred-year-old beams that matched the rustic look. She spent hours walking along the ocean, collecting driftwood to put on the walls and doors.

Melanie started frequenting flea markets. She'd arrive at four in the morning, holding a flashlight, and asking for the dealer's price. If she saw something interesting, she'd negotiate the price. She inherited her father's genes, so it had to be a good bargain. "We were antique and estate sale people," said Jeordie's older sister, Leilah. "I loved going on the hunt. You never knew what treasure you were going to find. I remember going with Mom to garage sales. We had so much fun."

A child of curiosity, Melanie loved to explore and discover new things. Everywhere she went, she'd see things that sparked her fascination. Purchasing a hot tub after a trip to Sweden, she'd run through the snow and ease her way in.

The cabin's expansion didn't involve an architect, or construction crew, but a carpenter who rejoiced as the budget grew. Melanie and Peter paid heavily for every intricacy. In one instance, the carpenter told Melanie that, in order to build a dining room, he would have to remove a tree. She refused to have the tree cut and had the room built, at great expense, around it.

A huge piece of stained glass made by Tiffany, picturing a woman at a table drinking a glass of wine, dominated the left wall of the room with the tree. There was an open, wall-to-wall fireplace in the room. Melanie collected building tiles from old brownstones in England. They were beautiful but very inexpensive. She bought a massive amount, shipped them home, and lined the fireplace with them. It was truly creative.

The fireplace had a cauldron for cooking, but it backed up with smoke. "No one told us it wouldn't go up the chimney," Melanie explained. "One man . . . said he could fix it for $5,000. We got rid of him. Now we're supposed to be getting some kind of fan to improve the draft."[2]

Melanie designed the kitchen, installing a heated brick floor. It was aesthetically beautiful, but she quickly discovered that standing on a heated floor barefoot burned your feet.

A room with an indoor swimming pool, that opened to a deck, overlooked the woods and a small creek. "I don't like to play up the pool," Melanie said. "I just have it because I love to swim. I do it every day."[3]

In addition to Melanie, Peter, and their growing brood, the house was home to their many pets. "[Melanie's] menagerie consists of a goat, a St. Bernard, a sheepdog, two sheep, and a spaniel called Roadie who goes on tour with her."[4]

Unfortunately, the Rag House wouldn't be where Melanie and Peter would spend the rest of their lives. While vacationing in Florida, Peter found a large house in Safety Harbor, a sleepy town south of Fort Myers Beach on Estero Island. At first, it was a second home, but Peter, Melanie, and their children ended up living there.

Melanie was thrilled to be near the ocean. She loved to swim, believing salt water to be incredibly healing. She'd go into the water and feel renewed.

Melanie and Peter always maintained an apartment in New York, whether they lived in it or not. It was where they told everyone they were from. "I think the city is where all the changes begin," Melanie said, "and I also feel it is the most desperate place. If you're aiming for peace of mind, the city is not the place to go, but, if you want life, then, the city is the place. I'm always getting new ideas from the buildings and the people."

Busy raising kids, playing music, and traveling, Melanie didn't know anything about mortgages or paying bills. Peter took care of everything, but he kept her in the dark. She was completely unaware of their financial situation. She had no idea that the Rag House was up for foreclosure. All she knew was that Peter told her that they were selling it and moving to Florida.

Melanie assumed that Peter understood business, but she was wrong. He wasn't about business; he was all heart. It's what drove him. He loved making a phenomenal deal and he loved having an escape clause. He got Melanie out of plenty of contracts legally. He trusted his gut and he lived for her. He was determined that nothing should ever hurt her, and he fiercely defended her. He saw greatness in her and wanted her to be recognized as the top singer in the world, but she was at odds with that. She wanted to live a little and experience a "normal" life. She wanted to be part of a group helping the planet, but Peter kept her sheltered and insulated. All she did was play shows and go back to the hotel.

Figure 1   Melanie and her Aunt Jeanne—Danbury, Palace Theater July 16, 2015
© Randy Morrison

Figure 2   Back by Popular Demand © Randy Morrison

Figure 3   Beau Jarred, April 8, 2016 © Randy Morrison

Figure 4   Beau, Melanie, and Craig © Randy Morrison

Figure 5   Melanie and Beau Jarred, Rhode Island © Randy Morrison

Figure 6 Melanie and Mr. Brzostowski © Randy Morrison

Figure 7   Melanie at Muckracker © Randy Morrison

Figure 8 Melanie Philadelphia Folk Festival, 1988 © Craig Harris

Figure 9   Wood burning in Rockport © Randy Morrison

Figure 10   Melanie and her Uncle George—North Truro, Payomet Theater, July 14, 2015 © Randy Morrison

Figure 11   Rock Hunting © Randy Morrison

CHAPTER 17
"ROCK AND ROLL HEART"

Investigative reporter Geraldo Rivera shocked ABC-TV viewers with his early 1972 Peabody Award–winning exposé of the abuse at the Willowbrook State Institution for Retarded Children in Staten Island. His report so moved John Lennon and Yoko Ono that they contacted him and volunteered their services. It turned into a once-in-a-lifetime event on Wednesday, August 30, 1972. In addition to a pair of "One on One" concerts by the ex-Beatle and guests at Madison Square Garden, activities in Central Park brought mentally challenged children together with unimpaired youngsters and adults and planted the seeds leading to the Civil Rights of Institutionalized Patients Act of 1980. The Willowbrook State School would shut down, with the last students leaving in 1987.

Accompanied by saxophonist Stan Bronstein's Elephant's Memory, and joined by Yoko Ono, Lennon performed what would be his only rehearsed full-length post Beatles show. Melanie participated along with Stevie Wonder, Roberta Flack, and Sha Na Na. When she came onstage for the full-cast finale of "Give Peace a Chance," Ono handed Melanie a black rose. She would invite her to a party, thirteen years later, giving her an acorn—"the secret pass key"—to get in.

Considering the massive success of *Gather Me*, it's incomprehensible that its follow-up, *Stoneground Words*, stalled in the eightieth chart position. "It took all of spring and summer to get it organized," Melanie said, "and I really didn't consider it was a very different style of work to anything I'd done in the past. It just so happens—probably because of [Kellaway's] arrangements—that the end product makes me sound as though I've come to a different bend in my career."[1]

125

Critics varied in their response to the album. *Melody Maker* called it Melanie's "most sophisticated album" and pointed out that "the essence remains, the emphasis on communal relationships is still quite evident, but the way she expresses her feelings has grown."[2]

New Musical Express complained that it was "a trifle over-arranged and more than a little corny" but admitted that it was "very soothing."[3]

Other reviewers were sharply critical. "Melanie's first two albums contained really nice material," said *Disc*, "but, of late, the lady appears to have floundered in a quagmire of self-pity, soul searching, and downright agony."[4]

"This is a sad album," said *Melody Maker*. "If you stripped away the music, and hid all the instruments, then the words alone would reek of pretty lonely misery."[5]

Stoneground Words reunited musicians who had recorded with Melanie in the past—DiTroia (acoustic guitar), McCracken (guitar), Don Payne (Fender Bass), Chuck Domanico (upright bass), Kellaway (piano/arrangements), Frangipani (organ, harmonium), and Donald McDonald (drums)—and added special guests Johnny Pacheco (congas), Bill Keith (steel guitar), Richard Davis (upright bass), and Al Cohn (tenor saxophone). Mel Lewis (Thad Jones/Mel Lewis Orchestra) played drums on "Here I Am."

Melanie believed *Stoneground Words* to be "the one." It included two of what she considered to be her best songs—"Together Alone" and "Do You Believe." "I originally wanted 'Together Alone' as a twenty-minute song to take up the whole of the first side," she explained. "Peter tended to be the stabilizer."[6]

"Melanie's plea to a lover to be 'Together Alone,'" said *Second Disc*, "sets the [album's] wistful, searching tone . . . ruminating on life, love and music itself . . . another well-crafted statement in song from the maturing artist. . . . 'Do You Believe' also expresses love with an undercurrent of ache as it builds to an explosion of gospel fervor."[7]

Pete Seeger's "My Rainbow Race" was the album's only cover tune. It resonated with Melanie's belief that love was the driving force.

"I'm Not a Poet" was another of Melanie's songs about being misunderstood. Due to the complexity of her lyrics, and her use of metaphors, some listeners failed to catch the absurdity of her songs. Melanie considered few pop songs more absurd than "Brand New Key," but some assumed that it was just a cute novelty tune, complete with roller skates and pigtails with bows. Others dismissed her without listening, thinking she was too pretty to have anything of substance in her head. "I'm Not a Poet" was her way of declaring that she wasn't going to put up with any of it. She might not be a poet, but she was living a life of poetry, beauty, and authenticity.

Melanie would regret the title of "Maybe I Was (A Golf Ball)." She originally called it "Maybe I Was" but when an interviewer asked her "Maybe, you're a what?" she spontaneously responded, "a golf ball," and it stuck.

Neighborhood's director of national promotion, Denny Zeitler, suggested releasing "Do You Believe" b/w "Stoneground Words" as a single in the United States. It would be a mistake. Melanie and Peter gave no thought to expense when it came to recording, but they lacked enough money to back their efforts with promotion. The single failed to break into the charts.

Sally Potts (née Dorgan) was in high school when she saw Melanie for the first time in Asbury Park in 1972. She had no interest in going to the concert until her brother and cousin talked her into it. She had a driver's license and a car. She wasn't excited about it though. Ushered into a seat far from the stage, she expected a loud rock band with background singers to come out and blast everyone away. Instead, a petite woman walked on stage, carrying an acoustic guitar, and sat down, alone. Sally was enchanted. When Melanie spoke, it was like she was speaking directly to her.

Seeking an intern position, Potts wrote Melanie a letter. It took detective work to know where to send it. As with most artists, Melanie's address was officially listed as Neighborhood Records, 15 Gulf and Western Plaza. The sheet music for "Brand New Key" offered an address in Long Branch, New Jersey, an hour away. Cutting class one day, Sally placed the letter in a mailbox marked "Schekeryk" and waited, hoping it would reach its destination.

After reading the letter, Melanie instructed a Neighborhood Records employee to phone her young admirer. Surprised by the call, Potts was nevertheless excited to talk about Melanie. Her enthusiasm was so apparent; she was given a part-time job answering Melanie's fan mail. Twice a week, she'd drive to Neighborhood's office and pick up the mail.

Neighborhood staffers—Dee Dee, Irene, and Karen—would fill a few bags with letters. Taking them home, Sally would read them and answer them.

Potts's efforts were rewarded with "promotional copies of albums and singles . . . great perks for a diehard Melanie fan."

Peter was in his office when Potts went to retrieve the mail in mid-January 1973. Peter surprised her with a pair of tickets to Melanie's Carnegie Hall concert. She was ecstatic.

Melanie's Carnegie Hall concerts, on February 2 and her birthday the following day, were recorded and released as her second live album, *Melanie at Carnegie Hall*, two months later. WNEW-FM's late-night announcer Alison "The Nightbird" Steele introduced her on the first night, and Scott Muni did the honors on the second. The eighteen-track double album presented "a very satisfying set though much of the material is familiar, and the overall standard of sound is good. What emerges most strongly is the quite astonishing rapport Melanie has with an audience."[8]

Melanie at Carnegie Hall included sixteen original tunes and covers of Pete Seeger's "My Rainbow Race" and Woody Guthrie's ode to Robin Hood-esque bank robber "Pretty Boy Floyd." "I'm probably one of the few pop artists," Melanie mistakenly bragged, "[to] put a Woody Guthrie song on [an] album."[9]

A live version of "Bitter Bad," which had been a Top 40 single, featured "a bright organ fill," said *Billboard*, "a strong vocal chorus, solid conga, and hot tenor surrounding Melanie's strong reading of a story about a nasty guy who's playing around with another gal."[10]

Melanie and Peter were constantly recording, whether a song made it to an album or not. When "Seeds" was released as a single, its sleeve suggested that it was "From a forthcoming album." It would wait to be included on an expanded CD version of *Stoneground Words* in 2015. "There are some good points to ['Seeds']," said *Disc*, "notably Melanie's delivery which fluctuates from loud to soft in her characteristic style, and some useful backing vocals."[11]

"[Melanie] sings in [a] less mannered style than usual," added *Melody Maker*, "and she is developing a shade more power."[12]

"Another slab of Safka whimsy," countered *Record Mirror*, "backed by humming, bongos, and the odd bit of full choral support."[13]

Melanie and Peter entered a new phase on the morning of October 3, 1973, with the birth of their seven-pound seven-ounce daughter, Leilah Schekeryk, in the Jersey Shore University Medical Center in Neptune, New Jersey. Alison Steele made an on-air announcement. Melanie opted for natural childbirth. In case Peter wasn't there when Melanie went into labor, Potts studied the Lamaze method of childbirth with its leader in the United States, Elizabeth Bing. Developed by French obstetrician Fernand Lamaze in the 1950s, the technique used controlled breathing and distraction for pain and anxiety reduction.

Melanie assembled a six-hour "birthing" mix tape to play while she was in labor. Tracks ranged from Handel, Bach, and Brittan to ragtime pianist Scott Joplin and new age flutist Paul Horn. There was Cat Stevens's "The Boy with the Moon and Star on His Head" and Mike Heron's "You Get Brighter" from the Incredible String Band's *Wee Tam*.

Pregnancy took its toll. "It's no fun performing when you're pregnant," Melanie complained. "It's hard to hold the guitar. It gets in the way and it's hard to breathe."[14]

Recording until two days before Leilah's birth, Melanie withdrew from the stage during her fifth month of pregnancy. It wasn't her choice. Walking up a hill before a Southern New Hampshire show, she started to bleed. She was rushed to a nearby hospital, where doctors warned that she might lose the baby. It was a turning point. Until then, she hadn't been so sure she wanted to become a mother. She was afraid she'd love her cat more than her baby. Potts, whose brother was fourteen years younger, was used to caring for toddlers. She spoke with Melanie about it for hours, assuring her that everything would be all right.

Seeking further advice, Melanie telephoned her health guru, Dr. Bernard Jensen. In addition to providing a list of healing teas, the doctor recommended vitamins, sesame seed butter, and molasses. Melanie smuggled everything he suggested into the hospital. She had to stay in bed for weeks, but she gave birth to a healthy baby girl. "I thought of calling her Melanie," she confessed. "I had thought [it] would be my daughter's name ever since I was about eighteen, but when it came to the point, I just couldn't. I mean, if I hadn't become famous, it would have been a good name, but I don't want my daughter to be seen by everyone as just the daughter of a singer."

Unsure of what to name the new arrival, Melanie thumbed through a book of possibilities until she came across Leilah. Its meaning was similar to hers. Melanie, in Persian, translates as darkness dressed in black, while "Leilah," in Arabic, means dark as the night. It was perfect.

Melanie didn't take much time to recuperate. Four months after giving birth, she brought Leilah on the road with her. It wasn't difficult. Leilah's nanny, Dorothy Godfrey, traveled with them. She had spent two and a half years training to become a caregiver—splitting her time between college classes and working in a children's adoption home—and she knew what she was doing. Melanie could nurse Leilah, hand her to Dorothy, and continue doing interviews and playing shows. She had special Bedouin wedding dresses made with side panels that unzipped. She was very comfortable. She also had a masseuse traveling with her and a cook who prepared special baby food.

Dorothy was well-established as a nanny when she hooked up with Melanie. She had spent a considerable amount of time in the United States. After working with a New Jersey family, she transitioned to a family in Pennsylvania. She continued in the position after the household moved to Newport, Rhode Island.

Dorothy was between jobs, visiting friends and family in England, when she saw Melanie's ad in a trade magazine, *Nursing World*. Going to the agency the day that Leilah was born, Dorothy started working with her two weeks later.

Dorothy traveled with Melanie and Leilah wherever they went. Then Jeordie was born and there were two babies needing attention. Dorothy didn't get to see much. One hotel looked like another. She got out more in Australia, but it was for taking the kids for a walk around the block.

Leilah and Jeordie didn't eat processed baby food. Dorothy cooked everything on the road. At the Hotel Adlon Kempinski in Berlin, she wasn't permitted to use the hot plate that traveled with them. She had to go into the hotel's kitchen with the chef and prepare her zucchini. She had to wear a white coat and chef's hat.

Dorothy enjoyed a great relationship with Peter. Peter was extremely friendly. He'd bring home the weirdest people. One time, he asked Dorothy to cook roast beef and Yorkshire pudding. Going to a garage sale, he met some people and invited them for lunch. They turned out to be vegetarians.

While a couple of lullabies and a few songs about being afraid of the dark filtered out, motherhood didn't inspire Melanie to write as many songs as she thought it would. She was convinced, however, that having a baby was the answer to the world's problems. She became much less self-conscious and introverted. She realized that many of the things she thought were urgently important really weren't. She was close to being at peace.

Renting a farmhouse in the Berkshire Mountain hill town of Ashfield, Massachusetts, Peter summoned Potts with clothes, books, and musical instruments. It would result in her meeting Melanie. Sally and Peter were unpacking the car when Melanie walked past them on her way to the kitchen. She stopped and introduced herself. Sally said she knew who she was. Wasting no time, Melanie asked if she liked cream cheese in her scrambled eggs.

That was that. Potts was supposed to leave that morning but somehow one day turned into a week. When Peter left for New York to finish mixing the Carnegie Hall double album, Potts stayed with Melanie in Ashfield. They found a true kindred spirit in each other and talked incessantly about music, books, cats, and kids. They'd talk when Melanie cooked or shopped in the middle of the night. Between takes in the studio, they'd kill time talking.

After he returned, Peter offered Potts a full-time job as Melanie's personal assistant. They'd give her plenty to do. She'd carry their suitcases and book their flights. She'd accompany them to the studio. She helped with set lists and assisted Melanie during sound checks. She'd prepare tea, honey, lemons, and cognac and place them on stage. During shows, she'd check the sound balance and lighting.

In celebration of her twenty-seventh birthday, Melanie performed a sold-out show in Lincoln Center's 3,750-seat Metropolitan Opera House on February 3, 1974. It was frigidly cold and snowing, but the Carnegie Hall concerts had been warmer in ways beyond temperature. The Opera House lacked the acoustics needed for the music that Melanie played— The Who's *Tommy* had been its only previous concert of contemporary music—but it was her first show in New York in six months, and she was thrilled to be back on stage. Opening with a traditional Christmas carol, "Oh, Come All Ye Faithful," she continued to play for nearly two and a half hours. In his review for *Melody Maker*, Chris Charlesworth claimed, "The lay-off hasn't affected Melanie's clear, ringing voice which resounded perfectly in this grandiose establishment."[15]

The concert signaled a change in Melanie's relationship with her audience.

"Hundreds of fans crawled up on stage," recalled Charlesworth, "standing and sitting around her so that it became impossible for the rest of the audience—unless they were viewing the show directly head-on—to see. . . . Between every number, a third of the audience took it upon themselves to . . . call out other equally pointless suggestions and ideas."[16]

Melanie recorded much of *Madrugada*, her first studio album in a year and a half, in Nashville. When it was released in May 1974, *Cash Box* wrote, "Melanie is a special person and everything she does has an attendant air of sensitivity and caring about it, and her latest is no exception."[17]

"Sit back and relax to Melanie's most accomplished effort to date," Australian BBC DJ John Beattie told *Record & Radio Mirror* readers. "The lady with plenty of guts and a 'liberated' image has finally come to terms with herself and settled down to realize her potential."[18]

"To listen to *Madrugada*," explained *Disc*, "one must think of Melanie as an album artist, not a pop singles composer. . . . This album features more orchestration than any of Melanie's previous albums and it does suit the lady."[19]

"Her vocals are starting to get melodic," added pre-Pretenders Chrissie Hynde. "Her lyrics are still pretty bland, but she does seem to be getting her chops down. Her trip is so openly autobiographic . . . but the way she's pulling it off lately has switched from the 'little lost cutie' angle to a kind of maternal 'take my hand' approach. The fact that I'm intrigued has my mind on edge."[20]

Barely breaking into the Top 200, *Madrugada* presented a wide range of emotions. "Whereas *Stoneground Words* revels in moody balladry, *Madrugada* balances the light and the dark. . . . 'Maybe Not for a Lifetime' juxtaposes a dark lyric that would have been right at home on *Stoneground Words* to a jaunty melody. 'Holding Out,' driven by Ron Frangipane's piano, has world-weariness to it. The funereal 'The Actress' echoes the themes of 'I Am Not a Poet' and 'Between the Road Signs' in exploring the life of a performer . . . and its sacrifices. The folksy 'Pine and Father' concludes . . . on a gentle, folksy note even if it's an anti-climactic one after the dramatic 'The Actress.'"[21]

A Spanish and Portuguese word, *madrugada* describes the time right before the sun comes up, the period between dark and daylight. Unlike most people, Melanie wasn't waking up in the early hours of the morning; that's when she went to sleep.

Frangipane replaced Kellaway partway through *Good Book* and arranged the songs on *Madrugada*. A student of classical composer Paul Creston, he had taken master classes with Igor Stravinsky and Aaron Copland and arranged and/or produced records by John Lennon, Diana Ross, the Monkees, the Archies, and the Rolling Stones.

Melanie experienced both sides of what Phil Ochs called the "chords of fame"—the ascent to the top of the music world and the sharp descent into obscurity—but stardom was never her motivation. Even when her career was spiraling downward, she managed to create. That was her purpose, not to be rich and famous. "Actress" reflected on that. Centered on the line, "When they asked him to be Jesus, he turned down the role," it left room for all kinds of discussions. It was another of Melanie's in-jokes.

"Actress" interpolated a British funeral hymn, "Sleep on Beloved" (Roud 15632). The original hymn had been rewritten, and renamed "Christian's Good Night," by Portsmouth, England–born novelist/poet Sarah Doudney in 1871. During a trip to Bristol, England, thirteen years later, Brooklyn-born gospel singer/composer Ira Sankey set Doudney's words to music and sang it, as "And We Bid You Goodnight," at the funeral of a prestigious British preacher. Joseph Spence and the Pindar Family recorded it on *The Real Bahamas in Music and Song* in 1965 and the Grateful Dead included it on their *Live Dead* album four years later. Melanie heard the Incredible String Band do it as part of "A Very Cellular Song" on *Hangman's Beautiful Daughter* (1968).

The American edition of *Madrugada* included a half-dozen cover tunes. Kellaway did a wonderful string arrangement of "Wild Horses," Melanie's third song by Mick Jagger and Keith Richards. She adored Kellaway's arrangement and played guitar along with it. She loved the tune's imagery and deep, haunting melody.

Melanie recorded several tracks at Jimi Hendrix's Electric Lady Studios in the basement of 52 West Eighth Street in Greenwich Village. Upstairs, there was a music club, the Eighth Wonder. Years before, Melanie visited B. B. King in the club's dressing room. As the legendary bluesman lectured her on how to sing the blues, she listened respectfully. Janis Joplin was on the stage, and she wanted to hear her, but she stayed in the dressing room. She would never see Joplin perform though she watched her leave the club, walk into the middle of the street, and hail a cab. She noticed that Joplin was by herself and thought it sad.

Melanie had a strong affection for Randy Newman, finding a whimsy in his writing that she admired. Newman's song, "I Think It's Going to Rain Today," haunted her, and she joined a long list of artists including Ricky Nelson, Dusty Springfield, Peggy Lee, Leonard Nimoy, Helen Reddy, Nina Simone, Mama Cass Elliot, Joe Cocker, Cleo Laine, UB40, Tony Rice, David Lindley, Bette Midler, Manfred Mann, Norah Jones, and Irma Thomas covering it.

On the British edition of *Madrugada*, Melanie's cover of The Shirelles' 1962 hit, "Will You Still Love Me Tomorrow," by Gerry Goffin and Carole King, replaced "I Am Being Guided." Melanie adored the Shirelles and sang "Mama Said," "Baby, It's You," and "Dedicated to the One I Love" since her teens. Released as a single, "Will You Still Love Me Tomorrow" peaked at number eighty-four in the United States but broke into the Top 40 in the United Kingdom, where it reached the thirty-seventh slot. The British record company spent money publicizing it but "the gamble doesn't pay off," said *Disc*. "It's a pleasant but unexceptional rendering of a song that is too well known to be a hit again."

Melanie's interpretation of Jim Croce's "Lover's Cross" was *Madrugada*'s second single. Croce was another who traveled against the tide. Reviewers derided him for not being poetic like Dylan or Leonard Cohen. He was from Philadelphia, and not New York or Los Angeles, and he was married. He didn't hang out or fool around. Listening to his album *I Got a Name*, Melanie fell in love with "Lover's Cross." She adored its refusal to be someone's martyr, though she changed "he'll have to be a super guy, or maybe a super god" to "she would have to be a super girl or maybe a Joan of Arc." She didn't think he would mind and never heard from him about it. Melanie struggled with the vocals for "Lover's Cross." Nothing she tried worked. She took a break to nurse Leilah. After she returned, with Leilah asleep in her arms, she knocked it out with the next take. It was perfect.

Leilah became Melanie's traveling companion. She brought her everywhere she went. They shared a child-like spirit, turning everything into a fun experience. Sometimes, the laughs were unexpected. Pretending to be lost in the woods one day, Melanie asked the child what they should do. Without hesitation, Leilah, accustomed to living in hotels, suggested ordering room service.

Leilah learned early on that people were cruel to those who had imagination. She was always the new kid in school, picked on for being creative. She decided to use reverse psychology. Rather than being defensive, she would counter their cruelty with warmth, openness, and friendship.

At first, Melanie answered every piece of fan mail. One fan started writing every day in handwriting that was so tiny she could barely read the words. Pages and pages and pages, he must have stayed up all night writing. When she recorded "Ruby Tuesday" and it became a hit, something clicked like a switch in his head. He became incensed and started writing vicious letters threatening her. She gave little thought to his threats when she embarked on a UK tour in June 1974, but when she performed at the Drury Theatre, he threw a brick onto the stage. It missed her by a half-inch. She thought someone had shot at her. The audience didn't know what was going on. Melanie continued her show. Security apprehended the obsessed fan but released him after he apologized. It wasn't over, though. Melanie's "admirer" presented her with a box of chocolates with shards of razor blades embedded in the chocolate. Again, he said that he was sorry, and security let him go. In their eyes, Melanie was the big American star in a small English town, and he was a fan expressing himself. She obtained a restraining order, and police were stationed at the doors of her concerts to ensure that he wouldn't get in. But they let her know they opposed keeping someone who wanted to see her show from coming. They treated her as though she was a lunatic. It shook her. There was a crazy person who wanted her dead, and he was allowed to run free. He pursued her as far as Florida. Somehow, she got wind that he was coming. Authorities knew which airline he was flying, and where he was supposed to be sitting, but the seat remained empty.

CHAPTER 17

Peter was a ball of energy, keeping up with the schedule of the entire world. He'd wake early in the morning to call a time zone and be up late calling another. He was always wheeling and dealing. He loved playing the game of business and making deals, but he made mistakes while thinking that he was doing the right thing. He wouldn't pay the electric bill, or a session player, and use the money to promote Melanie's record, hoping that the payoff would be big enough to pay the electric bill and the session player and make a profit. He was never in his comfort zone or anybody else's. He catapulted into having to run a mega-business and that wasn't within his scope. He was a record producer; he didn't make decisions based on business and he didn't get good advice from anyone. People told him what they thought he wanted to hear, nothing to do with reality. Clive Davis surrounded himself with knowledgeable people, but Peter trusted the wrong ones. He hired the Long Island City accountant who handled taxes for Melanie's parents, the local shoe store, and the community dentist. It might have been better to bring on someone more astute in the music industry, but Peter resisted sharing control of any part of Melanie's career.

Kept in the dark, Melanie lost perspective of reality. She had a working machine building her public image and she "could be as wacky" as she wanted. Celebrity privilege sometimes got the best of her. She refused to perform, for example, on the same day that she traveled. Peter respected that. If she played a concert on a Friday, for instance, she couldn't play on Saturday if it involved traveling. There were things she had to have on the road with her—like her dogs and cats. She tried to stay in hotels that allowed pets, but when she couldn't, she'd smuggle them in. Roadies carried cat litter with them.

Money was of little concern. "I did all the things you expect rock stars to do," Melanie told the *Toronto Globe*, "all the trivial things that you're not supposed to do. We just trivialized the money and gave it to people. I was embarrassed about it and didn't want it. We'd hire two floors of the hotels, give parties, [and] hire live-in weightlifters for the house, things like that."[22]

There were so many people in charge of Melanie's career, that she feared that she had "lost the freedom of flopping and [the ability to] look after me. So many people have said, 'You don't want to bother yourself with your money problems, let us handle all that ugly stuff for you.'"[23]

Complicating matters, Peter increasingly opted for distilled spirits over buttermilk, occasionally drinking too much after a show. He wasn't yet into biochemical drugs, cocaine, or marijuana—those would come later. "We don't see too much of each other," Melanie confessed, "because I travel a lot, but I think that's a good thing. We appreciate each other more. Since I've gotten myself together, my marriage has been extremely happy. I think any time a person improves within themselves, the person with them feels that security in them. You're adding something to the relationship because you're becoming a stronger person."[24]

CHAPTER 18

"CYCLONE"

Gulf and Western's split with Neighborhood Records came as a complete shock. It had expanded its stake in music, absorbing thirteen smaller labels, but the acquisition had left it financially unstable. It couldn't have happened at a worse time. Melanie was at her creative peak. She had great new songs but no outlet for her records. She needed to connect with another label. That connection, surprisingly, came through Clive Davis.

CBS terminated the attorney-turned-record executive on May 20, 1973, for allegedly misappropriating "$53,700 for alterations to [his] apartment; at least $20,000 for a bar mitzvah for his son . . . and $20,000 of reimbursements that CBS claimed he used to pay for renting a house in Beverly Hills. . . . In its legal complaint, the company also listed one alleged cash kickback."[1]

Davis denied using CBS's money to pay for his son's bar mitzvah and shifted blame to a former head of artist relations "in cahoots with a mobster." Pleading guilty to failing to pay $2,700 in taxes on $8,800 of contested travel expenses, he wasn't out of music for long. As soon as he became available, Columbia Screen Gems (unconnected to Columbia Records until 1988) hired him as a consultant to its music division, which included Bell, Colpix, and Colgems Records. When Larry Uttal left to start Private Stock, Davis took his place as president. The date was May 20, 1974, a year to the day after his dismissal from CBS. Wasting no time, he consolidated Columbia Screen Gems' subsidiaries into Arista Records. Releasing most artists from their contracts, he held on to the Bay City Rollers, Melissa Manchester, and Barry Manilow, whose second album yielded a massive international MOR hit, "Mandy." Addressing

139

the label's saccharine approach, British rocker Nick Lowe sang "Arista say they love it, but the kids can't dance to it" in his 1978 song, "They Called It Rock."

When Peter told Melanie they were signing with Arista, she protested. "Not Clive Davis. No!" They bickered back and forth, but Peter assured her that the record executive had changed. Reluctantly, she agreed to meet with her former employer. When they arrived at Davis's office, Peter and the record mogul shook hands and quickly negotiated an agreement. That was that—Arista and Clive Davis.

As promised, Davis refrained from being as brutal as he had been when Melanie was starting out. She had more clout now and he had to be careful. They were, however, destined to clash. When Davis learned that she was pregnant, he didn't tell Melanie to have an abortion, but he warned her that it might not be the best time for a baby, and he strongly suggested that she reconsider it. She didn't give any further thought to it. On March 27, 1975, she delivered her second daughter, Jeordie.

Davis had little understanding of what Melanie was doing musically. She rebelled against his suggestion that she record "Somewhere in the Night" by Richard Kerr and Will Jennings. It would be a Top 20 hit for both Helen Reddy and Barry Manilow, but Melanie considered it overly slick. Davis was insistent that she record it and recruited Rick Chertoff (who would produce hits for Joan Osborne and Cyndi Lauper) to play piano and supervise the recording. Tension continued to build. One night, as Melanie rehearsed, Chertoff demanded that she "sing on the beat." It completely shook her. She had no clue what it meant but she realized that, if she did what she thought Chertoff was asking, it would obliterate her phrasing, her uniqueness, what was truly her own. She reluctantly completed the demo but refused to do it the way Chertoff wanted her to do it.

Davis continued to be dismissive. When Peter sent him demos recorded with Melanie in Nashville, the mogul was livid. It wasn't what he was expecting. During a phone conversation, he asked Melanie why she was in Nashville playing "shitkicker music." Arista would become the hip, "new country" label, and Davis would sign Alan Jackson, Carrie Underwood, Brad Paisley, Pam Tillis, Steve Wariner, Michelle Wright, Deana Carter, and Tanya Tucker, but Melanie would be long gone by then.

While in Music City, Melanie, Peter, and their daughters lived next door to Country Music Hall of Famer Webb Pierce. On weekends, the honky-tonk/rockabilly superstar blasted loud music for passengers on tour buses. He built a ramp so fans could admire his guitar-shaped swimming pool and take pictures. Pierce's adopted son was a frequent visitor to Melanie and Peter's home. Melanie got the feeling that he didn't have a lot to do with his father. He was always by himself. Ray Stevens later sued Pierce because, when the tour buses drove up the ramp, they could look down onto his swimming pool, which he didn't like.

Melanie wrote a song with Ken Williams, Nashville-based composer of Randy Travis's country hit, "Three Little Crosses," but it didn't flow, and she soon forgot about it.

Released in February 1975, Melanie's sixth album, *As I See It Now*, included a "quality mix of ballads, mid-tempo, good-natured rockers; a wonderfully done Dylan tune ('Don't Think Twice, It's Alright'); and an interesting one from the good old days ('Yes Sir, That's My Baby'). . . . [It] stands as an album as well as a collection of potential singles . . . strongest item from the lady in a long while."[2]

"A pronounced country-rock influence permeates a number of the tracks," observed *Second Disc*, "including the reflective 'You're Not a Bad Ghost, Just an Old Song,' 'Sweet Misery' and 'Monongahela River' though other songs like the stomping 'Eyes of Man' (incorporating Native American-influenced chants) and the spare, near-sketch of a song, 'Stars Up There,' betray no country sound at all."[3]

The basic tracks featured Roy Yeager (drums, conga, tambourine, and sand block), John Mulkey (bass), Barry Harwood (electric guitar, acoustic guitar, angel guitar, pedal steel, and banjo), and Frank Franco (acoustic guitar, bottleneck acoustic guitar, xylophone, and sand block). Everyone but Franco sang. Keyboard duties were split between Steve Feldman (piano, electric piano, conga, bongos, celeste, tambourine), John Shane Keister (piano, electric piano, honky-tonk piano); and Sy Moon (tack piano). Additional players included George March (woodwinds); Gene Bianco (harp); Toots Thielemans (harmonica); George Ricci (cello); Harry Wimmer (electric cello); and Richard Davis (bowed bass). Cliff Nivison, Susie Watson Taylor, and Steve Feldman sang background vocals.

Originally titled *Small Town Desperation*, *As I See It* included three cover tunes. Uncle George used to sing Dylan's "Don't Think Twice, It's Alright" and he encouraged Melanie to do it. Melanie showcased her interpretative skills with Gus Kahn and Walter Donaldson's "Yes Sir, That's My Baby," one of Polly's favorite songs. It was introduced by Detroit-born Margaret Young in 1925; more than one hundred artists including Frank Sinatra, Ricky Nelson, Nat King Cole, and Count Basie covered it. Melanie also revisited her mother's era with "Stars Up There," an original song from "the mindset of a woman from the 1940s."

Melanie wrote "Eyes of Man" during a visit to Uncle George's cabin on Cape Cod. Waking early one morning, she walked across the street to the beach. Sitting on the sand, surrounded by dunes, her thoughts wandered. It was that magical time, that *madrugada* time, just before sunrise.

The astrology-themed "The Chart Song" was recorded at Theatre Royale in London, with Frangipane (piano) and the Incredible String Band's Robin Williamson (kalimba) and Mike Heron (Moog, acoustic guitar, background vocals). "I have an astrologer," Melanie told the *Sidmouth Herald*, "but I don't get daily word on what to do or anything like that. Just to get your chart is to know yourself a little more. . . . There is some strange energy following me around. I'm not kidding you. I've really got this strange kind of positive energy with me."[4]

Madrugada's closing tune, "Monongahela River," responded to Melanie's tour stop in Pittsburgh. Reading a biography of the Italian actor Eleonora Duse, who died in the Pennsylvania city in 1924, she recognized its harsh vibe—iron and coal, the mining industry. While she was there, pollution on the river became so toxic, it caught on fire. By the time that the album came out, however, a massive urban facelift had begun. Downtown Pittsburgh was becoming artsy. Melanie's song struck anger in the city. A reporter asked why she was slamming Pittsburgh. Didn't she know it had always supported the arts?

Released in October 1975, Melanie's second and final Arista album, *Sunset and Other Beginnings*, included Alan J. Lerner and Frederick J. Lowe's "Almost Like Being in Love" from *Brigadoon* (1947) and Jerome Kern and Oscar Hammerstein's "Ol' Man River" from *Showboat* (1927). Reinvented as a minor key, soft-rock ballad, "Almost Like Being in Love" was released as a single in 1975. It failed to chart. Three years later,

Michael Johnson borrowed from Melanie's recording and scored a Top 40 hit.

Sunset and Other Beginnings included covers of Lindisfarne guitarist Rod Clements's "Dream Seller (Meet Me on the Corner)" and a medley comprised of Diana Ross and the Supremes' "You Can't Hurry Love" and the Shirelles' "Mama Said." There was even a version of Muddy Waters's showstopper "Got My Mojo Working," composed by blues guitarist Preston "Red" Foster.

"Loving My Children," "Afraid of the Dark," "Sandman," and "The Sun and the Moon" were inspired by Leilah and Jeordie. Melanie's maternal instincts were piqued, and she had a different focus than she had in the past. It wasn't all about her. She was into living an organic, natural life and trying to control the environment around her children.

Leilah and Jeordie were close from the start. Jeordie often hung out with her older sister. Their lives differed from other people's, and they had a hard time finding anyone who understood what they were going through. It wasn't easy to find friends, but they always had each other.

As teens, the sisters became more independent. Leilah spent more and more time with her boyfriend, while Jeordie hung out with her own friends. They took their connection for granted until Leilah headed to college. Jeordie, still in high school, missed her sister badly.

The front window of Sam Goody's Record Store, on Forty-Ninth Street off Broadway in Manhattan, displayed *Sunset and Other Beginnings* when it was released. It wouldn't be there for long. Problems began after Clive Davis asked Melanie to write an endorsement of his autobiography, *Clive: Inside the Music Business*. She reluctantly agreed to do it but had serious second thoughts once she read the book. She found it so self-serving it made her ill. She didn't know what to do. Every other artist on Arista endorsed it. It would have been a standard career move, but she couldn't bring herself to do it. She kept stalling, repeatedly telling Davis's secretary that she would do it the following week. She used every excuse to get out of doing it. Finally, an ultimatum was issued, "You

WILL endorse this book, or we'll write something and put your name on it!"

With her continued refusal, Melanie's album came out of Sam Goody's window and Davis's book went in. The conflict would sever Melanie's connection with Arista. Again, Peter had a fabulous escape clause. Davis became another enemy in a high place.

CHAPTER 19

"LOOK WHAT THEY'VE DONE
TO MY SONG, MA"

Melanie and Peter were recording in Los Angeles when they received a phone call from Atlantic Records cofounder Ahmet Ertegun, the Istanbul-born son of Turkey's first ambassador to the United States. Attending Melanie's sold-out concert at Royal Alpert Hall, he had been enthusiastic about her performance. Peter invited him to the studio to watch her record Harold Arlen and Yip Harburg's "Somewhere over the Rainbow" from *The Wizard of Oz*. When Ertegun arrived, Peter got into his white Rolls-Royce, and they drove around for a few blocks. When they came back, Peter had a signed contract with Atlantic. He later bought a white Rolls-Royce for himself.

Ertegun took over Melanie's recording sessions after she moved to a larger studio, the Sound Factory, in Hollywood. It wasn't her favorite place. The control booth had the biggest mixing board she had ever seen and there were cocaine mirrors built right into it. She had absolutely no interest in the white powder and wanted nothing to do with it. She considered it an extremely unmusical drug.

At the time, the drug culture was going through changes. Pharmaceutical drugs were starting to emerge. People were constantly handing Melanie all kinds of pills. She'd throw them into the trash. "I don't think it was an accident that the PR against drugs was always so silly," she told the *Sidmouth Herald*. "People were . . . sold the idea that times were changing, and, instead of caring about the planet, the mood became 'Me first, right now!' But that wasn't any more real than the idea that everybody at the time of Woodstock was caring about peace and love—there are opportunists, political groups who seize on these tendencies as a way of manipulating large numbers of young people."[1]

Melanie considered Ertegun to be the real deal—authentic and fun. He oversaw a music empire with his brother, but he knew how to make artists feel good. That's where he came from; he had been Billie Holiday's roadie. He told Melanie that she reminded him of Holiday, the ultimate compliment. [Ertegun] was ecstatic about Melanie's voice. He not only admired her ability to sing original songs but also the way she could turn a jazz standard into her own.

Bassist Jerry Scheff had played for Elvis Presley, the Doors, Bob Dylan, and John Denver. The rhythm section included drummers Jim Gordon, John Guerin, and Jeff Porcaro and percussionist Milt Holland of Phil Spector's Wrecking Crew. Members of the Edwin Hawkins Singers sang harmony. Richard Greene, who had played with Bill Monroe and the Blue Grass Boys and Seatrain, was featured on violin. Robin Williamson took a mandolin solo on "Rain Dance."

David Paich played keyboards and handled the arrangements. The son of pianist, composer, music director, producer, and Barbra Streisand's string arranger Martin Louis "Marty" Paich, he divided his time between Melanie's sessions and starting a band with Steve Porcaro, Steve Lukather, Keith Carlock, and Joseph Williams. It was in the works behind the scenes. They took their name (Toto) from the liner notes of *Photograph*. Melanie referred to Dorothy and Toto from *The Wizard of Oz* and they took it from there.

Melanie found Paich's approach to music perturbing. She thought he had too clear a vision of how he wanted to design Toto. It was overly premeditated. Rather than building the group around the music, he was assembling it to appeal to a specific demographic. Melanie considered it overly Hollywood-ish. Romantically involved with Emmy-winning actor Rosanna Arquette, Paich would write Toto's top-five hit "Rosanna" for her.

Melanie was at a very high point vocally and energetically. She was going through a prolific period, producing tons of new songs. She'd wake in the middle of the night, grab a pencil and paper, and write.

It was a wonderful time. Melanie was in peak shape physically. She had gotten her weight down and was very high on life. She was the mother of two healthy daughters and thrilled about it. She recorded with that spirit, and it showed in her concerts. During shows at the Bottom

Line, she donned a blonde wig and called herself "Dolly McPharlan." "Sometimes . . . putting a stupid wig on your head, or screaming, or doing some rotten thing," she told *Rolling Stone*, "will break [the public's image]. I'm not out there creating musical masterpieces that only the few can listen to—I'm really a communicator."[2]

The Hand-Made Band accompanied Melanie on the road. Dave Doran had played guitar for Moby Grape and Barefoot Jerry. Jim Drennan (keyboards, piano, synthesizer, orchestron, and clavinet) played bass using the pedals of his keyboard. Symphonic percussionist and UCLA professor Angelo Mauceri added marimba and tympani. Unfortunately, the group failed to gel. Mauceri's orchestral approach wasn't right for Melanie's style.

Bassist Jay Wolfe looked good on stage but, in the studio, he couldn't keep a groove and wasn't steady. Melanie tried him on one or two songs but replaced his bass parts. Credited in the liner notes, Wolf was enraged that his playing had been eradicated from the final recording. Taking a lien on Melanie and Peter's house, he instituted a lawsuit "seeking an exorbitant amount of money for [their] failing to pay him for the recording sessions." On the road when Dorothy accepted the summons, Melanie and Peter were unaware of the lawsuit until it was too late. They lost by default.

It was an extremely difficult time for Peter. He had gone from producing records in small studios to the "big time," where he had to take a back seat to Ahmet Ertegun, David Paich, Marty Paich, and the recording engineer. In the past, he had been hands-on, talking with musicians and offering suggestions. Recordings reflected his input. Now he was outnumbered and outpowered; he wasn't one of "the guys." They gave him credit as a producer but took his power from him.

Soon after advance copies of *Photograph* went out to reviewers, Ertegun left for Turkey. Melanie and Peter didn't see him again until much later. The album was a critical success. John Rockwell of the *New York Times* called it one of the top releases of the year and pointed out that Melanie's "composing and phrasing are those of a major artist."[3]

"Melanie seems to have made the transition," added *Rolling Stone*, "from flower child to woman rather nicely and with her talents intact."[4]

Comparing *Photograph* to Joni Mitchell's *Hejira*, *Crawdaddy* proclaimed, "[*Photograph*] meets and beats . . . Mitchell on any songwriting terms they can now be seen to share."[5]

"[*Photograph*] shows the versatility—jazz, blues, gospel, [and] country—[Melanie] has always attempted," chimed in the *St. Petersburg Times*, "but with a new self-assuredness and control of the emotional excesses she was always criticized for."[6]

Considering such rave reviews, Atlantic's withdrawal of the album was incomprehensible. "For all the maturity [*Photograph*] revealed," said Rockwell, "Melanie is very clearly still a person easily hurt, one who moves intuitively, and moodily, through a world full of laughter and more cynical people than she."[7]

Peter frantically tried to contact Ertegun, but the record mogul was in Turkey and unreachable.

Stylistically, *Photograph* stood on its own. It wasn't pop like Barbra Streisand's, Helen Reddy's, or Karen Carpenter's records. There wasn't enough folk music for the folkies, but it wasn't totally artsy. It had plenty of bouncy rhythms and catchy, repetitive lines. It had the potential to be a breakthrough, but its emotional diversity and lyrical depth countered what record companies were promoting. Glamorous hairdos and sequined suits were in. Atlantic kept Melanie's album off the shelves. "Music should transcend marketing," she told the *Sidmouth Herald*. "People should be able to hear a lot more variety of music. Radio has a polarizing effect. People like 'this' music, they wear 'those' jeans, they have 'this sort of' hairstyle, [and] they wear 'those' socks."[8]

Hard-rocking opening track "Cyclone" should have been a hit single. Melanie and the Hand-Made Band did their best to promote it, performing scorching versions on Dick Clark's *American Bandstand* and ABC-TV's *Brady Bunch Hour* in March 1977. On the latter, Melanie sang "Somewhere over the Rainbow" in a medley of movie tunes with Florence Henderson, the Brady Kids, and impressionist Rich Little.

"Groundhog Day" was another example of Melanie's sense of humor. She had fun singing it.

"'Save Me' remains one of [Melanie's] finest pieces," said the *All Music Guide*, "a fiery, feverish song with a mesmeric David Campbell string arrangement. It puts her on a par with more respected peers like Laura Nyro."[9]

A tenor saxophone solo by Gardena, California–born Arthur Edward "Art" Pepper (1925–1982) featured during "I'm So Blue." Melanie was recording when Ertegun ran excitedly into the studio. He had gone to a jazz club, Billy's Baked Potato, where Pepper was playing with his small combo. He spoke with the saxophonist after their set and invited him to the studio. A sideman for Benny Carter and Stan Kenton in the mid-'40s, Pepper was a pioneer, along with Chet Baker, Gerry Mulligan, and Shelly Manne, of what became known as "West Coast Jazz." Drug addiction, however, left him a tragic character.

Melanie's mother measured success by how thin she was. If she was skinny, she was doing all right. If she gained weight, she wasn't. Melanie saw a correlation with music. If a musician was making money, and playing in big halls, they were doing well. If they were playing lower-echelon gigs, that was who they were, and that's where Pepper was. She felt bad for him. He played beautifully. She could hear it in his solo—a first or second take—but he had spent too much time in drug rehabilitation centers where they had beaten his sense of integrity out of him. He would die from a stroke in June 1982.

Melanie dedicated "I'm So Blue" to her mother. She had become famous for doing what her mother had always wanted to do but it left her depressed. Polly kept blaming Peter for widening the divide, but he was doing whatever he could to keep her connection with her daughter going. Melanie didn't have patience for it. She was working hard. She had no idea about what to do about her mother's problems, so she avoided her. When Polly called, Peter would answer the phone and say that she was too busy to talk. She couldn't take the constant attacks.

Melanie wrote the closing track, "Friends and Company," as a response to a born-again Christian movement emerging in Nashville. Reassessing her religious convictions, she pleaded, "Oh God, I need to swallow you whole again."

Ertegun thought the playful "Whomp-bomp" could be a hit, but it didn't make it onto the album; perhaps, as Melanie suspected, if it had been a hit, the label wouldn't have been able to suppress the album as easily as it did. The song would debut on *Photograph Double Exposure* in 2005.

A few months after Atlantic withdrew *Photograph*, Melanie and Peter met with Ertegun. Melanie was still shattered. Peter took a back seat during the meeting. He didn't want to start trouble, believing this could be his wife's big shot. Expecting to be discussing the postponed release of *Photograph*, Melanie was stunned when Ertegun started by asking about her plans for her next album. She sang a few songs before he stopped her and said, "Maybe you should put the guitar down and do other people's songs."

Rumors circulated that Melanie turned down an invitation to open for the Rolling Stones' American tour, a slot that went to Billy Preston. It would have been a natural connection; she recorded several Stones tunes. Peter dismissed the rumors. "If the Rolling Stones want Melanie to go on the road with them," he assured *Billboard*, "she would."[10]

Partway through the *Photograph* sessions, Potts resigned. She would become the first woman to graduate from the University of Miami's audio engineering program in 1980. The opportunity to go back to school was not the only reason for her resignation. The first year she worked for Melanie, she was paid well. Then, problems started to arise. She went two years without being paid. Melanie didn't know; Peter kept the truth from her.

"Peter kept people away from her," said Tomczak. "Deep down, he was an insecure man. He knew what he had with her—the talent—and it scared him. He wanted to be sure she wouldn't catch on with anyone but him. He kept her preoccupied and confused. She never knew where she was landing but you could never say anything about it to her. She was so caught up in it that she blocked it out."

"Melanie divorced herself from direct contact," added Uncle George. "You couldn't call her on the phone. Peter would answer every time and say 'What do you want? I'll tell her.'"

Even Melanie's children encountered resistance when they tried to call. Melanie went long periods without hearing from the kids. They tried calling, but Peter would answer and refuse to pass the phone to Melanie. He was afraid they would tell her bad news.

Phoning after Peter's death, Jeordie was amazed when her mother answered. It was the first time she could remember them talking without having to talk to her father first.

Though she understood that her father was shielding her mother from being hurt, Leilah believed things should have been more transparent. There were things her mother should have known, like her financial condition, but she was kept unaware.

CHAPTER 20
"PEOPLE IN THE FRONT ROW"

Richard Diamond's "You've Got a Brand New Pair of Figure Skates" used the melody of "Brand New Key" to poke fun at Tonya Harding's 1994 attack on US Olympic skater Nancy Kerrigan. The Irish Brigade, a rebel band from county Tyrone, rewrote it as "Kinky Boots" to protest British security in Northern Ireland. A scrumpy & western or novelty folk band from Somerset, England, the Wurzels adapted it for "I've Got a Brand New Combine Harvester." It became a chart-topping hit in the United Kingdom in June 1976.

"People in the Front Row" was interpolated, in 2003, into the Adelaide, Australia–based Hilltop Hoods' hip-hop track, "The Nosebleed Section." It broke into Australia's Triple J Hottest 10 upon its release; listeners voted it into the seventeenth slot on the Hottest 100 of All Time six years later. A list of the Hottest 100 of the past twenty years, compiled in 2013, placed it in the twentieth position. The holder of the publishing rights of "People in the Front Row" found out about its use and collected. Melanie didn't. By that point, she didn't own the song anymore, having signed away the publishing rights to all of her tunes before 1993. "[Peter] without my knowing sold my writer's share," she told the *Australian*. "In some countries that's not even legal. I didn't even know it had happened. That was in 2004. I found out about it right after he passed, and I was sure it was a mistake. I couldn't have signed away my writer's share, but I did."[1]

"Feeling a lot of pressure to be commercial and to keep under budget,"[2] Melanie delivered *Phonogenic (Not Just Another Pretty Face)*. The *Los Angeles Times* took a mixed view. Forecasting that "this LP should help dispel her outdated flower-child image," and suggesting that Melanie was

153

"a distinctive vocalist whose wistful, raggedy style has taken on a note of fully developed authority," it questioned why she had included "so many overworked standards [rather] than more of her own material."[3]

Phonogenic (Not Just Another Pretty Face)'s stark, black-and-white cover contrasted with the music industry's emphasis on glamour. Melanie had done a session with a professional photographer and the results had been beautifully stunning. Not wanting to be "just another pretty face," however, she vetoed a "visually striking cover" and instructed the art director to design "a simple black cover with the title in white letters."

Recorded at the Hit Factory, *Phonogenic (Not Just Another Pretty Face)* featured the Brecker Brothers—Michael (saxophone and flute) and Randy (flugelhorn and trumpet). The Philadelphia-born siblings not only collaborated on commercially successful jazz-fusion albums but also sported extensive résumés on their own. An original member of Blood, Sweat & Tears, Randy toured with Horace Silver's Quintet and Art Blakey's Jazz Messengers and recorded with Ron Carter, Billy Cobham, Aerosmith, Todd Rundgren, Lou Reed, and Frank Zappa. Michael played on records by James Taylor, Herbie Hancock, Chick Corea, George Benson, Charles Mingus, Jaco Pastorius, Pat Metheny, and Billy Joel, and he was a member of the *Saturday Night Live* band. The *Down Beat* Jazz Hall of Fame would posthumously induct him in 2007.

Richard Tee played keyboards. A Brooklyn-born graduate of the High School of Music and Art, his discography included records with Paul Simon, Art Garfunkel, Barbra Streisand, Diana Ross, Quincy Jones, George Harrison, Billy Joel, and Eric Clapton and eight albums as a bandleader. He was a charter member of jazz-funk supergroup Stuff in 1976. Chris Parker, also a member of Stuff, played drums.

Phonogenic (Not Just Another Pretty Face) included Eddie Floyd and Steve Cropper's "Knock on Wood," Lennon and McCartney's "We Can Work It Out," and Carole Bayer Sager's "I'd Rather Leave While I'm In Love." Melanie changed Jesse Winchester's "Yankee Man" to "Yankee Lady" and altered some of his lyrics. She loved the Memphis-raised and Montreal-based songwriter's tune, especially its images of autumn in New England where "decent folk live in the hills of Old Vermont" but needed to personalize it. Winchester sang about taking up with a woman; she changed it to a "full-grown man." The two songwriters met in Florida. Melanie was headlining at a large theater on the night that Winchester was appearing a few blocks away in a small club. Walking over after her show, planning to sing "Yankee Man" with him, she found him uncommunicative. He glared at her but didn't say a single word. His silence unnerved her. She tried to explain that, considering society's view of the role of a man and a woman, the person singing didn't "sound as much like a jerk if it was a woman taking advantage of a man rather a man taking advantage of a woman." Winchester hated what she was saying. He stared chillingly at her for a couple of seconds and then turned around and walked away. She felt humiliated. He hadn't said one nice thing to her. She thought he was going to snap.

Melanie's rendition of "California Dreamin'" unfolded spontaneously in the studio. She was in the vocal booth when Tee started to play the Mamas and the Papas' hit on piano. Melanie knew the words and she started to sing. Peter recorded it without them knowing that the tape was rolling. Some of Melanie's best recordings happened when she didn't know the tape was rolling. She'd be warming up or trying out a new tune, and Peter would flip the switch on the recorder.

"Melanie builds an impassioned vocal," said the *Boston Globe*, "that gives the song poignancy that the Mamas and the Papas' smooth harmonies could not pin down."[4]

"Melanie's strange phrasing allows her to get nuances out of songs," added the *New York Post*, "another reason why 'California Dreamin'' is so hauntingly beautiful."[5]

A top-ten love song for the Everly Brothers in 1960, "Let It Be Me" was composed by Gilbert Becaud with French lyrics by Pierre Delanoë.

Arthur Prysock's R&B cover of Melanie's "Spunky" was included on the Spartanburg, South Carolina–born saxophonist's posthumous CD, *Here's to Good Friends* (2013).

Musicians on *Phonogenic (Not Just Another Pretty Face)* were familiar to TV viewers. Will Lee played bass for Paul Schaeffer's World's Most Dangerous Band, the house band for *Late Night with David Letterman* from 1982 until 2015. He arranged for Melanie to be a guest on the show, but the producers canceled her appearance at the last minute. She was also scheduled to appear on *Saturday Night Live*, but they ran out of time. Neither show was rescheduled.

WNEW-FM broadcast Melanie's sold-out June 3, 1978, concert at Carnegie Hall. "Just as her performance before a million people a decade ago started the explosion that led to her becoming the top female new star in the American music scene," read the program booklet, "her performance here tonight is sure to make the evening nothing less than a major musical event."[6]

Melanie's band included Sal DiTroia (acoustic guitar), Robbie Georgia (lead and rhythm guitars), Tony Battaglia (lead, rhythm, and bass guitars), Louis Cabeza (keyboards), Stan Kipper (drums), and Bob Leone (bass). The concert was divided into two halves, separated by a fifteen-minute intermission.

The Brecker Brothers made a guest appearance during the second set. They would play several shows with Melanie including the Academy of Music in their hometown, Philadelphia. "We jammed our parts," remembered Randy Brecker. "We loved the way Melanie sang."

Critics remarked on Melanie's appearance at Carnegie Hall. She bought her cool 1920s dress and long, orchid-colored pants that flowed like a skirt and tied at the waist in a vintage dress shop on the Upper West Side of Manhattan. She found her "gorgeous, hand-painted silk shirt" in an art store. "Her freshly permed hair surrounded her noble, beautiful, radiant face," wrote one unnamed reporter. "her appearance is much more mature and sexual."[7]

"The audience gazed upon a young, beautiful, shapely woman," added John Lambo, "in a black sequined dress worn just below the knee, with a matching shawl and black, high-heeled shoes. Her hair, slightly curled, with a hint of gray, was worn up on one side."[8]

In his *New York Times* review, John Rockwell tore into Melanie's performance. "[She] didn't have a very firm notion of when enough was enough," he wrote, "letting her encores run on raggedly way past the emotional climax of the evening."

Rockwell was especially critical of Melanie's singing. "When she pushed it loudly toward the top, before shifting into the fluty, soprano, upper-extension she sometimes uses, it took on a hard, tense, forced quality. . . . Unless she takes vocal lessons, it could never hold up in the kind of day-in/day-out theatrical revue that her gifts would suit her for well."

Rather than rushing into another recording studio, Melanie and Peter rented a beachfront, five-bedroom, five-bath, 5,428-square-foot house at

461 Ocean Boulevard in Golden Beach, Florida (sixteen minutes north of Miami). Eric Clapton recorded one of his best albums in the house. A photo of the house is on its cover. Built in 1940, its location was supreme, amid one of Florida's most exclusive areas. Zillow valued it at more than $18,000,000 in March 2024.

The only single from the sessions was a cover of Buddy Holly's upbeat raver "Oh Boy" paired in the United States with a jazz redo of "Brand New Key." RCA released it in Germany with "Runnin' after Love" on the flip side. "When I was growing up," Melanie said, "[Holly] was the only one who meant anything to me. . . . 'Oh Boy' was just a thing we did to fill time."[9]

Ballroom Streets was released as a double album in November 1978. Tomato Records issued it in the United States and RCA in the United Kingdom. "Melanie is a contender to be reckoned with," wrote one critic, "and I reckon that the airplay out of the box will finally, and firmly, establish Melanie as the bright alternative to the female singers on the charts today."[10]

Ballroom Streets took four days to complete. Melanie sang to prerecorded tracks featuring Tony Battaglia (guitar, slide guitar), Louis Cabaza (keyboards), Robbie Georgia (Dobro, rhythm guitar), Stan Kipper (drums), and Bob Leone (bass) before an invited audience of roughly thirty people at Triad Studios in Ft. Lauderdale. Mary McCaffrey sang background vocals. The Persuasions harmonized on "Secret of the Darkness (I Believe)." "We had that low, haunting style of harmony," bass singer Jimmy Hayes (1942–2017) told me during lunch in Brooklyn. "Everybody loved it."

Kevin Eggers, the Brooklyn Heights–born owner of Tomato Records, launched his first label (Poppy Records) after signing Townes Van Zandt in 1966. Sid Bernstein's former assistant, he would work with Van Zandt until the Texas songwriter's death thirty-one years later. Eggers's labels released albums by Albert King, John Lee Hooker, Nina Simone, Doc Watson, John Cage, and Philip Glass.

Sparing no expense when it came to Melanie, Eggers was excited when her album was released. His enthusiasm quickly fizzled. He "promoted it heavily for a minute and then let it die." Tomato went out of business and *Ballroom Streets* went out of print. For Melanie, it was another "all-too-brief romance."

Part 6
HITS AND MISSES (1980–1990)

CHAPTER 21

"RUBY TUESDAY"

B eau Jarred Schekeryk was born on Thursday, September 11, 1980. Melanie had a powerful maternal instinct, but she was equally passionate about what she did as an artist. Being a musician was the only life she knew; having a family gave her a feeling of stability.

Beau's sisters remember him as a terror. There was no limit to what Beau was capable of doing. He'd run through the house dressed in all kinds of ridiculous costumes and screaming like a madman. One time, he threw a glass at his sisters watching TV. It came close to their heads and shattered. Dorothy had a hard time believing he would do such a thing.

In retaliation, Leilah and Jeordie chased their brother around the house with a vacuum cleaner.

Recording in a Bogalusa, Louisiana, studio until her eighth month of pregnancy, Melanie and Peter settled in Sarasota, Florida's exclusive Whitaker Estates to prepare for childbirth. Their house was one of the oldest homes on the Gulf Coast. Leilah and Jeordie had bedrooms on the second floor. Melanie prepared a room for Beau. She did artsy things like embedding ancient Japanese paper in polyurethane on the floors. It looked beautiful. Walt Disney had once resided in the house, and there was a board in one of the bedrooms with his scribbling.

The tranquility faded when the house, like the Rag House, was lost to foreclosure. Losing her second house was heartbreaking but Melanie was oblivious to the extent of the damage. Peter was digging deeper into debt while assuring her that everything was fine. Somehow, they managed to live in beautiful homes. Peter was a master at finding investors, but he spent money like it was flowing from a tap, thinking the good times would last forever. It was a sharp awakening when they didn't.

During a 1973 interview, Melanie told *Cosmopolitan* that she had been drug-free for five years. "I never lost control," she said, "but I had a dependency on speed, and it was horrible. . . . I couldn't go to sleep at night. I'd have to take something else to go to sleep. It was insane. I was living on one kind of pill after another."[1]

Forty-two years later, Melanie became an official ambassador for the Tennessee chapter of the Foundation for a Drug-Free World (FDFW). "I see people . . . my granddaughter's age," she said in a press release, "who feel they have to apologize for not taking drugs. They're being pressured into it."[2]

Melanie appeared to be recapturing her former glory when she starred in the musical *Ace of Diamonds*. She wrote twenty-seven songs for the show. Her old friend Ed Kelleher based its script on letters written by a woman, Jane Hickok McCormick (supposedly born 1873), who insisted that she was the illegitimate daughter of sharpshooter Martha "Calamity Jane" Canary and Wild West legend Wild Bill Hickok. During a Mother's Day 1941 radio show, McCormick claimed to have been adopted and raised in England by a wealthy sea captain, Jim O'Neil, and his wife. Her claims were widely disputed. Hickok biographer James McLaird alleged that the evidence she submitted—a diary, letters, and a marriage certificate—were forgeries.

Ace of Diamonds was slated to premiere on Broadway in late 1985 with Tommy Walsh (*Best Little Warehouse in Texas*) directing. Producer Seymour Vall was a master at attracting investors. A cofounder of the First Theater Investing Service, he had helped to finance *Fiddler on the Roof*, *Mame*, *How to Succeed in Business Without Really Trying*, *Carnival*, *Luv*, *A Thousand Clowns*, *Stop the World . . . I Want to Get Off*, and *A Funny Thing Happened on the Way to the Forum*. Taking an intense interest in *Ace of Diamonds*, Vall instructed Melanie about writing songs for a musical, reminding her that she wasn't writing for herself but for Captain Jim O'Neil, Calamity Jane, and Wild Bill Hickok.

Ace of Diamonds was on track for success. That's when things fell apart. Diagnosed with cancer, Vall withdrew from the project. By this time, the thrill for Melanie had passed. She felt stabbed in the back by the musical director. He had been "a real nightmare" who despised that she was coming from the world of pop music and not from a theatrical background. He hadn't bothered to find out that she had gone to the American Academy of Dramatic Arts.

For the show's finale, Melanie brought an expensive bottle of Dom Pérignon onstage. After singing "Champagne Song," she took a slug from the bottle. The music director and some cast members reported her to Actors Equity for drinking on the set.

Melanie later experienced problems with the music director of *Melanie and the Record Man* in 2012. She found his arrangements emotionally syrupy and feared they would ruin the audience's appreciation of her songs. Twenty-two-year-old Beau Jarred Schekeryk took over.

Beau's guitar skills came as a surprise. Leilah was amazed by how quickly he had mastered the instrument. She had gone off to study music in Denver at the University of Colorado, and by the time she came back to visit, he could play like a virtuoso.

Drawn to sports, Beau showed little interest in music. Melanie and Peter enrolled him in guitar lessons, but he refused to get out of the car. He'd pick up the guitar on his own, teach himself every chord, and start playing on his own. It happened quickly.

Melanie and Peter tried sending Beau to learn guitar, paying for eight lessons. Beau hated it. When Dorothy drove him to the music store for a lesson, he held tightly to the seat and refused to budge. He wanted to play keyboard.

Melanie and Peter went to a folk music convention and brought back some Doc Watson CDs. Beau didn't know who he was, but when he heard the CDs, something clicked. He realized that it would be a blessing to make people feel as good with his music.

Beau took a few lessons from Norman Rockwell (not the painter, but a "technically awesome country-rock guitarist" who briefly played with Melanie), but his attention was distracted by flamenco. Whenever Beau visited his grandmother, she'd have jazz records playing. One night, she played a flamenco recording by Carlos Montoya. Beau had never heard anything like it before.

Unaware that the long-playing 33⅓-rpm disc was playing at 45 rpm, Beau was mesmerized by what seemed like Montoya's impossibly fast playing. Admiring jazz guitarist Kenny Burrell's swift playing, Beau was equally drawn to lightning-fast rock guitarists like Eddie Van Halen and Alex Lifeson (of Rush). He realized, however, music was much about more than speed. It was great to be able to play fast, but the combination of virtuosity and simplicity is what he truly loved.

Beau practiced in the bathroom for hours and hours. Learning to read music was too much like following rules. When people asked him how he learned to play, he reminded them that he has his parents' ears. He listened intently to Segovia's records and picked out the notes by ear. He read Metropolitan Opera House guitarist Frederick Hand's books.

Drawn to steel-string guitars, Beau had a red, electric Fender. After hearing Montoya's record, he got into nylon strings, thinking that was the key. Melanie had an old guitar case in the corner of a room. Beau opened it one day and discovered a classical guitar. It didn't have much volume, but it had an extremely beautiful tone. Practicing on it, he developed a distinct style between classical and folk music.

Until then, sports was the driving force. Attending alternative schools since kindergarten, Beau dreamed of playing football. Transferring to a public high school, he played for a season. Realizing that he "didn't have the necessary 'killer' instinct," he handed in his uniform and resigned from the team. The coach had other plans. Recognizing the youngster's natural athletic ability, he arranged for him to compete on the wrestling team. Beau did exceptionally well. He received a trophy, but he despised wrestling. He hated hurting people. Beau realized he wasn't made to compete. Sports weren't what he wanted to do. It felt physically good, but he didn't have a competitive mentality. He felt sorry when his opponent didn't win. He told the coach he was going on the road to play music with Melanie, but they didn't comprehend what he was telling them. They tried persuading him to continue wrestling, but he made up his mind. He appreciated sports, but music was on a much more spiritual level.

Beau opted for a homeschooling program. "I wasn't used to how the public school system worked," he said, "doing things just to pass a test even if you didn't understand it. Where I had been going, they made sure that you knew what you were learning."[3]

Playing a difficult Segovia piece in an audition for a prestigious guitar school, Beau was so nervous his hands shook, and his playing was horrendous. The director could see how much he was doing, especially being self-taught, and was impressed. Inviting Beau to his house after the audition, he taught him some things on the guitar. Later, Beau ran into Norman Rockwell, his first guitar teacher, and proudly showed him what he learned. Beau kept practicing the classical technique, determined to master it.

Beau was still in high school when Jeordie went on the road, singing backup for their mother. Leilah left to study music at St. Petersburg Junior College. She started writing songs when she was twelve, drifting further and further away from her schoolwork. Teachers called her a dreamer. Melanie came to the school to protest. She was a sight to see; her hair was purple and blue. She angrily addressed school administrators. They were recommending that Leilah take drugs to stay more focused, but Melanie resisted, insisting it was okay to be a dreamer.

Leilah struggled with her college classes. She wasn't a trained musician. With her limited understanding of theory, she was ill-prepared for college-level music.

Two months into her sophomore year, Leilah had to make a tough decision. She had been singing with her mother and a guitarist she called "Mr. Bean," and she loved it, but studying music was not her calling. She had half a semester left, but classes left her miserable. Peter told her that if she wanted to sing with her mother, she should do it. She would for the next four or five years.

Beau began touring with his mother in 1997.

Audiences raved about Beau's playing, They'd tell him he sounded like Segovia. His virtuosity was apparent, but he wanted to be creative and get into composition. He was in awe over how Peter brought out the magic in Melanie's singing. Going to a Sam Ash music store, they looked at guitars. Suddenly, Beau's eyes caught a computer with Acid (one of the first commercially available pre-sampled loop programs). He thought it'd be a good place to start. He experimented until he taught himself to put together tracks to use as beds for his guitar playing.

Doing his first recording on a four-track recorder as a final project for the Cambridge Academy's homeschooling program, he recorded Segovia's "Guardame Las Vacas (Protect My Cows)," the piece that inspired him to play classical guitar.

Beau's debut solo album, *Scrapbook*, came out in 2004. "This is a collection of compositions, songs, and colors of flamenco," he said in its liner notes. "It represents me from the moment I began to create and perceive a life communicating with music. I am different now. I am transforming. My voice has changed. I'm emerging. This is my beginning. This is not an apology. It's just important that you know."[4]

Beau has yet to release a second solo album. While he could easily headline concerts of his own, with dozens of masterful releases, Beau remained devoted to his mother and has not yet followed his debut.

Beau produced *About You*, the second album of Leilah and Jeordie's group, Safka, in 1998. They recorded in a St. Petersburg studio that lacked running water, air-conditioning, or a bathroom. It didn't matter. They got it done and the album sounded good. It had a unique style with interesting songs and solid production.

Safka's first CD, *Foreign Film*, had come out three years before. Leilah built a small but loyal following in Denver with her music. Jeordie came to visit. She had written a few songs, and they worked on them. Their harmonies were uncanny. They were born to sing together. Jeordie extended her stay, and the sisters began performing shows as a duo.

Assembling a solid band, Safka started playing out every week.

Leilah's first husband was hoping to manage Safka, but their marriage fell apart. In 1995, Leilah and her second husband, Daryl Hayman, became parents with their daughter Christiana's birth. A year later, they relocated to Safety Harbor, Florida. Jeordie followed. Resurrecting Safka, Leilah and Jeordie became one of the busiest acts in Tampa, opening for the Indigo Girls, Jewel, and Sade, and appearing at lots of festivals. They wanted Beau to join them, but he was busy working with their mother. Instead, they joined him and Melanie for several tours.

Jeordie continued to search for a home. She lived in Fort Lauderdale for a while. Falling in love with a concert promoter, she followed him when he was transferred to Arizona. Although they broke up, she remained, enchanted by the weather and the many opportunities to play music.

Jeordie's debut solo album, *Can I Ask You Something*, came out on her independent label, Learning Curve Records, in 2003. She followed with a live album, *Bootleg*, in 2006, and a studio recording, *XO*, in 2011. Forming a duo, Harmony Drive, with Ashley Norton in 2007, she assembled a six-piece band, Jeordie & the Mixology Project, two years later.

Safka's albums weren't the first time that Leilah and Jeordie recorded without their mother. They had scored a hit in Canada, in 1983, when their single, "Grandma, We Love You," produced by Peter, sold a quarter of a million copies. As "There's No One Quite like Grandma," the song had been a chart-topping UK hit during the Christmas 1980 season for the primary grade St. Winifred's School Choir and its director, Terry Foley. They went to a "real" studio to record, but they weren't intimidated in the least.

Despite their youth, the sisters were seasoned entertainers. When their previously recorded accompaniment suddenly stopped on the *Joe Franklin Show*, they kept singing and didn't miss a beat.

CHAPTER 22
"TUNING MY GUITAR"

Idle for a couple of years, CBS/Portrait resurrected with Melanie's single, "One More Try" b/w "Apathy," in 1981. A string section accompanied Melanie's full-bodied, confident vocals on "One More Try." She would record her ode to indifference, "Apathy," multiple times. The label would return to the top with platinum-selling albums by Cyndi Lauper (*She's So Unusual*), two years later, and Sade (*Diamond Life*), a year after that, but again Melanie was too far ahead of the curve.

Melanie's twentieth album, *Arabesque*, came out in August 1982, on Blanche Records in the United States and RCA in the United Kingdom. Its music director/keyboardist, Paul Harris, had been a member of Stephen Stills's Manassas and Souther-Hillman-Furay. Melanie covered Chip Taylor's "Any Way That You Want Me," Liberty DeVito's "Fooling Yourself," and Cathy Evans's "Imaginary Heroes." Michael MacDonald's publishing company sent Melanie the demos of two songs; she loved both of them. One was "It Don't Matter Now." Alison Krauss covered it.

Melanie recorded "Detroit or Buffalo" by Barbara Keith, a western Massachusetts singer-songwriter who played in an "AC/DC-meets-Patsy-Cline"[1] country-rock band, the Stone Coyotes, with her husband and son. "She had one album," said Melanie, "and that was it. I got it in one of those record stores with all these obscure albums. . . . I hope I can make her a million dollars and meet her."[2]

Peter was in the studio with an Australian soft rock duo, Air Supply. He wanted Melanie to cover their song "Chances." It seemed an odd tune for her, but he was insistent that she do it. Going through its lyrics, she had a few questions. Calling its writer, Graham Russell, she expected an enthusiastic reception—she was recording his song. Instead, she got the complete opposite. Annoyed by her call, Russell snapped, "What difference does it make? It's a pop song," and he hung up.

There were five originals on *Arabesque*—"Too Late," "Standing on the Other Side (of Your Love)," "Love You to Loathe Me," "When You're Dead and Gone," and two versions of "Roadburn"—a cabaret-like ballad and a straight-ahead rocker.

Seventh Wave was released in late 1983. Neighborhood Records released it in the United Kingdom, and Ballophone, owned by Ralph Bierley, released it in Germany. It wasn't released in the United States and has never come out on CD. At the time, Melanie and Peter were living near the beach and Melanie was spending hours by the ocean. Counting waves one day, she discovered that the seventh was always the strongest. "That's the wave that can take you to shore or destroy you," she said. "I just feel that something very positive is happening in my life now."[3]

Seventh Wave combined covers and original songs. Chip Taylor's "Son of a Rotten Gambler" was recorded in Bogalusa, Louisiana, and Eric Clapton's "Lay Down Sally," written with George Terry and Marcella Detroit, in Miami. There were six original tunes—"Didn't You Ever Love Somebody," "Lovin' the Boy Next Door," "Dance to the Music," "If You Go Your Way," "Lovers' Lullaby" and a second recording of "Apathy." "Lovin' the Boy Next Door" could have been sung by girl groups of the 1960s. "Didn't You Ever Love Somebody" questioned why people suppressed their impulses. "Every Breath of the Way" was an up-tempo, acoustic guitar–driven rocker.

In October 1972, Melanie performed for a capacity crowd at London's 5,272-seat Royal Albert Hall. "Truly the concert contained its feeble moments," *Melody Maker* reported, "when sweet innocence was unrestrained. The miracle was that Melanie, in one shape or form, got through to everybody."[4]

Selling out the prestigious venue again in October 1975, Melanie was booked to return on October 13, 1983. The promoter had a serious problem distributing tickets, however, and canceled the concert. Melanie and Ed Kelleher were "dining on anchovies and toast and drinking cocktails—a classic English breakfast" when she found out. Peter was on the phone trying to book other dates. After he hung up, he said that two hundred people hadn't heard about the show's cancellation and were outside the

Royal Albert Hall. Melanie boldly announced that she was heading there to sing. She didn't dress for a concert; she stayed in her street clothes. When she arrived, she took her guitar from its case, strummed a few chords, cleared her throat, and started to sing. People were ecstatic. They were going to get their Melanie show after all. As she was playing her songs, thinking she was doing a wonderful thing, she heard sirens in the distance. They came closer and closer and closer. Sure enough, it was the police. A couple of officers got out of a patrol car, walked to where Melanie was playing, interrupted her song, and threatened to arrest her unless she stopped immediately. They waved the crowd to disperse. Photographers and reporters arrived, and it turned into a media event. Expecting them to report how she so wanted to please her fans she was playing a free show, she read that, because she couldn't sell out Royal Albert Hall, she sang for "stragglers."

Peter heard Melanie singing "Rag Doll" by Bob Crewe and Bob Gaudio and suggested that she cover the Four Seasons' 1964 chart-topper. She added a new verse to the end. Peter had always wanted to do a production like it: a Phil Spector–esque wall of sound.

In October 1984, Melanie paid an on-air visit to the WNEW-FM studios. The first radio station to play her records, its DJs continued to be supportive of her music. She sang "Tell Me What to Do (Right About Now)," "I Just Can't Do It If I'm Not in Love," and "Lovers' Lullaby." She believed that you didn't need to have an agenda when you appeared on the radio. You didn't have to be promoting an album or an upcoming show. "You sang what you felt like singing, something you had just written, or a song you truly loved. More than likely, you didn't do your hits; you did things people wouldn't normally hear and that's what made it special."

Buffalo-based Amherst Records released Melanie's twenty-second album, *Am I Real or What*, in the United States, with Ballophone Records releasing it in Europe. "Melanie certainly deserves credit for sticking to her trade," said *People*. "At a time when everything from her heyday is, suddenly, back in style, Melanie may find paisley-clad fans at her feet once again."[5]

"We started out, not with the idea of doing an album," Melanie explained, "but to put down certain songs that I had written and see what kind of direction they were going to take. The album came later. It just

171

continued and I had enough material. In fact, that whole project was very reminiscent of my first album because it had been so long since I had been in the recording studio."

Some people refer to *Am I Real or What* as Melanie's "disco album." "A pounding beat accompanies most of the songs," said *People*. "That innovation in her style often drowns out Melanie's most appealing trait: simplicity."[6]

A year before the album's release, Amherst Records had begun branching out to dance music, acquiring Hugo and Luigi's AVCO and H&L record labels and disco artists including the Stylistics and Van "The Hustle" McCoy. The company's promotion director escorted Melanie to a Manhattan loft where dance club DJs gathered to preview new records. Singing to a prerecorded track, she felt completely out of place. The vibe was so not her. "I'm gonna do a [disco] album," she joked, "I'm gonna call it *Disco Plague*."[7]

Daniel LeMelle (saxophone), Erskine Williams (keyboards), and Tom McDermott (guitar) of Rick James's Stone City Band played on *Am I Real or What*. McDermott insisted that he was no "punk-funker."

"Somebody's Been Sleeping in My Bed" sported a solid funk groove. An extended version was released as a twelve-inch vinyl single with a special club mix on one side and a radio edit on the other.

Winter in Buffalo could be brutal. Not only was there a blizzard hampering recording sessions but there was a hotel fire on the night of the blizzard. In their third-floor Holiday Inn room, Melanie couldn't wake Jeordie, who kept telling her to leave her alone. Filling the bathtub with water, she wet towels and put them at the bottom of the door. She peered out the window at the fire engines in the street below and prayed they'd be safe. It was terrifying.

Leilah, Jeordie, and Beau sang on "Crack Seeks the Edge." They were accustomed to singing at home, but Melanie preferred that they continue their education. She hoped they'd go to college and become teachers or veterinarians, anything but musicians.

Leilah and Jeordie loved making up songs and singing. Pretending they were at a recording studio, they took turns being the musician, the producer, and the receptionist who answered the phone and took messages.

Joking that she was raising her own backup singers, Melanie would bring the kids to the studio. They were accustomed to a rock 'n' roll life. They didn't eat at six o'clock; they had ten o'clock dinners. Although they stayed in Buffalo so long they started looking at houses, Peter shuttled Melanie to the Hilton Hotel in Niagara Falls when he started postproduction. Leilah, Jeordie, and Beau visited her on weekends. There may have been reasons Peter didn't want her around, but she didn't worry about it. She occupied herself with exercising, swimming, jogging, and walking near Niagara Falls. The hotel had a health spa, and she was determined to lose weight and get in shape. Taking aerobic classes every morning and every evening, she tried a variety of routines. Jumping up and down on a cement floor, however, proved detrimental to her knees and back. She paid the price for the rest of her life.

Melanie's show at Gerde's Folk City, in October 1985, closed with "Soldiers of the Heart." Long Island–born songwriter David Pomeranz composed it after attending the dedication of the Strawberry Fields Memorial, in Central Park, a year after John Lennon's December 8, 1980, assassination. Melanie had been in Sarasota when she heard of the former Beatle's death. She received a hysterical phone call from Ed Kelleher informing her. It felt even more surreal than the death of Marilyn Monroe or the assassinations of the Kennedys and Martin Luther King Jr. Lennon had been her favorite Beatle, and they had a great deal of affinity for each other. She linked his murder to what she believed was going on in America, suspecting that Jimi Hendrix had also been the victim of foul play.

Melanie filmed her first video, "Rock and Roll Heart," in the Kaufman-Astoria Studio, a couple of blocks from where she grew up. In preparation, she went to a hairstylist before leaving Buffalo to get a perm. She didn't want to put in too much curl, just puff her hair up a little, but the stylist wound up burning her hair. It was really upsetting. Melanie's long, flowing locks had always been part of who she was. Instead of its luscious shade of brown, it was now a burnt orange. The beautician added dark coloring to it, hoping that it wouldn't look so fried, but it didn't work. Melanie looked as though somebody had put shoe polish on her head. She didn't know what to do. She tried putting her hair up, tried using hair combs to cover it, but nothing worked. With her hair in such impaired condition, she was wary of doing the video. She reluctantly changed her mind after screening the video the production company had done for Canadian singer-songwriter Jane Siberry. Filmed on a beach, it was very '80s, but also extremely artsy. She agreed to the project. The production crew returned soon afterward with storyboards, but what they presented disappointed Melanie. She hadn't had a story in mind when she wrote "Rock and Roll Heart," but she knew that the song had more substance than what they were showing her. The song was not about someone obsessed with her as they proposed.

Melanie tried to have the damage to her hair repaired. She went to an "expensive French hairdresser in downtown Manhattan who took a unique approach to hair styling." After examining her shoulders, he handed her a sheet and instructed her to remove her clothes. As she sat there, wearing nothing but the sheet, wondering what it was all about, he pranced around and gave her a haircut. She wanted the burnt part removed but he left her hair shaved on one side and long on the other. It saddened her deeply. She spent the rest of the year in hair combs.

Problems with the video continued. Melanie lobbied for an actor she thought would make a good "love interest," but the producers instead hired someone she thought looked "like a psycho killer or stalker."

Despite its huge budget, Melanie found the video embarrassing. The producers had her put her guitar down, telling her that it would look funny in the shot, that it was not the right guitar, and that it did not have the right look. She felt weird without it.

Once she saw the finished video, Melanie thought it abhorrent. She told Peter that she didn't want it to come out. She didn't want anyone to see it. She got her wish.

"RING THE LIVING BELL"

Cliff Eberhardt accompanied Melanie between 1988 and 1990. Born in Berwyn, Pennsylvania, in 1954, the songwriter/guitarist/ vocalist spent his teens haunting the Main Point Coffeehouse in Bryn Mawr and touring the East Coast with his brother, Geoff. Moving to Carbondale, Illinois, at twenty-one, he was immersed in a songwriting scene that included Shawn Colvin. After a brief stay in Colorado, he arrived in New York in 1978. Supporting himself as a taxi driver, he became involved with Jack Hardy's Songwriters Collective and, along with Colvin, Hardy, Suzanne Vega, John Gorka, and Rod MacDonald, recorded songs for sampler albums accompanying the monthly *Fast Folk Music Magazine*. He also spent time as Richie Havens's accompanist. "I opened for Melanie at Folk City," Eberhardt remembered from his home in the foothills of the Berkshire Mountains.

> We hit it off and she asked me to come up to the stage and sing "Lay Down (Candles in the Rain)" with her. Sometime later, we got together in my manager, Doug Yeager's office. She told us that she was going to be playing at the Philadelphia Folk Festival. I was already booked to play there. She asked me if I wanted to play with her. We met at her hotel room before the festival and practiced. Then she came over to my brother's house for dinner.
>
> It was a joy to play with her. She's a great musician and songwriter. We came from the same songwriting arena so I could predict what she was going to do. She was like Richie Havens. She wasn't into rehearsing. She'd write a new song and play it on stage that night.

Amid a European tour with Melanie, Eberhardt signed a solo singer-songwriter contract with Windham Hill Records and returned to the United States to record his album. "Peter didn't like that," he said.

Eberhardt last played with Melanie in Canada. "At the end, I was also roadie-ing," he said. "We would sometimes be paid in cash. I wouldn't take anything extra, even though Peter still owed me money, but he called me on the phone and threatened me because I had taken out the $500 that I was supposed to be paid."

Released in England on Food for Thought Records in 1988, and Bairle Records in Germany a year later, Melanie's twenty-third album, *Cowabunga—Never Turn Your Back on a Wave* didn't come out in the United States. The title came from a 1964 movie, *Pajama Party*, starring Annette Funicello as a typical teenager, Tommy Kirk as an alien, and Buster Keaton as a stereotypical American Indian. Beau designed the album's logo. Melanie sang Malvina Reynold's "What Have They Done to the Rain," a new version of "Ruby Tuesday," and nine originals— "Racing Heart," "Show You to Be a Star," "On the Lam from the Law," "Another Lie," "Prematurely Grey," "Window Pane," "Chosen Few," and the jovial "Lovin' the Boy Next Door."

Recording most of the album and its follow-up, *Silver Anniversary*, in a downtown Tampa studio, Melanie and her accompanists jammed through one song after another. They recorded Dylan's "Hard Rain" at Richard Kaplan's Indigo Ranch Studios in Malibu, California. Garth Hudson of The Band played the organ. Bryan Ferry's version of Dylan's song about nuclear proliferation inspired Melanie's recording.

"What Have They Done to the Rain," Malvina Reynolds's song about a similar subject, was recorded at Long View Farm in North Brookfield, Massachusetts. Melanie heard Joan Baez's version on *Joan Baez in Concert*, in 1962, and the British Invasion group the Searchers' folk-rock hit two years later. She knew little about Reynolds. She heard the San Francisco–born songwriter/political activist's "Ticky-tacky (Little Boxes)," in the early '60s, but Pete Seeger recorded the version that she knew.

Most of the tracks on *Cowabunga—Never Turn Your Back on a Wave* were released in the United States on *Precious Cargo*. "I had the luxury of not having to please anyone other than myself," Melanie explained, "[and] the luxury of totally indulging each song. . . . That's why I called this album *Precious Cargo*. I've carried these songs for a long time."[1]

CHAPTER 24
"TOGETHER ALONE"

On September 17, 1989, Melanie received an Emmy Award for writing the lyrics of a song ("The First Time I Loved Forever") featured in an episode ("A Distant Shore") of the CBS-TV series *Beauty and the Beast*. She had been recording in Artie Ripp's Renegade Sound Studio in Los Angeles when she first learned that Ron Koslow, the show's director, wanted to speak with her. She invited him to the studio. When he arrived, Koslow asked if she'd be interested in writing the lyrics. He had heard her song "Racing Heart" and thought its words were gorgeous.

Lee Holdridge composed the music for "The First Time I Loved Forever." Melanie had given him one of his first breaks after he immigrated to the United States from Haiti; he arranged her recording of "Ruby Tuesday." She was expecting him to help her as she had done for him, but it didn't turn out that way. Writing the lyrics wasn't a done deal yet. Melanie had to compete with a husband-and-wife songwriting team, Marilyn and Alan Bergman, who were very politically connected. They had written "The Windmills of Your Mind" (Noel Harrison), "You Don't Bring Me Flowers" (Barbra Streisand), and "Yellow Bird" (Harry Belafonte). Marilyn also wrote the lyrics for Marvin Hamlisch's "The Way We Were," the title track of Barbra Streisand's 1973 album. Holdridge was pushing for the Bergmans. Melanie could tell. He rejected her initial lyrics, which she thought were perfect. She had listened to his melody and immediately written the lyrics. She handed them in and went back to Florida. Then she got a phone call. The producers wanted her to come back to LA to finish writing the song.

Melanie submitted other lyric ideas, but she knew the first lyrics were perfect. Everyone involved with the show took a personal interest. Overanalyzing every word, they made suggestions for improving them. It became overwhelming. Melanie was ready to throw in the towel, return the advance, and refuse to work any further on the song. She kept with it, though, and tried to keep up with everyone's suggestions. Expecting to be singing the song (though Lisa Angelle wound up doing it), Melanie wanted the lyrics to represent herself. She filled a legal pad with lyric ideas and submitted what she thought were the best. The show's producers kept sending them back, telling her to think about this verse, think about that verse. Finally, out of absolute frustration, she resubmitted the first lyrics she had written. The producers sent word that they loved them, suggesting that her hard work had paid off.

When they heard about the Emmy nomination, Melanie and Peter were at a low point. Peter was constantly running somewhere without letting her know where he was going. She suspected something not so good was afoot but had no idea what it was. Creatively, she was at a lull. Nothing seemed right. She detested the way she looked. She didn't like her hair, didn't like the shape of her body, and was unsure about what to wear to the awards ceremony. At the last minute, she told Peter that she didn't want to go. She didn't think she had a chance to win. The other nominees were the theme songs of *Sesame Street: 20 and Still Counting* (NBC), *Dadah is Death* (CBS), *Shining Time Station* (PBS), and *Roseanne* (ABC). Staying home, watching the ceremony on her living room TV, she perked up at the opening of the envelope with the winner's name for "Outstanding Achievement in Music and Lyrics." Sure enough, she had won. Artie Ripp accepted the award, standing onstage with Lee Holdridge. It would be one of the most brutal experiences of Melanie's life—to watch someone else get her award for no reason other than her feelings of unworthiness. Ripp would fail to deliver the award to her. She'd wonder why anyone would want an Emmy with someone else's name on it.

"PEACE WILL COME
(ACCORDING TO PLAN)"

V iolinist/vocalist Alana MacDonald had been singing with Tom Dean and Herb Ludwig in a folk-rock trio, Devonsquare, since 1976. Their first two albums scored Maine Music Awards and led to a two-album deal with Atlantic in 1987. The title track of their debut, *Walking on Ice*, broke into the top twenty on the adult contemporary charts. Its follow-up, *Bye Bye Route 66*, spawned two singles—"If You Could See Me Now" and the title track—as well as a Boston Music Award nomination as "best new act of 1992."

MacDonald was a passionate Melanie fan. Devonsquare's attorney, who had begun working with Peter (and dating Melanie's sister Stephanie), introduced them. Hitting it off, they talked long into the night and agreed to collaborate. Within a few weeks, Melanie and Beau traveled to Orchard Beach, Maine, where MacDonald and her husband ran a bed-and-breakfast. They stayed in a cabin on the beach. Melanie loved beach towns, especially during the off-season. She and Beau were the only ones there.

Melanie didn't have a clue about what was happening on the home front. All she knew was that she was in a beautiful place singing with an amazing group. Rehearsing with Devonsquare for weeks, Melanie and Beau prepared to tour. She wanted to call the group the Vendetta, with a slogan saying, "When they couldn't get backing, they got even." Despite their efforts, the project fell apart.

Melanie reworked Ben E. King's "Stand by Me" during the Gulf War (August 1990–February 1991) and performed it as "We Stand by You" at the MacDill Air Force Base in Tampa. It was an intense time. Americans had to either take a stand or face annihilation, but it wasn't a clear-cut decision like the Vietnam War. Even people who had taken a strong pacifist stance questioned what was right. One afternoon, Melanie's phone rang. Peter answered and handed the phone to her. Joan Baez was calling. It was the first, and so far only, time that they'd spoken. Baez quickly got to the point of her call. She was planning a protest demonstration and wanted Melanie to participate. Melanie didn't feel comfortable. She considered war evil but if it was to defend your country, family, or friends, there was a difference. She turned down Baez's invitation.

Covering Jimi Hendrix's "Purple Haze" on *Silver Anniversary*, a double CD of "unplugged" tracks, Melanie performed it during Woodstock's thirtieth anniversary in 2009. The album also included a cover of "Estate Sale" by Cheryl Wheeler. People assumed Melanie had written it because it was so quirky. "I thought it was just funny," she said. "When I performed it, I thought I would hold up something old like a pair of roller skates. It was a reminiscent thing."[1]

Melanie explored a more tender side of Wheeler's songwriting with "Arrow." Lydia Carole DeFretos described her interpretation as "delivered sensitively and with just the right amount of emotion."[2]

Cape Cod–born Jess Leary introduced Melanie to Wheeler's songs. Playing guitar and writing songs from the age of ten, Leary toured the East Coast with a country-rock band, Caravan, in her teens and built her reputation, in her twenties, as a solo singer-songwriter. The regional winner of the Wrangler Country Star Search, she participated in a special showcase at the Grand Ole Opry. While in Nashville, she signed a songwriting deal with Reba McIntyre's publishing company. She would go on to pen chart-topping hits for Tim McGraw ("Where the Green Grass Grows") and Pam Tillis ("Mi Vida Loca [My Crazy Life]") and sing background vocals during McIntyre's 1992 tour. She also sang and played guitar for Garth Brooks and Faith Hill. Melanie was the reason that Leary had become a singer and a songwriter. They bonded instantly and collaborated on several tunes. Leary wrote additional words for "Freedom Knows My Name." She had the idea for "Something Warm," but didn't have the lyrics. She and Melanie wrote them together. Leary also added words to "Someday, I'll Be an Old Record." Melanie recorded that version, but she wasn't crazy about the lyrics.

Comprised mostly of tracks previously released in Germany, Austria, and Switzerland, *Freedom Knows My Name* came out in the United States on Peter and Melanie's independent label, Lone Star Records. DeFretos praised Melanie's "smooth, immediately identifiable, acrobatic voice" and claimed, "the change from dreamy ballads to charming mid-tempo rockers are professionally carried out with lots of sense and fantasy . . . a treasure chest of ideal songs."[3]

Entertainment Weekly took a different view. "You'd think it was still 1971," it complained. "Though she has the occasional good sense to cover writers like Cheryl Wheeler, her own tunes are stuck in Woodstock-era reverie, and her soft-boiled versions of Bob Dylan's 'Hard Rain' and (no kidding) Jimi Hendrix's 'Purple Haze' sound as if she got tossed off their tribute albums."[4]

A sharp reaction to freedom, peace, and humanity reduced to commercial entities, the title track could be "the theme song of the Libertarian Party." Melanie didn't consider herself political, but she identified with the party's commitment to getting the government out of people's lives. Introduced to Libertarian tenets by a woman she met at a Woodstock reunion, Melanie became an invited speaker during the party's national convention, in Anaheim, California, on July 1, 2000. Walking to the podium, she looked at the crowd, took a deep breath, and said, "This is a lot of fun. . . . I think I'm going to run for something."

Melanie was booked to perform at a Communist rally in Portugal. There was a large banner with a hammer and sickle on the back wall of the stage. She looked at it and questioned why she was even there. That wasn't the message she wanted to promote.

On May 4, 2012, Melanie participated in a Kent State University concert in memory of the four students killed by the National Guard forty-two years before. In her journal, she wrote of learning that one of the two women who died had sung "Beautiful People." It hit home.

Part 7
SEEDS (2000–2001)

CHAPTER 26
"WORKING LEGEND"

R eturning to acting, Melanie appeared in a revival of *As Is*, one of the first plays about HIV/AIDS, at the Beacham Theater in Orlando. It had been a phenomenal success when it premiered at the Lyceum Theater, Broadway's oldest continuously operating venue, in 1985. William Moses Hoffman, a Lehman College (CUNY) professor of theater, scored an Obie Award for playwriting. The original production received a Drama Desk Award for Outstanding Play and Tony Award and Pulitzer Prize nominations. Michael Lindsay-Hogg, director of videos by the Beatles, the Rolling Stones, and the Who, adapted it for television.

Melanie considered pursuing acting further but realized, as she told *New Musical Express*, she wasn't a "normal person who could get some acting experience by portraying a whore."[1]

Released in February 1996, Melanie's twenty-eighth album, *Old Bitch Warrior* ranged "from the scary title song, about a fearless woman who 'sleeps in the grave' to the lament 'No Time to Smell the Flowers.'"[2]

Covers included David Buskin and Robin Batteau's "These Nights," and Lennon and McCartney's "Any Time at All." Melanie felt compelled to record Freddie Perren and Dino Fekaris's "I Will Survive." A multi-million-selling disco hit for Gloria Gaynor in 1978, its title was Melanie's mantra. The song gave it a voice.

Melanie recorded "I Don't Know What Love Is" with cowriter Jonathan Edwards. Born in Minnesota in 1946, and raised in the Appalachian Mountains of Virginia, Edwards dropped out of college and headed to Boston in 1967 with a folk-rock band, Sugar Creek. After releasing a quickly-out-of-print album with the group in 1969, Edwards signed a solo deal with Atlantic-distributed Capricorn Records. He spent a year at Intermedia Sound Studio, in Boston, recording his eponymous debut album. After an engineer accidentally erased one of its intended tracks ("Please Find Me"), the uplifting "Sunshine" was substituted in its place. Released as a single, backed with "Emma," in November 1971, it reached #4 on the *Billboard* Hot 100 and established Edwards's still-thriving career.

Edwards came to Melanie's house, and they had dinner a couple of times. They tried writing songs together but found that their approaches to music were too different. Preferring technical precision, Edwards chastised her like a stern English teacher.

Melanie wrote several tunes with David Bruen. "Rock in the Road" and "Ballerina" came out on *Old Bitch Warrior*. Bruen was married to the heir to the American Express fortune and Peter thought that having him cowrite songs would lead to financial backing. Melanie always had a backlog of songs-in-progress, so she gave a couple of unfinished tunes to Bruen to write the lyrics. It didn't feel right to her, though. She added Bruen's name to the song credits but, for the most part, didn't use what he wrote. Their styles weren't compatible.

A more formidable collaboration resulted when Melanie revived "Beautiful People" with Belgian vocalist Meredith Vets's psychedelic-rock band, Pop in Wonderland. It was included on *Old Bitch Warrior* and Pop in Wonderland's second album, *Barbarella Butterfly*. Pop in Wonderland's management had contacted Peter and asked if Melanie would be interested in singing it. Promising to promote the record, they sent a tape of what they had recorded. It was different from the way she did the song, so she agreed to overdub her vocals onto the recording. Peter produced it.

Booked to perform at the ZAMU Awards (Belgium's equivalent to the Grammys), Pop in Wonderland invited Melanie to make a guest appearance. She thought it would be fun. Placing a long-distance call to Belgium, she spoke with Vets, who assured her that she and her bandmates were excited that she would be singing with them. Melanie and Peter stayed in a luxurious hotel along Belgium's shore. Pop in Wonderland came to their room. Melanie was anxious to show them her new songs. She was sure they'd be eager to hear them. Vets listened enthusiastically but her partner, songwriter and guitarist Rudolf Hecke, "considered himself artsy and modeled himself after Leonard Cohen and

(Parisian pop songwriter) Serge Gainsbourg," and dismissed her songs. Shaking his head, Hecke insisted that he and his bandmates weren't "pop artists." Melanie felt insulted but she had met musicians like that before, so overly concerned with how people were going to see them that they forgot about being creative.

Unchained was recorded in Florida and Connecticut and sold through Melanie's fan club. She recorded her next album, *Low Country*, in Raymond "Jake" Jaekle's Gemini Studio in Summerville, South Carolina, about a half hour from Charleston. A step up from Weissman's studio, it was fully stacked with the latest equipment. There was even an isolated vocal booth.

In South Carolina, Melanie made up a fictional history for herself about growing up in the low country and drinking sweet tea. On weekends, she frequented a farmers' market where a group of black women made baskets. She started to collect them.

Driving back and forth between studios and their home in Florida, Melanie and Peter racked up thousands of miles on their car's odometer. When they recorded, the entire family and Dorothy would stay in a Holiday Inn for weeks. It cost a small fortune.

Recording sessions lasted long into the night. One early morning, around 3:00 a.m., a car pulled into the driveway, its headlights shining through the front window. Jaekle said, "That doesn't look good." Then, another car pulled in and stopped next to the first car. A group of vicious-looking brutes got out of the cars. Jaekle called his wife who was in the house and said, "Cleoma, get the gun." Cleoma did what he asked. Walking out to the parking lot, she pointed the gun at the invaders, and said, "Can I help you?" The thugs got back into their cars and drove off. It was the first and only time Melanie felt glad that someone had a gun. She wrote a song about it, but nobody heard it because of its "political incorrectness."

Christmas was always a special time. Melanie's first full-length yuletide album *Antlers: A Christmas for True Believers* was her second release of 1997. Reissued in 2004 as *Yes Santa, There Is a Melanie*, it included holiday classics like "Good King Wenceslaus, "I Saw Three Ships," "Silent Night," O Come All Ye Faithful," "We Wish You a Merry Christmas," "What Child Is This?" "The First Noel," "Oh, Holy Night," and "The

Coventry Carol." Melanie covered Murray McLaughlin's "Tin Star," Tom Paxton's "The Marvelous Toy," and "It's Christmas" by Cindy Church and Nathan Tinkham. She rerecorded "Merry Christmas," from *Born to Be*, and introduced two other originals—"Ships in the Harbor" and "True Believers," written with Jaekle, who supplied most of the lyrics.

CHAPTER 27
"APATHY"

P eter was constantly coming up with new ideas. He'd meet someone and immediately start thinking about what they could do together. Meeting an executive of the Melitta Coffee Company, he decided that what they should do is have celebrities choose a blend of coffee and market it with their names and faces on the packages. It was an ambitious plan, but he signed the Blues Brothers (Dan Aykroyd and John Belushi), Tommy James & the Shondells, Richie Havens, and Melanie. Martha Stewart backed out at the last minute. Melanie spent an afternoon at Melitta's plant, in Clearwater, sampling coffee blends. She opted for one that tasted to her like "a perfect European cup of coffee." The project fell apart when the coffee executive tried to wheedle Peter out of the deal; things like that were always happening to him.

Another time, Peter got an idea for something he called "Dial-a-Record." Few people had computers at the time, but he planned to provide internet access to recordings that were out of print and no longer available. He rented office space that took up an entire floor of a large building in downtown Clearwater, but the funding didn't come through.

Peter arranged for the Moscow Circus to tour North America, but Scott Leber (Aerosmith's manager) and Scott Sanders of Radio City Music Hall Productions stepped in, handled the negotiations, and negotiated him out.

One of the most ambitious projects was a restaurant and café, Melanie's, at 310 Tarpon Avenue, in Tarpon Springs, about twenty minutes north of Safety Harbor. Opening on May 5, 1998, in a Victorian house built in 1905, it was as much about aesthetics as it was about taste. Melanie hand-painted the exterior a pale apple green and yellow-tinged chartreuse and lined it with a bright, multicolored border. The interior was just as beautiful. Local artists, including Todd Ramquist and Kiaralinda [Whimzey], hung their paintings on its walls. Jeordie painted a landscape in the bathroom while Beau Jarred took care of the men's room. A sign with hand-printed lyrics of "Beautiful People" greeted diners.

A large wooden board, on which Melanie had written the lyrics of some of her songs, was displayed in a prominent location near the front. People would bring in all kinds of unusual things and glue them to the board. Melanie started it with her own "junk"—things that she didn't want to throw away, like earrings she couldn't find one of or things that the kids had made. She put her entire collection of buttons up, using black silicon that came out of a caulking gun. As the board filled up, the lyrics became less and less recognizable.

Original plans called for fine "Floribbean-style" dining. Melanie loved to create new dishes, but she had no intention of doing the restaurant's cooking. A five-star chef whose restaurant had gone bankrupt was hired. It didn't take long, however, before the chef's sanity was in doubt. Deciding that he needed more room in the kitchen, he kicked down a wall. He didn't last at the restaurant long. Other chefs followed, but none worked out. Melanie ended up being the cook. People loved her cooking. She wasn't a five-star chef, but she made up for whatever culinary skills she lacked by concocting unique things like signature salad dressings and coleslaw made with purple cabbage. She grilled a marinated portobello mushroom, stuffed it with three kinds of cheese, broiled it, topped it with tomato sauce, and served it to very satisfied diners. She took lavash (a very thin bread that's thinner than pita bread) and spread it with tzatziki. She stuffed sun-dried tomatoes with chicken or tuna salad. "I love garlic," she said. "It's a soulful food and I find that people who like it are people who have a passion for life. It's a natural purifier; it helps eliminate the toxins in your body."[1]

Melanie's restaurant was a hit. Culinary magazines praised it and investors expressed interest in franchising. It would be so crowded, at times, people would get angry when they couldn't get in. But Melanie and Peter had no idea about running a restaurant and they made mistakes. They had a very conservative lawyer handling the business, but he didn't know much more about running a restaurant than they did. It was the most stressful thing Melanie had ever done. She'd go to sleep thinking of things she had to do in the restaurant and dream about them for the rest of the night. She'd wake up feeling as though she hadn't gone to sleep. It was nonstop, twenty-four hours a day. Music became an afterthought. She was still being creative; she just didn't get any rest or peace.

Melanie chose the restaurant's staff as though she were casting characters for a situation comedy. Of course, she needed a punk rocker with pins in his ears and a shaved head. She had to have a server with a bun on top of her head who would say, "Okay, honey, what do you want?"

Theft became chronic. Things kept walking out the doors. Melanie ordered glasses with guitar-shaped stems, but they kept disappearing. Bottles of expensive champagne vanished through the back door.

Melanie and Peter hadn't anticipated another major problem when they opened the restaurant. Located in the heart of the city's Greek district, it was surrounded by Greek restaurants whose owners were angry not because Melanie's represented competition, but because it was getting all the media attention. Police were constantly raiding the restaurant. They would receive anonymous reports of excessive noise, or the parking ordinance being broken. It became too much for its owners and closed after a year.

CHAPTER 28
"SOMEDAY I'LL BE A FARMER"

The 6ths is a side project for Yonkers, New York–born songwriter and multi-instrumentalist Stephin Merritt of the Magnetic Fields, the Gothic Archies, and Future Bible Heroes. On its CDs, a different guest vocalist is featured on every song. Melanie appeared on the album *Hyacinths and Thistles*. Merritt sent her the instrumental tracking of "I've Got New York" and she went to a studio in Nashville and added her voice to it. Jess Leary helped her record it.

Disky Communications, a Netherlands-based record label with offices in Los Angeles, proposed an intriguing project. Tony Bennett agreed to be involved. They planned to present a list of twenty songs to participating artists who would pick ten and put their distinctive slant on them. The label promised to pitch the tracks to producers of movies, TV shows, and advertising jingles. Melanie considered the list of songs "hysterical," but Beau came up with ear-catching arrangements. Melanie chose songs by the Rolling Stones ("As Tears Go By"), Kansas ("Dust in the Wind"), Bill Withers ("Ain't No Sunshine") the Bee Gees ("To Love Somebody"), and the Supremes ("You Keep Me Hanging On"). She sang Stephen Stills's "For What It's Worth," Cat Stevens's "Peace Train," the Youngbloods' "Get Together," the Rascals' "People Got to Be Free," and Cyndi Lauper's "Time After Time." She did Boy George's "Do You Really Want to Hurt Me?" bluegrass style.

Giving little thought to the tracks as she embarked on a European tour, Melanie was startled when a reporter reached into his backpack and pulled out a copy of *Moments of My Life*. Disky Communications released without her knowledge. She considered the recordings a creative exercise, not as tunes intended for release.

A more meaningful collection, *Victim of the Moon*, released in the United States in 2002 on Afterglow Records with three new songs—"You Can Find Anything Here," "Till They All Get Home," and "The Punishment Fits the Crime"—and a thirtieth-anniversary rerecording of "Brand New Key." There were three songs cowritten with Beau—"And We Fall," "Smile," and "Jamming Alone." *Victim of the Moon* evolved into *Crazy Love*, released on Pyramid Records in the United States, and on Smith & Co. Sound & Vision in Europe, with eight tunes in common. Melanie was at an artistic peak. Following a period of soul-searching following the tragic events of September 11, 2001, she had "had this creative explosion," she told *Billboard*, "and I have been going full-steam ever since."[1]

Crazy Love introduced four new songs—"This House," "Prone to Wander," "Come Away Come Go," and "Poet Is King"—and a rerecording of "The Wanderer," which had been on the 1987 Dutch CD *Melanie*. Melanie was especially proud of the title track, written with her son. She found Beau's melody so compelling that she felt obligated to write the lyrics. She envisioned it being performed by a jazz trio. "It's about our situation in the world," she said. "As you get to the years where it's a countdown, you start thinking about things like wait a minute, I just got here. I've always had a sense that we are spiritual beings, not just these bodies. It's a glimpse into a moment of soul searching."[2]

Part 8
LOSS AND SURVIVAL (2001–2023)

CHAPTER 29
"MOMMA MOMMA"

I n the predawn hours of November 9, 2003, Melanie woke to the
ringing of her bedside telephone. Her mother had died at the age of
seventy-seven. They had just begun to reconcile. For years, Melanie
had suffered the sting of her mother's criticism and had been made to
feel as though she could never do anything right. Now, just as they were
coming back together, her mother was gone.

A little more than a month before, on October 3, Polly had attended
Melanie's concert at Monmouth University. She wrote her daughter a
letter afterward complimenting her performance and suggesting that she
do an album of jazz standards. She told her that other singers were trying
to do it, but they were botching it up. Melanie could do it right. Polly had
never said anything like that to her daughter before. It meant a lot.

Melanie called her mother the day that she died. Polly promised to
look through her fake books and put together a list of songs that she
should do. The next morning, Melanie got the phone call.

Writing "Falling Awake" to sing at her mother's funeral, Melanie
repeated it a few times in concert, as an introduction to "My Rainbow
Race," but she didn't record it.

Despite their differences, Dorothy and Polly had a great relationship.
Polly was a quick-tempered Italian woman while Dorothy was patient,
laid-back, and British. The month before she died, Polly hosted Dorothy
who was caring for Peter's mother.

Two years after divorcing Melanie's father, Polly became involved
with Newark-born Salvatore P. Bertolo (1929–2008). They would be
together for almost thirty years, working together at Paint-N-Place and

sharing a love of music. Playing piano from the age of seven, Bertolo performed regularly (often accompanied by Polly) at Sirianni's Friendly Café, Ron's West End Pub, My Way Café, and Ocean 20.

Polly recorded an album of jazz standards, *Yesterdays*, in 1976. "Stephanie's friends took me [to a recording studio]," she said, "and I sang sixteen songs—old favorites—stopping only for coffee. My husband listened and said they should be on a record. . . . Instead of just one as a keepsake for my grandchildren, I have a thousand."[1]

Assembling a jazz quartet, Yesterdays, with bassist Richard Gaffney and drummer Dick White, Polly and Bertolo performed a Fourth of July 1976 weekend gig at Jimmy's Jetty, a popular restaurant on the Long Branch boardwalk. It turned into a weekly engagement. "It's so much fun," Polly told the *Asbury Park Press*. "I had thought about selling the shop because I was getting bored but, now that I'm singing, I feel better about it. My first love was singing, and it all comes back to me."[2]

Polly's relationship with Peter grew increasingly strained. "She said, in her own words," Stanley Tomczak claimed, "that he was always what he was—a person who tried to get away with things. Polly was usually nice and didn't mention anything about it, but sometimes, she'd let things slip out. She had a serious problem with Peter."

"Peter was constantly borrowing money from Polly," asserted Uncle George. "He once told me that relatives were there to lend you money that you didn't have to pay back. Polly was living on her savings. She didn't have a pension. She had always thought of Paint-N-Place as her retirement, but Freddy told her that she should hold on to it and issue stock. It ended up that she didn't get any money out of it."

At one point, Peter and Melanie were about to lose their house. They owed the bank $15,000. "[Polly] gave them the money," said Uncle George, "and saved the house, but they lost it after the next batch of payments, along with a lot of their belongings. I reminded her that she had promised that before she gave them the money she would talk to me. Do you know what she told me? She said, 'If I had talked to you, you would have explained why I shouldn't give the money.' Pretty strange logic, hunh?"

Melanie and Peter's financial problems caused Polly to be "stressed out sometimes," said Jeordie. "She was always worried about my mom, always worried about us. She had differences with my father and there was a lot of turmoil with my mother. She would have liked it if my mom had been with somebody a little more stable. Anytime she could talk about my father, she would. She had to get things off her chest. She probably shouldn't have been speaking to eight-year-olds, but she did. We had our problems [with our father] as well. As much as he wanted not to be an old-school Ukrainian man, he was. He was a survivalist, and children were just children."

Polly's death widened the family gap. The funeral was uncomfortable; there was a lot of tension.

Melanie dedicated her next album, *Paled by Dimmer Light*, to her mother. New songs included "Elements," "Make It Work for Me," "Extraordinary," "You Call Yourself a Writer," "Lover of My Friend," and "They Can Find You in My Dreams." "Nothing Is Real" was a revised version of "Hearing the News" from *Melanie at Carnegie Hall*. The only cover was a version of U2's "I Still Haven't Found What I'm Looking For." The album closed with an instrumental composed by Beau, "Deserts of Blue."

Another new song, "I Tried to Die Young" approached a dark theme with a sense of playfulness. "I love irony and playing with words," Melanie said. "I was a very self-destructive person in my youth. Not in the ways of ['60s] youth culture, I wasn't a druggie and didn't abuse myself in those ways. I did crazy things that could've been risky, and I didn't play the music business game very well."[3]

Twenty-nine years after Atlantic withdrew *Photograph*, Time Warner–owned Rhino Hand-made Records released an expanded two-CD version, *Photograph: Double Exposure*, in September 2005. In addition to the previously withdrawn album, it included unreleased tracks and outtakes, including a ten-minute-plus "Groundhog Day." Melanie loved recording it with the Hand-Made Band in Artie Ripp's Renegade Studio. David Campbell played viola and Chick Corea played piano. It couldn't have happened in the LA studio, which was much more sterile, but most of the songs recorded at Renegade didn't make it onto the original album.

The heartbreak of leaving loved ones addressed in "The Saddest Thing" resonated strongly with listeners in Korea, who identified it with the divide between North and South. Numerous Korean artists covered it. Melanie had no idea; there were no royalties.

Melanie first traveled to South Korea during the 1972 UNICEF tour. Returning in 2006 and 2008, she came close to the DMZ (demilitarized zone) both times. Days before the October 2006 Three Divas tour, with Karla Bonoff and Rita Coolidge, North Korea announced that it had become a nuclear weapons state. It was an extremely tense time. On their way to sing at the border, Melanie peered out of the car's window with binoculars. She could see guns aiming at them. It was a North Korea/South Korea face-off.

Far less terrifying, Melanie's May 2008 tour climaxed with a peace festival at the Jamsil Olympic Stadium in Seoul. Organizers told her that it was "Melanie's Flower Power Festival" and presented her as an ambassador of peace.

Devotees of Hindu spiritual leader Amma (Mātā Amritānandamayī Devī) claim that her hugs are life-changing experiences. Born to a poor family in a remote south Indian village along the coast of the state of Kerala, in 1953, the "hugging saint" had been gaining the world's attention with her embraces since the early '80s. Melanie fought against getting a hug for years. She had received a letter from Mira, one of the people who publicly spoke for the holy woman (Amma speaks Sanskrit and very little English). Hailing from South Africa and well-educated, Mira had been listening to Melanie's songs since she was a preteen. In her letter, she explained how she had been inspired to pursue spirituality by listening to her. Like Melanie, she had searched and questioned various religions, hoping to find an answer. Then, she found Amma. To her, Amma was the answer. She encouraged Melanie to get a hug, explaining how people hugged by Amma had all kinds of insights revealed to them. She told her how people who were sick would get well after Amma hugged them.

Melanie continued to resist. She had no interest in getting a hug and kept finding reasons to avoid it. Mira remained persistent. At one point, Amma was planning a trip to New York. Mira called Melanie, who said that she would be in the Big Apple at the same time. Mira explained that a meeting with Amma wouldn't be difficult to arrange, but Melanie insisted that she'd be busy on the day that the holy woman would be in New York.

Soon afterward, Melanie was booked to perform in the Netherlands. By chance, Amma would be in the area on the day before the show. This time, Melanie had no way out. She would have plenty of time. She reluctantly agreed to have Amma hug her.

On the day of the hug, Melanie and Beau moved to the front of the line quickly. As they entered a large tent, they could smell burning nag champa, an Indian fragrance containing frangipani and sandalwood. Melanie continued to hesitate. She hated being there. She didn't want to get a hug. Resisting until the very second she reached the stage, she approached Amma slowly. Noticing the holy woman's diminutive physique, she knelt down. Amma hugged her and started to say something in Sanskrit. Sensing soothing, unconditional love in the resonance of Amma's voice, Melanie started to cry. It was a purging of tension, an affirmation of the spirit she believed was inherent in all human beings. Amma handed her an apple and she took it as though it was an apple from God. Beau had a similar thing happen to him. Amma was definitely in touch with something amazing. She rarely talked about the people she hugged, but she told Mira that she and Melanie were from the same wellspring.

CHAPTER 30
"PREMATURELY GREY"

Melanie's father was living near her sister in North Creek, New York, when he died, at the age of eighty-four, on January 29, 2009. It was traumatic. When her mother died, Melanie was working in a studio in Orlando. She had her whole family around her. When her father died, she was on the road. It felt surreal. Melanie's children cherished their time with their grandfather. Before they moved to New Jersey, he'd join them for spaghetti dinners at Polly's house. He reminded them of their father, always involved in some scheme to make a lot of money. He was always in good mood and made them feel good.

Like his daughter, Freddy was into early morning flea markets. He'd look for things he could refurbish and sell for a profit.

For a while, Melanie's father owned and operated a seafood restaurant in a northern Vermont inn. He didn't know much about cooking, but he knew what he liked and he loved tasting.

Melanie's playfulness helped her raise her kids. To convince four-year-old Jeordie to order fish instead of lobster, she'd have a quarter placed under her daughter's plate. The child got to keep it if she ordered fish. It did the trick.

Melanie's father left her boxes of ribbons. She'd take them out at Christmas. They reminded her of when he got the idea to manufacture pre-decorated bows and ribbons and color-themed Christmas trees. He drew his plans out for her on a napkin, and she told him that she thought it was a good idea. He could sell them in department stores and clean up.

Freddy's passing was a harbinger of things to come. After touring the Netherlands and Germany, Peter, Beau, and Melanie flew back to the United States on October 30, 2009. They planned to go through customs in New York and continue to Florida, where they were renting a house. The airplane had begun its descent when Melanie noticed a commotion a few rows ahead of her. At first, she thought it was Peter, who was sitting with Beau, trying to get the steward to smuggle him more drinks. She could see him, collapsed in his seat, but she assumed that he was drinking too much and passed out.

The steward kept asking for aspirin. Melanie looked in her pocketbook but came up empty. She started asking everyone for an aspirin, not realizing why. Beau was running around the plane, trying to get aspirin, when the steward stopped him and said, "You have to take your seat. We're about to land." Melanie thought Beau was going to punch him, but he answered the steward, "No! I think something is wrong with my father. We need an aspirin."

The pilot made an announcement, asking if there was a doctor onboard. Melanie panicked. She realized that this was serious. Peter wasn't waking, and he was cold and gray. She didn't know what to do. She had been uncomfortable the entire flight. There had been an extremely tall man with long legs sitting in the row in front of her. He pushed his seat back on takeoff, and she felt like he was practically sitting in her lap. Even when he was eating, he sat back. Every time that she had to get out of her seat to use the bathroom, or get something out of the overhead bin, she had to lean sideways and backward to get out. She hated him and cursed him under her breath, but she desperately asked him if he had an aspirin. He held her hand and told her that it was going to be all right. It comforted her. She thought about how life could be so crazy, how someone could spend nine hours hating somebody only to find that he's a decent, caring person.

Someone on the plane finally came up with aspirin and put it in Peter's mouth. The doctor later said that it saved his life. After that day, Melanie carried aspirin in her pocketbook. It sat in a little plastic bag. She figured that if anyone else had a heart attack, she'd be prepared.

By the time that the plane touched the ground, an ambulance was waiting. Beau helped carry Peter to a stretcher. Taken to a nearby hospital unequipped to handle him, Peter continued to North Shore University Hospital in Manhasset, Long Island. Melanie and Beau followed in a taxi. Melanie tried to gather her belongings before leaving the plane but the steward who had been so nasty to her snapped that she had more serious things to worry about.

At the first hospital, Melanie told the doctor that Peter had been drinking before the plane landed. The doctor yelled at her, stressing the seriousness of the situation. "This isn't about alcohol," he roared. "Your husband had a heart attack!"

By the time Melanie and Beau arrived at the second hospital, Peter was in the CCU (critical care unit). Melanie had no idea what or where that was, but she and Beau continued to follow the signs. Melanie thought to herself that it was a nice, quiet hospital. She didn't know that the CCU was where critically ill patients went. Peter made it through the night.

Melanie and Beau had no fresh clothes. They had been on their way to Florida and their suitcases had continued going there. She didn't have money, credit cards, or her checkbook. She began to panic. The head nurse recognized her and said, "Oh my God, I have all of your albums!"

The nurse suggested that Melanie and Beau get a room at a hotel, close to the hospital, but Melanie explained her dire financial situation. The nurse said, "You must have friends near here." Melanie confessed that she didn't know anyone close. She didn't want to go too far while Peter was in the hospital. Empathizing, the nurse led her and Beau to a room where "fathers wait for their wives to have babies." It had a La-Z-Boy chair with a footrest. Beau put sheets on the floor and he and his mother took turns sleeping on the chair and the floor. Melanie woke every couple of hours to check on how Peter was doing. At any moment, he could be gone.

Accustomed to Peter handling everything, Melanie felt very alone. She no longer had a mother or a father or anyone she could rely on for support. The following night, the nurse arranged for her and Beau to share a room in a house for patients' families. They slept in twin beds. It was like being in a dorm. They were there for weeks.

Peter needed a triple bypass. The surgery took an entire day. Melanie spent hours on the telephone, trying to figure out what to do.

Before leaving for Europe, Peter and Beau had begun working on tracks that would comprise *Ever Since You Never Heard of Me*. It would be Peter's last album. In addition to Beau's instrumental "Deserts of Blue," it included "A Kiss from the Heart," "Angel Watching Over You," "Hushabye," "I Tried to Die Young," "Smile," "Ordinary Rain," and Melanie's tributes to Johnny Cash ("Working Legend") and Amma ("Motherhood of Love"). The title track, Melanie told the *Phoenix New Times*, was "tongue in cheek. . . . I have a very strange career. I had some number one records and there were times [when] I [was] a household word. . . . Some people just don't know who I am, which is natural, especially now, because you have to do bizarre things to have people know who you are."[1]

Father and son took different approaches to production. "Peter was all about [capturing] the feel," Melanie explained. "He would let the artist reign. That was his gift—to let the artist come out with the album they wanted. . . . Beau is much more in control of everything. . . . The magic part is making that appear as if it happened with the spontaneity and magic of a live session."[2]

Melanie altered her usual method of recording. "[The album] began with my voice," she said, "whereas so many productions begin with the band. This one was Beau and me sitting there and just playing the songs; and he, with such detail, duplicated the exact rhythm, the exact groove from the original from what I sang."[3]

A year passed before Peter showed signs of recovery. Released from the hospital, he went to Nashville with Melanie and Beau to recuperate. Doctors warned him against flying, so Melanie rented a van and Dorothy flew to New York to drive them to Nashville.

Peter wasn't the same. He had a hard time seeing, and it took a long time for him to be able to walk correctly again. Within a few months, however, he seemed to be back to his old self. He had a new outlook. "He said he wasn't afraid to die anymore," Melanie recalled. "He said it was really beautiful and that the only reason he came back was to make sure that our son Beau and I were okay."[4]

The last thing Melanie was thinking about was paying rent for their home in Florida. She called the property owner to inform her that they would be going to Nashville, but she neglected to mention that they would be returning. When she didn't receive the rent check, the property owner entered the apartment and gathered Melanie, Peter, and Beau's possessions. Cosmetics, books, paint, Melanie's collection of shells, and Beau's guitars were thrown into a storage shed and garage. The property owner gave little thought to what she was doing. Then, she started the eviction process.

Determined to regain his health, Peter stopped drinking, changed his diet, and exercised daily. He lost a lot of weight and looked good. His rebound, however, was deceptive. Four days short of the anniversary of his heart attack, he experienced a second attack on October 26, 2010. Melanie and Beau had started the Working Legends Tour at Norfolk, Connecticut's Infinity Hall three days before. They arrived in Framingham, Massachusetts, a couple of days in advance of the show and checked into a Residence Inn. The morning of their final day together, Peter wanted to go to Best Buy to upgrade his cell phone. Melanie asked if he wanted her to go with him, but he told her that he could handle it. Instead, he dropped her off at a Whole Foods market and promised to pick her up after he was done. It was just like that—very casual. He told her that he'd see her in an hour and headed off to get the cell phone.

When she finished shopping, Melanie waited for Peter. Sipping soup in the market's café, she waited for hours. She sensed that something was wrong. It was getting late, and the store was preparing to close. She wavered between anger and nagging fear. "Where is he?" she thought to herself. She decided to wait outside. Rolling her overloaded cart to a decorative haystack, she sat down and waited. She tried distracting herself by looking at the store's Halloween decorations—the pumpkins and the mums. The store's manager came over and asked if she needed help. Melanie borrowed his cell phone and tried calling Peter. It rang once and went right to voicemail. Melanie saw a man walking across the parking lot and thought for a moment that it was Peter. It wasn't. A car passed by. That wasn't Peter either. Melanie began panicking. Two police cars pulled up in front of the store. Melanie thought it odd and wondered why they were there. Nothing bad was happening at Whole Foods, was it? Getting out of the patrol car, one of the police officers walked over and asked, "Are you Melanie Schekeryk?" Taking a deep breath, Melanie asked if Peter was all right. She knew the answer before she asked, and she wasn't surprised when the officer told her, "No."

Praying that the officer was wrong, and crying hysterically, Melanie climbed into the back of the patrol car. Reports of Peter's death had to be mistaken. She was positive he was still alive.

Beau remained at the hotel when his parents went shopping. Police phoned to inform him that they'd be picking him up and taking him to the hospital to identify the body. He thought that both of his parents were gone. It wasn't until he got to the hospital that he realized that his mother was still alive.

Melanie and Beau identified Peter's lifeless body. He had "a soft, self-satisfied expression on his face, almost a smile, but his life force, his energy, was gone."

Returning to the hotel, Melanie and Beau received a very nurturing reception. The entire staff knew Peter. He spent the short time they had been there making friends. "I spoke to Peter two days before he died," said Dia Huizinga. "He was really excited. Hewlett-Packard used 'Brand New Key' in a television commercial and he was convinced that it was going to be a hit again. He said, 'I'm going to be a millionaire again.' That was the last talk that I had with him."

Melanie and Beau played the scheduled show at the Amazing Things Arts Center in Framingham, Massachusetts. Informing the audience about Peter's passing, Melanie concluded her remarks with a self-reassuring reminder that "everybody dies." She then poured her grief out in song. The venue sent her flowers and told her that she didn't have to do the show, but she was determined to fulfill her contract.

It was a very tense time. The day before the show, Melanie lost her voice. She couldn't talk, couldn't sing, could barely whisper. A doctor friend of Jess Leary prescribed prednisone, a powerful steroid usually used to treat severe allergies and chronic diseases. Melanie took it though she claimed that she would "normally never take anything like it." She was that driven to do this show. Sure enough, her voice came back. "Melanie bared her soul," said the *Metrowest Daily News*, "summoning what must have been the lessons of her own life in music, the skyrocketing success, inevitable letdown, the struggle to earn a living doing what you love, to reach out with unrestrained emotion at once raw and touching."[5]

Beau opened on solo guitar. A group of doctors, nurses, and hospital staff were in attendance. Jeordie flew in to Boston to sing with her mother. Leilah wanted to come but Melanie advised against it. She told her that there was no need; they weren't going to be doing any kind of ceremony. She assured her that they'd do something after she got home but they never did. There wasn't a funeral.

After leaving the hospital, Melanie went back to her hotel room and sat by herself. The telephone rang. It was the hospital calling to ask what she wanted them to do with Peter's remains. She didn't know. Locating a funeral parlor that handled cremations, she and Beau brought the box of ashes back to the hotel afterward. Then, they took it to Jess Leary's lake house, about an hour southeast of Framingham, and spent a few days figuring out what they were going to do. Melanie and Beau cried the whole time. They had been three people Beau's entire life and they had always traveled together. Now, it was just the two of them.

Melanie and Beau decided to drive to Arizona. Jeordie was moving to a new apartment, and they'd be able to help. Hiring a woman driver, they headed west on Route 66 with Peter's cremains in the car. Beau and the hired driver took shifts. Beau had never driven before. He had always been an "artist in residence" passenger in the back seat of the car. Melanie had a driving license and a perfect driving record, but she hadn't driven in decades. Peter or one of his assistants always handled the driving.

For the first time since she was a teen, Melanie was on her own. She had been free to focus on songwriting, recording, touring, and motherhood while Peter was responsible for everything else. "Right after [Peter] died," she told *Life After 50*, "I cried all the time. Grief took over—big grief. . . . [It] buffered me from the sharp edges of his loss but, while I was in a cloud, I never wallowed in the grief. I never spent a day in bed. I just kept going. To deal with it, I just started being as busy as I could be. I would do a tour and come home and paint and write and be creative."[6]

"[Peter] hurt [Melanie] more than he helped her," said Artie Kornfeld. "He wasn't systematic or organized by any stretch of the imagination. He took control of her career, but he should have just let her run and do the music that she wanted to do. She could have expanded a lot more creatively. Peter was a hustler, and that's what she needed in the beginning, but after she got to a certain point, he should have let go."

Peter often confided in Potts. During one post-session meal, he went on about his love for Melanie and his family. There was tenderness as he spoke.

On the other hand was the Peter who emerged after the financial problems began, the one dependent on drugs, the one sometimes embarrassingly drunk, the one who liked getting into bar fights. He kept Melanie from what was going on. He'd take out a second mortgage without telling her. He thought he was protecting her, but there were things she should have known.

"Unfortunately, [Peter] did leave us in a big ol' mess," Melanie told *US Weekly*. "He loved playing the game of making the deal . . . but he wasn't good at keeping [money] or accumulating [it]. He loved artists. If every artist could have a Peter, there'd be world peace. I believe that art and music could change the world, but artists are so screwed up most of the time mostly because they don't have someone really supporting who they are. I was fortunate for the forty-five years that Peter was in my life that I was buffered from a lot of what the industry has to dish out."[7]

Leilah did her best to make sense of the financial mess. She had just started to perform with a band but put that aside and went to help her mom. She didn't have any idea about what was going on. Everything stopped dead in its tracks—the release of Melanie's new album, tours that were already booked. She was dealing with life as best as she could, and she wanted to get back to touring.

A large suitcase filled with her father's papers arrived at Leilah's house. She spent weeks organizing them. Her kids thought she was crazy. Her husband thought she should take some time off. It was overwhelming.

As her dining room table filled with paper, Leilah got to work. The times were intense. Leilah did her best piecing things together, but it was a struggle. Terrified, Melanie phoned repeatedly, crying. Leilah tried to keep her from knowing how bad things were, how Peter had sold the publishing rights of her songs, but she couldn't sleep and was worn out.

As much as she tried to straighten out her father's finances, Leilah found the task nearly impossible. There were scores of people contending that Peter owed them money. Leilah tried to explain that he had died, expecting compassion, but instead met with fierce hostility. Unable to take much more, she put her foot down and declared that, unless someone had the paperwork, it was just too bad—she would do nothing about it. It was inconceivable how Peter could act so optimistically while everything crumbled around him. He was supposed to be taking care of things so that Melanie could concentrate on her art. Instead, he was running it into the ground.

Leilah discovered her mother hadn't been paid royalties for songs she had written before 1993. When McDonald's or Hewlett-Packard used "Brand New Key" in television commercials, or someone like Miley Cyrus covered one of her songs, Melanie didn't receive a dime. "I think [Peter] gambled my writers' royalties," she said, "[and he] stuck a piece of paper under my nose. I never read it, but I signed it. . . . I didn't know I was signing away my writers' share."[8]

The United States is one of the few countries where it's legal to sell a songwriter's publishing rights. When someone covers their tune, they reap the benefits. It's their retirement plan. Peter needed the money, but he had no right to sell Melanie's songs.

Unknown to Melanie, Peter hadn't paid taxes for a decade. He and his accountant had been filing extensions instead. When she phoned the accountant, he told her not to worry and promised to take care of everything. She believed him but she didn't feel good about it. Wanting to resolve the situation, she asked him about her next step. Again, he assured her that he would handle it. Unsure of how much trouble she faced, she went to the IRS office in Phoenix. She was terrified. After she heard her name called, she walked into a large room. A glass door shut automatically. She realized that there was no way out unless she jumped over a desk and ran out the door. She noticed an extremely long table that extended from one wall to the other. A man who appeared to be an

IRS auditor was sitting behind the table. Melanie was shaking, but she was told that she didn't need to be so nervous. She started by explaining how she didn't know anything about taxes. She tried to make a joke, saying that all she knew about the IRS was that they had shot a dog in Ruby Ridge. The auditor didn't laugh. She told him her name and her Social Security number. He looked them up on a computer and told her how much she owed. She explained how she had thought her taxes were paid. He phoned the accountant who confirmed that he was handling it. Then he disappeared. Melanie was unable to reach him, so she had to hire another accountant—the one who did the local shoe store's taxes. He filed all ten years in a way that prevented her from being responsible for Peter's share.

Melanie and Beau stayed in Arizona for a very difficult year. Flying to Arizona, Potts and her son, Brian, spent a week with Melanie and Beau. She hadn't seen Beau in eight years. A frame drummer who plays Brazilian music, Brian jammed with Beau for hours.

Dorothy remained in Nashville with Peter's mother, who she considered strange. She hadn't been to the Ukraine since 1947, but she talked about it a lot.

Peter's mother died shortly before her eighty-ninth birthday in January 2012. Just before she passed, Leilah, who was with her at the hospital, heard her say that she heard a flauta (flute) being played. At the time, in Arizona, Beau was playing for his grandmother. Somehow, she heard him playing all that distance away.

Melanie returned to Tennessee after the unplanned birth of her first grandson, Kingston, in 2012. She loved being with her grand-daughters—fifteen-year-old Christina and ten-year-old Analisa. She pondered about the irony of Kingston's birth being so close to Peter's passing. She saw her departed husband in the newborn.

On May 15, Melanie performed for the American Society of Composers, Authors, and Publishers (ASCAP)'s annual "We Write the Songs" event in Washington, DC. Congressman Joe Crowley of the House of Representatives' seventh Congressional district, which encompasses parts of Queens and the Bronx, introduced her. "Not only is Melanie Safka a talented and accomplished singer-songwriter," he said, "she is also a product of Queens. From performing at the legendary 1969 Woodstock festival to writing and performing multiple chart-topping hits, Melanie's talent is nothing short of amazing."[9]

Keeping a journal since Peter's death, Melanie published selected entries in *Tales from the Roadburn Café*. Peter had given her a blank, leather-bound journal and told her that he wanted her to write something every day. He told her how much he loved the way that she wrote and suggested that she write about Woodstock, the Vietnam War, and how she had performed for the United Nations General Assembly. She told him that she would never get the chronological order right, that it would be too overwhelming. Where should she start? When she was a little girl or when she was already famous?

Embarking on the Working Legends tour, in October 2010, Melanie brought the journal with her. After losing Peter, she looked at the empty book and thought back to their life together. How could they have lasted together for so long? They had such contrasting views, but they survived despite them. Words crystallized in her head, and she wrote them down—"Sometimes you don't know you have a story until it has an end."

It burst open the dam. From then on, the memories flowed. She wrote about how Peter had been a refugee, how he had come to the United States with his parents, and how Stalinists shot his dog. She wrote about how Peter's father had run the village mercantile but lived an incredibly hard life anyway and about how his mother survived World War II by eating sawdust. A Jewish family trying to escape persecution hid in the basement of his father's mercantile. Peter's mother spoke about it for years. She was sure somebody had ratted on them. The Stalinists came in the middle of the night. Peter's dog started barking so his family knew something was wrong. They sneaked out the back. They were running when they heard the dog being shot.

As she wrote, Melanie realized that her story was Peter's story. There wouldn't have been a "Melanie" without him. He was bigger than life. He wasn't self-conscious. He didn't think about what people thought of him, but, to her, that was the charming thing about him. Whatever he wanted to say, he would say. He wasn't careful about being politically correct. He wasn't as diplomatic at times as he should have been. He was just very authentic, not prompted by what the outcome could be. He made enemies, but he got along with people. They may have hated him, but they loved being around him. He made them feel good.

Melanie's journal writings inspired *Melanie and the Record Man: A Musical Memoir*. "This is an intimate show," proclaimed the souvenir booklet for the musical's staging at Blackfriars Theater in Rochester, New York, from October 19 to 28, 2012. "You don't have to be a former hippie or even a folk music fan to appreciate [it]. The themes of love, remaining true to one's self, pitfalls of fame and fortune, and angst of aging are there for all to ponder. But, if you are a music fan or former hippie (or child of them!), Melanie is the jackpot of '60s nostalgia and legends, a magic carpet ride back to a time that has the chance of being forgotten or misunderstood in the next generation without living history opportunities like this."[10]

"It was surreal," Melanie reflected. "It told Peter's story; he was the P. T. Barnum of the music business in the '60s, the extrovert. I couldn't wait to leave. I'm one . . . who goes to a party and gravitates to the farthest corner. Peter would make the room. He'd come out with fifty business cards and know the names of the children and all their birthdays."[11]

"We had ups and downs for sure," she added. "We constantly disagreed but he was the most dynamic and charismatic person. He always woke earlier than I did, and he would come into the room and yell 'Guess what, great news!' He just started the day with that. Even if he didn't have any news, he was always positive like that. The endless possibilities were just dancing above his head, and it was quite a life."[12]

Melanie and the Record Man proved an enormous success. "We sold every ticket," said John Haldoupis, who directed, designed, and cowrote it with Melanie and script consultant Katharine Fischer. "People came from all over the world to see it. Broadway producers came. We got some very good feedback."

Haldoupis proposed the musical to Melanie by telephone. After she agreed to the project, he flew to Nashville to begin work. "I stayed at her house for a week," he said. "Dorothy made breakfast in the morning. I was amazed that there were so many mementos given how much they moved around. They wound up leaving some places in the middle of the night."

A guitar case in Melanie's living room caught Haldoupis's attention. "It had a drawing of a woman and a rose on it," he said. "I asked about it and Melanie said, 'That's my guitar case from Woodstock.' I asked her what had happened to the guitar, and she told me that her father had backed his car over it."

Melanie and the Record Man wasn't a joyful musical but extremely dark and dramatic. "We didn't shy from the darker side of things," Haldoupis said, "like Peter's involvement with drugs and the mob. Melanie wanted me to know that money wasn't important to Peter. He made money and he gave it away. In his mind, he was justified. In the musical, there's a story of how someone brought Melanie a box of her baby pictures that he bought at an auction. She said to me, 'Do you know what it's like to be playing a concert and have someone say, 'Here, I bought these'?"

Le Roy Junior/Senior High School music teacher Andy Pratt accompanied Melanie and Beau on piano. They mixed songs written for the musical and a variety of hits. Remaining onstage through the entire show, Melanie would recall some incident, and young Melanie (Mandy Hassett) and young Peter (Nick Feruch) would act it out. Sometimes, the two Melanies would interact. Melanie would talk about going to New York and mention that she didn't remember traveling by bus or train. Hassett would remind her that it was a train.

Seeing "Peter" walk again, hearing him talk, and remembering their life together made Melanie feel like a voyeur in her own life. "I met [Peter] when I was eighteen," she told *OC Weekly*. "We had hits, and we went through the historic phases of the Vietnam War, protests and pro-peace demonstrations. . . . I wrote this musical with that in mind."[13]

Fans traveled great distances to see *Melanie and the Record Man*. A regular at Melanie's shows since 1971, Margaret Corby "called for tickets as soon as they went on sale. . . . It's a small theater," she said, "only 125 seats. John Haldoupis answered the phone, took my order, and told me, 'You're the second person to call today. Somebody from Germany beat you to it.'"

CHAPTER 31
"BITTER BAD"

M elanie and Beau spent the summer of 2014 touring Australia with a band that included Andrew Worboys (piano), Dave Hatch (drums), and Tina Harris (bass). Concerts in Adelaide, Brisbane, Lismore, Melbourne, Newcastle, and Sydney were sold out. Before the first show, Melanie told *AU* Magazine what audiences should expect. "They don't have to fear that I'll do a jazz version of 'Brand New Key.' . . . It'll be a good cross-section of hits and things that were maybe not even released. . . . I've sometimes got real die-hard Melanie people who don't want to hear 'Brand New Key' and want to hear the newer or more obscure things. For them, there will be something too."[1]

It was Melanie's third trip to Australia. She had brought her daughters in 1976 and 1977 and did the usual tourist activities like watching koala bears and kangaroos in the wild. Accompanied by Beau, Melanie returned a fourth time in 2019, climaxing with a headlining slot at the Port Fairy Folk Festival.

On October 24, 2014, a few weeks after returning to the United States, Melanie and Beau flew to Boston for a show in Worcester the next night. Melanie felt a little pain before they left for the airport. She had sustained a hernia when a car in which she was a passenger was rear-ended. She could feel a tear in her stomach when the other car hit them. She went to a doctor, who suggested surgery but warned her that she'd have a couple of months of downtime. When she balked at the idea, he assured her that the hernia was nothing to worry about. He told her to keep an eye on it, but she wasn't sure what that meant—keep an eye on it. She had a bump on her stomach. She could push it back in, but she followed the doctor's advice and didn't worry. The pain continued to

217

intensify. By the time she got to the airport, Melanie was unable to walk and had to use a wheelchair. She tried acting normal when she boarded the plane, not wanting anyone to tell her that she was too sick to fly, but she was in severe agony. As soon as the door closed and the plane began to taxi, she collapsed in her seat. The flight attendant brought her a bottle of water and it revived her enough to make it the rest of the way to Boston. When her driver, Lauren Schultz, picked her up at Logan Airport, Melanie was in intense pain. Beau listened as his mother and Schultz discussed whether to go to a hospital's emergency room or drive to the hotel and see how things were in the morning. Finally, he interrupted their debate and announced that they had to go to the hospital—now!

Schultz drove Melanie to Massachusetts General Hospital. After examining her, the surgeon explained that he had something to tell her that she wasn't going to want to hear—she needed emergency surgery. He was right. It wasn't what she wanted to hear, and she argued against it. She told him that she wasn't from Boston, she didn't know anybody, and she had three gigs to play. Couldn't she wait until after the gigs? The surgeon was insistent, explaining that her colon was strangulated, her intestines were dying, and surgery was her only option.

Phoning her in Nashville, the hospital asked Leilah to speak with her mother. Without the surgery, she was in danger of dying, and she was resisting. They needed her consent. It was life or death. There was no choice.

Still resistant, Melanie told the surgeon to push the bump back in and that would be that. She took a painkiller and two enormous hospital workers pushed on her protruding bulge. Her insides felt like they were coming out but no matter how hard these behemoths pushed they couldn't get the bulge back in. Melanie finally agreed to undergo surgery.

Beau needed a place to stay while his mother was in the hospital. I hooked him up with my friends, Kimball and Neysa Packard, who lived a short train ride from the hospital. Owners of the Eagle Mountain House, in Jackson Village, New Hampshire, in the late '70s and early '80s, they presented shows by Leon Redbone, David Crosby, David Bromberg, Dave Mason, Jesse Winchester, and many others. They currently own and operate the Farmstand Bed and Breakfast and continue to produce concerts in Chocorua, New Hampshire.

One night, Kimball mentioned to Beau that he had an archival board mix from Melanie's Eagle Mountain House show in 1984. Going into his basement, he located the ancient cassette, blew off decades of dust, and put it on his stereo. It sounded muffled but there were some great performances. When he visited his mother at the hospital, Beau told her about the recording. He was especially enthralled that she had mentioned her four-year-old son during the show. That was him, thirty years before.

As documented by *1984*, Melanie's band, the Bruizers, provided extremely empathetic accompaniment. Stanley Sheldon, Peter Frampton's bassist since 1976, had played with Melanie on *Am I Real or What* and toured with Warren Zevon. Drummer Ernest "Boom" Carter and keyboard player George Meyer came out of Asbury Park's music scene. Carter had been the E Street Band's drummer in 1974 and played on Bruce Springsteen's first big hit, "Born to Run." He also played with David Sancious, the Butterfield Blues Band, and John Lyons's Southside Johnny & the Asbury Jukes. Meyer had been a charter member, along with Lyons, of the Blackberry Blues Band—the group that would become Southside Johnny & the Asbury Jukes after the arrival of Little Steven Van Zandt—and he toured with Corky Laing (Mountain) and Ian Hunter.

The *1984* album included "Look What They've Done to My Song, Ma," "Brand New Key," "Beautiful People," "Lay Down," "Psychotherapy," and "Ruby Tuesday," along with "Cyclone," "Lovers' Lullaby," "Didn't You Ever Love Somebody," "Roadburn," "It Don't Matter Now," "Lovin' the Boy Next Door," and "Groundhog Day." "Just Can't Do It If I'm Not in Love," "Taking It Easy," "If You Don't You Love Me," "It's Not a Job," "Damn Old Apathy," and "Champagne Song" from *Ace of Diamonds* were previously unavailable. You get a glimpse of Melanie at her best—playing live for an appreciative audience. "When it comes right down to it," she told me, "I want to get up in front of people, sing, and interest them in some of the bizarre or humorous or serious or sad ways I see something. I want to go away knowing I've really put out more than I even needed to, you know?"

CHAPTER 32
"LEFTOVER WINE"

"When people want to talk only about the good old days," Melanie said in 1992, "there's this horrible implication that you're nothing now. But I know I'm better than I used to be."[1]

Melanie and Beau continued to work together in the studio. Taking over the production duties of his father, Beau brought a new sensibility to Melanie's music. He arranged "Live One" for a string quartet, played on synthesizer and acoustic instruments. They recorded it for an EP that went unreleased.

Beau and Melanie planned a live album, realizing they were at their best before an appreciative audience.

The enthusiasm of Melanie's fans remained strong on both sides of the Atlantic. In September 2015, London-based Cherry Red Records released remixed CDs of four of her 1970s albums. All four included bonus tracks. The expanded *Stoneground Words* added "Bitter Bad," which had been a single in 1973, and a lengthy version of "Seeds" that interpolated the "Gather Me" poem. "I Am Being Guided," which was substituted by "Will You Still Love Me Tomorrow" on the original UK release, was restored to *Madrugada*. A live recording of "Beautiful People" from Melanie's October 6, 1975, Royal Albert Hall concert was added to *Sunset and Other Beginnings*. The expanded *As I See It Now* included Melanie's cover of "La Bamba." "I recorded [it] when I was on Arista," Melanie said, "but we never mixed it, never finished it, and never released it. It came out in Italy, and it was a number-one record. . . . I didn't know."[2]

Playing two-hour-plus shows with her son, Melanie gave new meaning to classic hits, and resurrected rarities. She continued to build on her legacy with masterful new compositions. "My new songs are by the same person who wrote the old ones," she told the *Australian*. "I am fortunate that my husband gave me that space to be creative. I am the oldest little girl in the world—a free spirit. I continue to create; that's the important thing."[3]

On Tuesday, January 22, 2024, that little girl joined her husband, parents, aunt, uncle, teachers, and sidemen on the other side. She had been suffering from a variety of ailments for years and was no longer the petite songstress of her youth. No cause was given for her death. She and Beau had been working on an album of cover songs, tentatively titled *Second Hand Smoke*, for Cleopatra Records. Over the previous two years, Brian Perera's Los Angeles–based label had released a rerecording of "People in the First Row," a live rendition of "Lay Down (Candles in the Rain)," and a five-track single that included a cappella, instrumental, slowed-down, and sped-up mixes of "Brand New Key." Leilah, Jeordie, and Beau Jarred posted a message on Facebook. "We are heartbroken but want to thank each and every one of you for the affection you have for our Mother, and to tell you that she loved all of you so much! She was one of the most talented, strong, and passionate women of the era, and every word she wrote, and every note she sang reflected that. Our world is much dimmer, the colors of a dreary, rainy Tennessee pale with her absence today, but we know that she is still here, smiling down on all of us, on all of you, from the stars."

The trio directed their mother's fans to light a candle in her memory. "Raise, raise them high, high up again. Illuminate the darkness and let us all be connected in remembrance of the extraordinary woman who was wife, mother, grandmother, great-grandmother, and friend to so very many people."

"I don't regret any of my life," Melanie once said. "It was all amazing. Who would have thought I would become a part of history?"[4]

NOTES

Chapter 1

1. Bernard L. Collier, "200,000 Thronging to Rock Festival Jams Roads Upstate," *New York Times*, August 16, 1969.
2. Collier, "200,000 Thronging to Rock Festival."
3. Collier, "200,000 Thronging to Rock Festival."
4. Tony Green, "Music Is Key for Melanie," *St. Petersburg Times*, August 12, 1994.
5. David Laurell, "The First Lady of Woodstock," *Life after 50*, January 8, 2013.
6. See http://popcultureaddict.com/interviews/melanie/.
7. See http://www.staythirstymedia.com/201507-089/html/201507-griffel-melanie.html.
8. Mike Boehm, "On Stage at Woodstock: Laguna's Nancy DeJongh, Who Sang in Sweetwater, Recalls Festival's Chaos," *Los Angeles Times*, August 15, 1989.
9. Nancy Burns Fusaro, "Meet the 'Brand New' Melanie," *Westerly Sun*, March 19, 2015.
10. Ray Sasho, "Melanie Safka Exclusive: 'My Mother Drove Me to Woodstock,'" *Classic Rock Here and Now*, http://www.classicrockhereandnow.com/2013/08 /melanie-safka-exclusive my mother-drove_18.html.
11. Phil Symes, "Melanie," http://melaniemusicsociety.tripod.com/PSSOP.htm.
12. Mike Evans and Paul Kingsbury, *Woodstock: Three Days That Rocked the World* (New York: Sterling Publishing, 2003).

Chapter 2

1. Judith Simons, "Mum's the Word for Melanie," *Daily Express* (UK), June 21, 1974.
2. Debra K. Minor, "New LP May Be Melanie's Brand New Key to Success," *Orlando Sentinel Tribune*, June 19, 1991.

Chapter 3

1. Judith Simons, "Mum's the Word for Melanie," *Daily Express* (UK), June 21, 1974.
2. "Melanie: Not So Wide Eyed," *Scene*, 1972.
3. See http://popcultureaddict.com/interviews/melanie/.
4. See http://popcultureaddict.com/interviews/melanie/.
5. Marybeth Allen, "First She Was Melanie's Mother: Now She's Polly, Her Own Singer," *Sunday Register*, July 24, 1977.
6. Jennifer Dodge, "Melanie Safka: 'I Went Out and Tried to Imitate Joan Baez and I Got It Wrong!'" https://mccartneyfans.wordpress.com/2015/07/03/melanie -safka-i-went-out-and-tried-to-imitate-joan-baez-and-i-got-it-wrong/.
7. Nat Hentoff, "Cosmo Listens to Records," *Cosmopolitan*, 1971.
8. Hentoff, "Cosmo Listens."
9. Carl Dallas, "Melanie: Certainly a Professional," *Melody Maker* (UK), April 19, 1969.
10. "Melanie: Not So Wide Eyed."
11. "Melanie: Not So Wide Eyed."
12. "Melanie: Not So Wide Eyed."

Chapter 4

1. Phil Symes, "Melanie," *Disc and Music Echo*, December 18, 1971.
2. Edwin Miller, "Melanie: On the Edge of Greatness," *Seventeen*, June 1971.
3. Jane Gaskell, "Melanie on the Troubles of Not Being a Flop," *Sketch*, 1971.
4. BBC Radio 1.
5. Richie Unterberger, *Eight Miles High: Folk Rock's Flight from Haight Ashbury to Woodstock* (Milwaukee, WI: Hal Leonard/Backbeat Books, 2003).
6. "Melanie: Prematurely Blond," *DISCoveries*, January 1990.

Chapter 5

1. Edwin Miller, "Melanie: On the Edge of Greatness," *Seventeen*, June 1971.
2. Miller, "Melanie."
3. See http://melaniemusicsociety.tripod.com/cosmo.htm.
4. *Folk and Blues* (Paris), March 1969.
5. Roy Carr, *New Musical Express*, October 1971.

Chapter 6

1. Edwin Miller, "Melanie: On the Edge of Greatness," *Seventeen*, July 1971.
2. Brett Ermilio and Josh Levine, *Going Platinum: Kiss, Donna Summer, and How Neil Bogart Built Casablanca Records* (Lanham, MD: Rowman & Littlefield, 2014).

3. Fredric Dannen, *Hit Men, Power Brokers, and Fast Money Inside the Music Business* (New York: Knopf Doubleday, 2011).

4. Ermilio and Levine, *Going Platinum*.

5. Ermilio and Levine, *Going Platinum*.

6. Ray Sasho, "Melanie Safka Exclusive: 'My Mother Drove Me to Woodstock,'" *Classic Rock Here and Now*, http://www.classicrockhereandnow.com/2013/08/melanie-safka-exclusive-my-mother-drove.html.

7. "Melanie: Prematurely Blond," *DISCoveries*, January 1990.

8. Roy Carr, "Voice of Experience and the Look of Innocence: Melanie," *New Musical Express*, October 14, 1972.

9. David Boldinger, "Roger Kellaway," http://melaniemusicsociety.tripod.com/rkellawy.htm.

10. See https://soundcloud.com/melanie-safka-1/i-tried-to-die-young.

11. Album review, *Hi Fi Magazine*, March 1969.

12. Carl Dallas, "Melanie: Certainly a Professional," *Melody Maker* (UK), April 19, 1969.

13. *Late Night Tune Up*, BBC2, January 17, 1969.

14. Jack Bentley, "Mystery Girl: Melanie, a New Pied Piper or a Big Fraud?" *Sunday Mirror* (UK), July 13, 1969.

15. Margaret English, "Melanie: Take Her Home with You," *Look*, May 19, 1970.

16. MIDEM, *Journal of Show Business* (Paris), February 7, 1969.

17. Melanie Safka, "Labor Day," *Journal*, September 5, 2015.

18. "Bob Dylan Live 'Friends for Chile' Benefit 1974, Carnegie Hall 1962," *The Amazing Kornyfone Label*, https://theamazingkornyfonelabel.wordpress.com/tag/bob-dylan-live-friends-for-chile-benefit-1974-carnegie-hall-1962/.

19. Melanie Safka, "The Elusiveness of Christmas," December 14, 2015, http://www.melaniesafka.com/journal/.

Chapter 7

1. David Martindale, "Where Are They Now?" *Biography*, August 1998.

2. *Journal of Show Business* (Paris), February 7, 1969.

3. *Variety*, March 5, 1969.

4. Hubert Saal, "The Girls—Letting Go," *Newsweek*, July 1969.

5. Saal, "Girls."

6. Dennis Schwartz, "Movie Reviews," October 12, 2013, http://homepages.sover.net/~ozus/rpm.html.

7. Phil Symes, "What Have They Done to My Song—It's a Hit!—Says Melanie," *Disc and Music Echo*, November 14, 1970.

8. Phil Symes, "Melanie," *Disc and Music Echo*, December 18, 1971.

9. Colin Irwin, "Melanie: Still a Beautiful Person," *Melody Maker*, October 4, 1975.

Chapter 8

1. *Times-Herald Reporter*, Middletown, New York, August 17, 1987.
2. Roger Moore, *Boston Herald*.
3. Fredrik King, "Melanie at Green Wood (A Postscript to the Garden)," April 7, 2000, http://melaniemusicsociety.tripod.com/FKGWAH.htm.
4. Stephen Israel, "Rock 'n Roll Legends in Garden Reprise," *Orange County Times Herald-Record*, August 16, 1998.
5. See http://amarillo.com/stories/081598/new_LA0750.shtml#.Va_JU_lViko.

Chapter 9

1. Mary Callahan, "Powder Ridge Music Festival Resurrected From 1970," *Record-Journal* (CT), October 5, 2014.
2. See http://www.ukrockfestivals.com/isle-of-wight-1970-setlists.htm.
3. Ibid.
4. Ibid.
5. Roy Carr, "Through the Good Book with Melanie," *New Musical Express*, April 3, 1971.
6. Sam Tweedle, "Little Sister of the Sun: A Conversation with Melanie," http://popcultureaddict.com/interviews/melanie/.
7. Michelle Miller, "Look What Melanie's Done to the House, Ma," *St. Petersburg Times* (FL), April 20, 1998.
8. Glyn Lomax, "Don't Live in the Past Says Heroine of Woodstock," *Sidmouth Herald* (UK), August 5, 1994.
9. Kevin Bryan, *Express and Echo*, Exeter.
10. Eddy Lawrence, "Jarvis Cocker and the Meltdown Festival," http://www.timeout.com/london/music/jarvis-cocker-and-the-meltdown-festival.
11. See http://intermezzo.typepad.com/intermezzo/2007/06/jarvis_cockers_.html.

Chapter 10

1. Vicki Sufian, "Melanie Lays Down Her Candles," *Rolling Stone*, March 10, 1977.
2. Lee Zimmerman, "Melanie: A Reluctant Superstar Reflects: 'I Never Wanted to Be a Celebrity,'" *Broward/Palm Beach New Times* (FL), February 21, 2013.
3. Jacoba Atlas, "Melanie: I'm Not Holding Back Anymore," *Melody Maker*, October 16, 1971.
4. Melanie, liner notes, "Lay Down (Candles in the Rain)," Buddah, 1970.
5. Sam Tweedle, "Little Sister of the Sun: A Conversation with Melanie," http://popcultureaddict.com/interviews/melanie/.

6. Linda Tuccio-Koonz, "Woodstock Legend Melanie at Danbury Palace," *Ctpost*, http://www.ctpost.com/entertainment/article/Woodstock-legend-Melanie-at -Danbury-Palace-6383746.php.

Chapter 11

1. Philip Norman, "Make Noise Not Love," *Sunday Times Magazine*, June 29, 1969.
2. John Scarborough, "Melanie Plus a Guitar Equals Instant Minstrel," *Houston Chronicle*, February 29, 1972.
3. Edwin Miller, "Melanie: On the Edge of Greatness," *Seventeen*, July 1971.
4. Margie English, *Look*, May 19, 1970.
5. Margie English, *Look*, January 12, 1971.
6. English, *Leftover Wine* liner notes.

Chapter 12

1. *Record World*, October 1971.
2. Robert Sobel, "Thousands Hear Melanie Preview Her New Single and Album at the Saratoga Springs Arts Center," *Billboard*, October 2, 1971.
3. Jim Smith, *New Musical Express*, October 1971.
4. Smith, *New Musical Express*.
5. Roy Carr, "Melanie: She's the Perfect Answer to Boob-Baring . . . the Queen of the Lonely Hearts Club," *New Musical Express*, October 14, 1972.
6. Mopsy Strange Kennedy, "Melanie: I Want to Buy a Mountain," *New Ingénue*, September 1974.
7. John Lambo, *Melanie: The First Lady of Woodstock* (self-published, 2012).

Chapter 13

1. *Rock*, 1971.
2. *Record Mirror*, 1972, https://melaniemusicsociety.tripod.com/unicef.htm.
3. Debra K. Minor, "New LP May Be Melanie's Brand New Key to Success," *Orlando Sentinel Tribune*, June 19, 1991.

Chapter 14

1. Phil Symes, "What Have They Done To My Song—It's a Hit!—says Melanie," *Disc and Music Echo*, November 4, 1970.

2. Vicki Sufian, "Melanie Is Changing Her Image," *Rolling Stone*, February 19, 1977.
3. Paul Solotaroff, "Trump Seriously," *Rolling Stone*, September 25, 2015.
4. See http://www.kissfaq.com/discography/assoc.html.

Chapter 15

1. Maureen Donaldson, "Melanie: Getting Straight," *Teen*, February 1972.
2. Andrew Furnival, "Melanie Today," *Petticoat*, October 15, 1972.
3. *West Australian*, June 2014.
4. Furnival, "Melanie Today."
5. Lillian Roxon, "The Top of Pop," *Sunday Times* (London), September 12, 1971.
6. "Melanie: Not So Wide Eyed," *Scene*, 1972.
7. Donaldson, "Melanie: Getting Straight."
8. Paul Freeman, "Melanie: Still One of the Most Beautiful People," http://popcultureclassics.com/melanie.html.
9. BBC Radio 2.
10. Mopsy Strange Kennedy, "Melanie: I Want to Buy a Mountain," *New Ingénue*, September 1974.
11. Mark Voger, "Melanie Recalls Red Bank High ('Miserable') and Woodstock ('Incredible')," *New Jersey Advance Media*, July 27, 2014.
12. Tony Traguardo, "Catching Up with Melanie—Eurodisc Agenda, 1994," http://www.traguardo.com/melanie-safka-1994---1.html.
13. Review, *Record and Radio Mirror* (UK), November 24, 1973.
14. Traguardo, "Catching Up."
15. Jason P. Woodbury, "Melanie Talks 'Brand New Key,' Starting Over, and McDonald's," *Phoenix New Times*, January 9, 2012.
16. Nat Hentoff, "Cosmo Listens to Records," *Cosmopolitan*, 1971.
17. Jim Smith, *New Musical Express*, October 16, 1971.
18. Jacoba Atlas, "Melanie: I'm Not Holding Back Anymore," *Melody Maker*, October 16, 1971.
19. Cameron Crewe, "Review: Melanie—*Gather Me*," http://www.theuncool.com/journalism/melanie-gather-me-review/.
20. *Fusion*, June 1972.
21. Jane Gaskell, "Melanie on the Troubles of Not Being a Flop," *Sketch*, 1971.
22. Ed Kelleher, "Insight and Sound," *Cash Box*, October 30, 1971.
23. Sean Piccolo, "Melanie's No Hippie Today—And Never Was," *Sun Sentinel*, January 13, 2001.
24. Freeman, "Melanie: Still One of the Most Beautiful People."

Chapter 16

1. Barbara Schoeneweis, "Melanie's Rustic 'Rag House' A Cozy Home Sweet Home," *Asbury Park Sunday Press*, January 28, 1973.

2. Schoeneweis, "Melanie's Rustic 'Rag House.'"
3. Schoeneweis, "Melanie's Rustic 'Rag House.'"
4. Phil Symes, "Melanie," http://melaniemusicsociety.tripod.com/PSSOP.htm.

Chapter 17

1. Anne Nightingale, *Sketch.*
2. Andrew Means, *Melody Maker* (UK), January 1973.
3. Charles Shaar Murray, *New Musical Express*, December 16, 1972.
4. Rosalind Russel, *DISC*, January 1973.
5. Means, *Melody Maker.*
6. Penny Valentine, "Melanie's White Gospel," *Sounds*, March 27, 1971.
7. Joe Marchese, "Brand New Melanie: Morello Label Reissues Four of Melanie's Rare Albums On CD," *Second Disc*, November 4, 2015.
8. *Record Mirror,* July 28, 1973.
9. Brandy McDonnell, "Woodstock Legend Melanie Finds Another 'Brand New Key,' Plays Saturday at Woody Guthrie Folk Festival," *OKNews*, July 13, 2012.
10. *Billboard*, February 3, 1973.
11. *Disc*, August 1973.
12. *Melody Maker*, July 1973.
13. Nick Kent, *New Musical Express*, August 4, 1973.
14. Colin Irwin, "Melanie: Still a Beautiful Person," *Melody Maker*, October 4, 1975.
15. Chris Charlesworth, "Melanie Lingers On," *Melody Maker* (UK), February 14, 1974.
16. Charlesworth, "Melanie Lingers On."
17. *Cash Box*, May 1974.
18. John Beattie, "Mellow Melanie," *Record & Radio Mirror* (UK), 1974.
19. Erica Bogart, "Musical Shirley MacLaine, a Warbling Édith Piaf or Just Plain Melanie. . . ," *Disc*, March 30, 1974.
20. Chrissie Hynde, "Safka Meets Hynde—and Live!" *New Musial Express*, May 18, 1974.
21. Marchese, "Brand New Melanie."
22. Bryan Johnson, *Toronto Globe.*
23. Johnson, *Toronto Globe.*
24. Maureen Donaldson, "Melanie: Getting Straight," *Teen*, February 1972.

Chapter 18

1. Ben Fong-Torres, "Clive Davis Ousted; Payola Cover-up Charged," *Rolling Stone*, July 5, 1973.
2. *Billboard*, January 18, 1975.

3. Joe Marchese, "Brand New Melanie: Morello Label Reissues Four of Melanie's Rare Albums On CD," *Second Disc*, November 4, 2015.

4. Glyn Lomax, "Don't Live in the Past Says Heroine of Woodstock," *Sidmouth Herald* (UK), August 5, 1994.

Chapter 19

1. Glyn Lomax, "Don't Live in the Past Says Heroine of Woodstock," *Sidmouth Herald* (UK), August 5, 1994.

2. Vicki Sufian, "Melanie Lays Down Her Candles," *Rolling Stone*, March 10, 1977.

3. John Rockwell, "10 Favorite Disks of 1976 and Why They Were Picked," *New York Times*, December 31, 1976.

4. Billy Altman, *Rolling Stone*, January 13, 1977, quoted in Discogs, https://www.discogs.com/release/4801145-Melanie-Photograph-Double-Exposure.

5. Fred Schruers and Joni Drones, "Melanie Finds New Key," *Crawdaddy*, February 1977.

6. Vickie Sufian, "The 'New Melanie' Trying Hard to Shed that 'Old Twit' Image," *St. Petersburg Times*, February 22, 1977.

7. John Rockwell, *New York Times*, March 17, 1978.

8. Lomax, "Don't Live in the Past."

9. See http://www.allmusic.com/album/photograph-mw0000546219.

10. Roman Kozak, "Melanie Convinced Hitting the Road Is Surest Way to Move Her LP," *Billboard*, April 15, 1978.

Chapter 20

1. Iain Shedden, "Look What They Did to Her Songs," *Australian*, June 5, 2014.

2. John Rockwell, "The Pop Life," *New York Times*, March 17, 1978.

3. Kristine McKenna, "Pop Album Reviews," *Los Angeles Times*, April 16, 1978.

4. Marianne Myers, "Melanie Is Still Making Music," *Boston Globe*, April 27, 1978.

5. Carl Arington, "4 Ladies Launching Comebacks," *New York Post*, April 24, 1978.

6. Program, Carnegie Hall, New York, June 3, 1978.

7. See http://arpeggioentertainment.com/forums/ubbthreads.php?ubb=showflat&Number=5887.

8. John Lambo, *Melanie: The First Lady of Woodstock* (self-published, 2012).

9. *Good Times of South Florida.*

10. Tomato Records promotional biography.

Chapter 21

1. Harvey Aronson, "Melanie Sings and Zings It," *Cosmopolitan*, 1973.
2. Press release, http://www.1888pressrelease.com/musician-melanie-safka-signs-on-as-drug-free-ambassador-pr-567957.html.
3. Ibid.
4. Beau Jarred Schekeryk, Liner notes, *Scrapbook*, 2004.

Chapter 22

1. David Jeffries, http://www.allmusic.com/artist/barbara-keith-mn0000787735/biography.
2. Tony Traguardo, "Catching Up with Melanie—Eurodisc Agenda, 1994," http://www.traguardo.com/melanie-safka-1994---1.html.
3. Ernest Leogrande, "Melanie in Play," *New York Daily News*, December 21, 1981.
4. *Melody Maker*, November 1972.
5. Michael Small, "Picks and Pans Review: *Am I Real or What?*" *People*, October 28, 1985.
6. Small, "Picks and Pans."
7. John Robson, *Good Times of South Florida*.

Chapter 23

1. Craig Harris, "Melanie," *Dirty Linen*, October/November 1991.

Chapter 25

1. Elizabeth John Deal, *Township Voice*.
2. Lydia Carole DeFretos, *Unknown Source*, http://melaniemusicsociety.tripod.com/freedom.htm.
3. DeFretos, *Unknown Source*.
4. Bob Cannon, "Melanie; Freedom Knows My Name," *Entertainment Weekly*, 1993.

Chapter 26

1. Roy Carr, "Melanie: She's The Perfect Answer to Boob-Baring . . . the Queen of the Lonely Hearts Club," *Melody Maker*, October 14, 1972.
2. Stephanie Shapiro, "Rediscovering Melanie," *Baltimore Sun*, February 12, 1999.

Chapter 27

1. "Melanie: Not So Wide Eyed," *Scene*, 1972.

Chapter 28

1. Charles Daugherty, "Melanie Returns After 17 Years with Pyramid Set," *Billboard*, October 19, 2002.
2. Linda Tuccio-Koonz, "Woodstock Legend Melanie at Danbury Palace," *Ctpost*, http://www.ctpost.com/entertainment/article/Woodstock-legend-Melanie-at-Danbury-Palace-6383746.php.

Chapter 29

1. Marybeth Allen, "First She Was Melanie's Mother: Now She's Polly, Her Own Singer," *Sunday Register*, July 24, 1977.
2. Ellen Carroll, "Melanie's Mom Making Her Comeback," *Asbury Park Press*, August 25, 1976.
3. Ray Sasho, "Melanie Safka Exclusive: 'My Mother Drove Me to Woodstock,'" *Classic Rock Here and Now*, http://www.classicrockhereandnow.com/2013/08/melanie-safka-exclusive-my-mother-drove.html.

Chapter 30

1. Jason P. Woodbury, "Melanie Talks 'Brand New Key,' Starting Over, and McDonalds," *Phoenix New Times*, January 9, 2012.
2. Mike Ragogna, "Conversations with Melanie and Steve Forbert, Plus Noah Chenfeld's 'Suddenly End,'" *Huffington Post*, September 24, 2012.
3. Lemia Leval, "Redefining Melanie: The Interview," *Lovely County Citizen*, (AR), June 28, 2012.
4. "Folk Icon Melanie: 'Michael Bolton Is Evil!'" *US Weekly*, March 21, 2011.
5. "Bergeron: Music, Memories and a Family's Grief," *Metrowest Daily News*, November 3, 2010.
6. David Laurell, "The First Lady of Woodstock," *Life after 50*, January 8, 2013.
7. "Folk Icon Melanie."
8. Ray Sasho, "Melanie Safka Exclusive: 'My Mother Drove Me to Woodstock,'" *Classic Rock Here and Now*, http://www.classicrockhereandnow.com/2013/08/melanie-safka-exclusive-my-mother-drove.html.
9. Official statement, Congressman Joe Crowley, May 15, 2012.
10. Carrie Putnam, program booklet, *Melanie and the Record Man*, October 2012.

11. Lee Zimmerman, "Melanie, A Reluctant Superstar, Reflects: 'I Never Wanted to be a Celebrity,'" *Broward/Palm Beach New Times*, February 21, 2013.

12. L. P. Hastings, "Melanie Visits OC and Talks on Woodstock, Love, and Finding Peace," *OC Weekly*, April 27, 2013.

13. Hastings, "Melanie Visits OC."

Chapter 31

1. Paul McBride, "Interview: Melanie Safka," March 27, 2014, https://paulmcbride.me/2014/03/27/interview-melanie-safka/.

Chapter 32

1. "Melanie: Flower Child Chanteuse," *People Weekly*, July 27, 1992.

2. Steve Eaton, *Central Maine Morning Sentinel* (Waterville, ME), August 1996.

3. Iain Shedden, "Look What They Did to Her Songs," *Australian*, June 5, 2014.

4. Brandy McDonnell, "Woodstock Legend Melanie Finds Another 'Brand New Key,' Plays Saturday at Woody Guthrie Folk Festival," *OKNews*, July 13, 2012.

INTERVIEWS

All quotes are from personal interviews, spring 2014–winter 2015, except where otherwise notated.

George Altomare

Miriam Berg

Randy Brecker

Margaret Corby

Ruthie Dytches

Cliff Eberhardt

Tom Finn

John Haldoupis

Jimmy Hayes

Dia Huizinga

Jeanne Altomare Iarrobino

Bill Jerome

Roger Kellaway

Alana MacDonald

Annie McGreevey

INTERVIEWS

Randy Morrison

Bruce "Cousin Brucie" Morrow

Sonny Ochs

Rich Pell

Stephanie Safka

Ira Stone

Janey Street

Stanley Tomczak

Eric Weissberg

SELECTED DISCOGRAPHY

Born to Be (Buddah) 1968
Melanie (Buddah) 1969
Leftover Wine (Buddah) 1970
Candles in the Rain (Buddah) 1970
Gather Me (Neighborhood) 1971
Stoneground Words (Neighborhood) 1972
Melanie at Carnegie Hall (Neighborhood) 1973
As I See It Now (Neighborhood) 1974
Madrugada (Neighborhood) 1974
Sunset and Other Beginnings (Neighborhood) 1975
Photograph (Atlantic) 1976
Ballroom Streets (Tomato) 1978
Phonogenic: Not Just Another Pretty Face (Midsong International) 1978
Am I Real or What (Amherst) 1985
Cowabunga—Never Turn Your Back on a Wave (Food for Thought) 1988
Precious Cargo (Precious Cargo) 1991
Crazy Love (Orpheus Music/Pyramid) 1993
Freedom Knows My Name (Lonestar) 1993
Silver Anniversary (Ariola/Hypertension Music) 1993
Antlers (Blue Moon) 1996
Victim of the Moon (Afterglow) 2002
Ever Since You Never Heard of Me (Arpeggio) 2010
1984—Live at the Eagle Mountain House (Arpeggio 2014/Chameleon 2024)

GENERAL INDEX

SONG INDEX

ABOUT THE AUTHOR

Melanie and Craig Harris © Randy Morrison

A music historian, educator, storyteller, percussionist, photographer, and Washington, DC, radio show host, **Craig Harris** is the author of *Rise Up! Indigenous Music in North America* (2023), *Crossing Borders* (2021), *Bluegrass, Newgrass, Old-time and Americana Music* (2018), *The Band: Pioneers of Americana Music* (2014/2017), *Heartbeat, Warble, and the Electric Powwow: American Indian Music* (2016), and *The New Folk Music* (1993).

A skilled percussionist, he's played with the Gaea Star Band for over a decade and has cohosted the weekly syndicated *Gaea Crystal Radio Hour* since 2014. He's also appeared onstage with C. J. Chenier, Greg Brown, Jonathan Edwards, Rod MacDonald, Melanie, Mustard's Retreat, Merl Saunders, Rick Danko (The Band), and Los Texmaniacs. After more than a quarter of a century as a music teacher in public/charter schools, Harris launched the *Drum Away the Blues* program in 2009. Since then, he's presented multimedia programs in Massachusetts, Connecticut, Rhode Island, New Hampshire, Maine, Vermont, North Dakota, Indiana, Kentucky, Arkansas, Michigan, New York, New Jersey, Pennsylvania, and Florida. *The Craig Harris Show* airs Fridays (10:00 p.m.–1:00 a.m. ET) on Washington, DC's WAMU-FM/Bluegrass Country Radio.